LEARNING TO
DRAW / A HISTORY

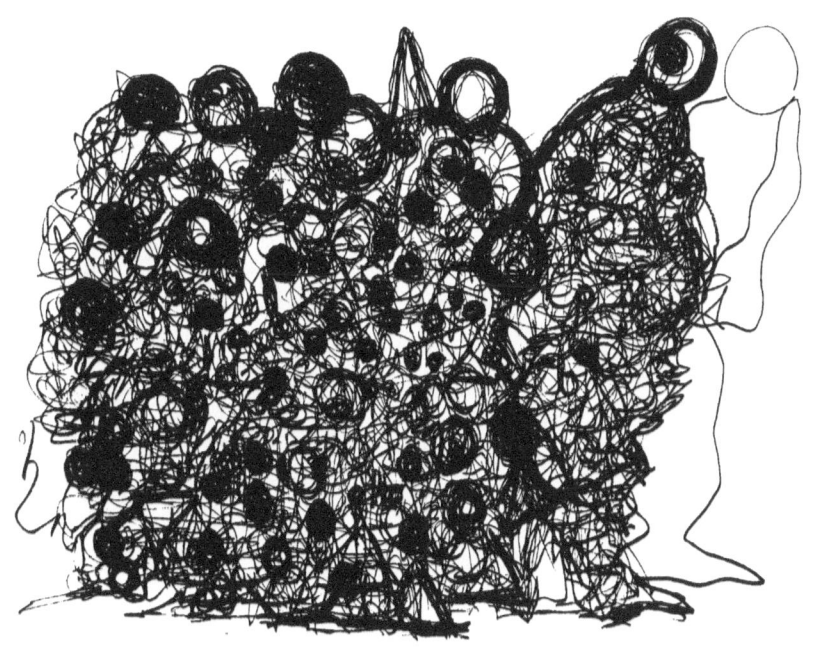

LEARNING TO DRAW / A HISTORY

BASIL KING
EDITED BY DANIEL STANIFORTH

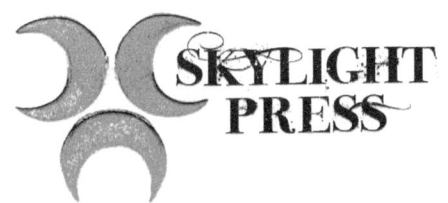

© Basil King 2011
Foreword © Daniel Staniforth 2011

This collection first published in Great Britain in 2011 by Skylight Press,
210 Brooklyn Road, Cheltenham, Glos GL51 8EA

All rights reserved. Except for the quotation of short passages for the purposes of criticism and review, no part of this publication may be reproduced, stored in a retrieval system or transmitted, in any form or by any means, electronic, mechanical, photocopying, recording or otherwise, without the prior consent of the copyright holder and publisher.

Basil King has asserted his right to be identified as the author of this work.

Designed and typeset by Rebsie Fairholm
Half-title page drawing by Basil King
Photo on p.7 by J. Kazimer

Cover artwork: "The Kings," mixed media on poster board, 40"x32", Basil King, © 2011 (www.basilking.net)

Text typeset in Minion Pro. Titles typeset in P22 Underground, a licensed recreation of Edward Johnston's 1915 type design for the London Underground.

Printed and bound in Great Britain by Lightning Source, Milton Keynes

www.skylightpress.co.uk

ISBN 978-1-908011-30-5

CONTENTS

EDITOR'S FOREWORD Daniel Staniforth	6
INTRODUCTION	11
ACROSS AND BACK	14
IT'S A DAY IN A DAY OF MY CHILDHOOD'S DAY BOOK	22
QUARTET	32
DICTATION	50
IN THE FIELD WHERE DAFFODILS GROW	58
SOLO	69
A HUNDRED AND ONE BEASTS	76
IN THE MOVIES	88
SHORT STORIES	97
PSALMS	102
THE TRUSTING CHILD	107
WINDOWS	118
14 EYES – DESIRE	130
CLOUDS	140
THE REAL THING HAS FOUR PARTS	153
BRING IT HOME	182
WILD CARDS	198
AMERICA KNOCKS	217
TWIN TOWERS	232
BASIL'S ARC	244
PURPOSE	260

EDITOR'S FOREWORD

As has been my experience, transplanted Brits in America have a unique magnetism to each other and this was the case when I met 'Baz' in the summer of 2009. We quickly established that we both had London childhoods; his during the Blitz and mine during the Brixton riots, and cockney repressions were wont to intersperse with our conversations. Rather in reverse to his temporal development, I came to Basil King the poet first, having recently stormed through his long versal memoir, *Mirage*, and was only casually aware of his existence as a painter, which came to the fore later in our correspondence. Fascinating to me, even beyond his sojourn at the famous Black Mountain College, was the fact that his genesis as a poet was a result of a trip back to the old Albion in 1985. And when I came to discover his paintings, I was struck by the English folk soul pouring through his biomorphic "Green Man" series.

Coming to Basil's *Warp Spasm* one quickly realizes that they are in the presence of the time honoured painter-poet, following such luminaries as Michelangelo (a famous sonneteer in his day), William Blake, Dante Gabriel Rossetti, Henri Michaux, and Jean Arp. As a musician-poet, I have always found the dual machinations of multi-disciplinary artists and how they find synthesis and expression within their hybridity makes for a riveting study. Of course, the idea of art in concert with poetry has a long and rich history gong back to Horace's *Ars Poetica* (and Plato before him), culminating in great works of ekphrasis like Shakespeare's descriptions of paintings in *Cymbeline*, or Keats' great *Ode on a Grecian Urn*, or more recently Paul Eluard's artist homage in *Donner à Voir*. Such follows the Renaissance ethos *ut pictora poesis* – "as in painting so in poetry." One can see this at work in Basil's formative years at Black Mountain where the combined teacher/student roll call is a veritable tribute to muti-disciplinary art – John Cage, Willem de Kooning, Robert Duncan, Franz Kline, Charles Olson, Robert Motherwell, Josef Albers, Robert Creeley, Ed Dorn, Robert Rauschenberg, and Peter Voulkos – to name but a few.

Although his art has been included in poetry books by Paul Blackburn, Allen Ginsberg and Amiri Baraka, Basil's true ekphrastic poesis is naturally automated in his own work where all is captured and processed through the artist's roving eye. His narrative scope is anchored in the abstract expressionism of his training but continually wanders to the expressive abstraction of a painter on the verge of a new creation, resulting in what Roland Barthes might call "painterly textuality." In his astute article

Thoughts on Basil King's Learning to Draw (alluding to previous partial editions), the poet Laurie Duggan draws a corollary between the poet and the painter where the poem being "tenacious about the tales it wishes to tell" is a parallel to "the processes he makes use of in paintings and drawings." The brushstroke works in equilibrium with the syntax where both become one utterance.

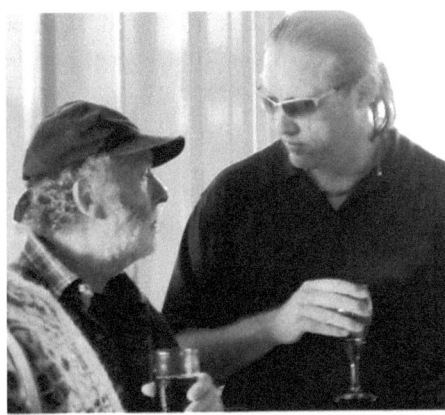

Basil King and Daniel Staniforth, Summer 2009

When Basil approached me about editing and compiling *Learning to Draw / A History* in the autumn of 2010 he insisted that I re-sequence the various sections according to my own reading of the work. In that it is a work he has been intermittently writing and publishing his whole adult life he said that he was "too close" to its separate parts to come to some organic whole. Upon going through the fragments it became clear to me that it did indeed comprise "a history" (one of many possible) rather than some definitive biography. In linear form, the 'story' (if it may be called such) takes the reader from London's East End during the 76 days of Luftwaffe bombing, through his own great crossing, to the glory days of Black Mountain College and the New York art scene. Peopling his textual canvas as he travelled through life, whether real or imagined, Basil followed the old Frederic Jameson mantra to "always historicize." In being asked to shuffle the cards in the King deck I initially felt a bit guilty of historiographic impingement, the sort of meddling or systematizing of history that Ortega y Gasset warns of. But as I read though the sections I realized that history itself is public, communal, and cooperative. As with his paintings, this loosely rendered autobiography was pliant and malleable, never misshapen as neither time nor memory is ever concrete or linear. Laurie Duggan puts it helpfully: "The question of autobiography looms large over *Learning to Draw*, but what sort of autobiography? The artist does not appear as an exemplar (though we might learn from his example). There is no false modesty at work, nor is King a kind of Zelig who comes into shot while the camera focuses on the famous others." Thus, I simply shaped the final manuscript as if I were learning to draw, through intuition and exploration.

The work before you already has a unique history as its various parts have been serialized over a number of years by various small presses and online zines. The current compilation, which is the first assemblage of its kind, does not follow the chronological publishing dates of the separate sections. On behalf of Skylight Press I would like to thank and acknowledge Marsh Hawk Press, Libellum, Skanky Possum, Talisman, Cy Gist Press, Local Knowledge, Cricket Press, Capilano Review, and House Organ for their previous printed excerpts of *Learning to Draw* – and to Jacket, Big Bridge, Sugar Mule, and Fieralingue for online renditions. Also, this collection would not be possible without the gracious help of Basil's beloved, Martha King, a wonderful poet in her own right – and the contributions of Rebsie Fairholm, Laurie Duggan, Andrei Codrescu, Nathaniel Tarn, and Amiri Baraka.

As Baz likes to say – "To the Future."

Daniel Staniforth
Autumn 2011

I dedicate – Learning to Draw / A History

    To all the men and women who have and those who will leave home, meet strangers and learn to draw.

INTRODUCTION

I use "I" – in my book *Warp Spasm* and again in *Mirage* and continue to use it in my new book *Learning to Draw / A History*. "I" is to tell the truth, tell the truth. And "I" helps me to do this. "I" changes the expected and repudiates the demand that we only progress in linear obedience, that we not be personal. "I" is a citizen. "I" is an artist and as an artist "I" disappear. The tapestry that "I" create doesn't need me to sign my name to it so that my ego will be assured of a place. My ego like my "I" is made up of many internal and external threads and for me they are all personal. *"Everything that has been painted and said about painters is part of art history."*

During the Second World War the fog in London could be as thick as lemon curd. On Sundays a Watusi stood in a corner of Petticoat Lane dressed in his warrior robes. He sang and he danced for money. He told fortunes. I remember that he was over seven feet tall and he'd pick me up and tell me I could touch the sky.

When I stayed home from school I read history, looked at art books, and copied with pen and ink music scores, Hebrew, and Arabic. I never was able to do the same with Japanese calligraphy. I didn't know then that it was done with a brush. With wooden matches, I constructed a model of the *Queen Elizabeth*. With pencils and crayons I drew flowers, gangsters, German and British planes fighting in the sky.

A year after I came to this country at the age of twelve I gave a presentation in auditorium talking about Van Gogh and Cézanne. The talk lasted the whole period. The teachers were mystified. My classmates wanted me to do something every week so that they wouldn't have to present anything of their own.

Lo, the line comes from outside. Sometimes it comes as a fastball and at other times it meanders making circles and repeating things that are remembered. It shouldn't surprise you that my contradictions reinvent inheritance. I have fourteen eyes, and am seven different people. As for meaning, my muse, my migrant, she sips tea and has me pass her a biscuit.

History is yesterday. And the day before that and the day before that I woke up saying to myself, "I don't want to be a third generation Abstract Expressionist. I don't want to ride a dead horse." I was twenty-seven and I had been trained from the age of sixteen to paint nothing but Abstract

Expressionism. I was at a dead end. It was the early 60s. The Beats, flower children, Viet Nam, civil rights, Pop Art, Minimalism. Allen, Roi, John, Jim, Dorothea. Everyone was moving. I wasn't able to.

In this city that I call home I spoke to no architects, framers, journeymen, or poets. I wore shirts, coats, shoes and pants. I looked like everyone else. But I wasn't. I was different. I crashed and almost became anonymous.

In the late 60s I saw a show of Olmec sculptures of children at the old Rockefeller Museum on 54th Street. I was so taken with them that I went back again and again. The Olmecs worshipped children with Down's Syndrome. They believed that these children who were not like other children had power. When they sculptured them there was no attempt to transform their deformities into the beauty that we understand, Greek mythology, Renaissance saints. I went home and drew hundreds maybe thousands of circles. Sunflowers, eyes, lips, Bosch. The Temptation of St. Anthony. I was smitten. I was mixing paint, climbing ladders, visualising tapestries.

It was the early 70s and my parents were living in the garden apartment of our house. I told my father that I was going to publish a magazine (*Mulch*) with Harry Lewis and David Glotzer. He said: "Like Hogarth Press." I asked him what he meant and he said, "Like Leonard, Leonard Woolf, you shook his hand, you talked to him." "When was that." "At a Fabian Society meeting." "Dad, I was four years old."

I began writing poems for *A Painter's Bestiary* in 1985, the year that Martha and I visited England for the first time since I had left with my parents in 1947. I wrote Bestiary poems for George Ault, Emily Carr, Rothko, de Kooning, Titian, Twombly, Warhol, and many many more.

Today we have corporations that have fallen in love with a Dada that promotes the female Christ, pickled lambs, and porcelain Scotch Terriers for the broker's mantelpiece. Once The Blue Rider covered the sky with red intentions and my mother's sister always covered her furniture with plastic slipcovers.

Rembrandt. Giotto. Misery and Kindness. The fortitude of artists. The smell of Gericault's raft and Ryder's Jonah, Medusa and Eros, Winslow Homer's pressed pants.

All of these things make me acutely aware that history is yesterday. And the day before that and the day before that there was the Holocaust. Forget the Holocaust. The Jews are not unique. Like all victims they become plagues, emotions, memories that are reinvented and reinvented. Stalin had millions of his own people killed. Mao did the same. Today there are people who worship the shoes and hair of the Holocaust victims. Their teeth like those of Stalin and Mao's victims cannot be distinguished from the garbage that litters the floors of American and European galleries and museums. Who pays the rent. Who tells us that we are free to do anything we want, that we can make anything we want.

I wrote the poet H.D. into *Learning to Draw / A History* and she became my muse. Her book, *The Gift*, edited and annotated by Jane Augustine, was written in London during the Second World War. In it H.D. internalizes her Moravian upbringing, her daily fears, her love of Ezra Pound, D.H. Lawrence, Bryher, Freud, Paul Roberson. The line circles to David Rattray. David interviewed H.D. when she was an old lady and he was a teenager. And years later I drew David in my studio on 39th Street in Brooklyn. Lo, the line comes from outside. It follows painters, jailed birds, dancers, writers, war heroes, photographers, and migrants. Cross the street, turn the corner. Cross. The metamorphosis is understated. Lo, the line comes from outside. Check the weather. It always comes from outside.

My muse migrated to London to marry Pound. They didn't get married, but she stayed. Pound changed her name from Hilda Doolittle to H.D. Her tapestry is full of faces, prose, poems, and the waters that leave home, meet strangers, and learn to draw.

With her I draw straight lines, thick and curved lines and the ever-essential circle that brings me back to where. Lines lack meaning. They are weightless until the space surrounding them is activated. This is as true of Watteau as it is of Cy Twombly. My muse, my migrant, sips tea and has me pass her a biscuit.

ACROSS AND BACK

H.D. composes her legs. She rarely crosses them. She never shows her teeth. H.D. changes her clothes, washes her face. And goes to the window. The wall across the street is lit up like a movie screen. H.D. reads, I saw your teeth. I'd never seen them before. I saw you on a horse. You were kicking the horse. You were naked. I'd never seen you naked. I saw you cross your legs. I'd never seen you cross your legs. You tell me that you are not lying. You tell me that you don't know what the truth is. She reads, I saw you looking out of the window. You looked surprised.

H.D. continues to look out of the window. She doesn't know it but D.H. Lawrence has joined her. He takes a seat in the far corner of the room and begins to draw H.D.'s shoulders. Her hair covers her ears. Lawrence cannot see the back of her neck. She wears shoes. They cover her feet. Her arms and her hands are bare. Lawrence says to himself, drawing is always contemporary.

The sky covers half of the movie screen. Trees are seen noises are heard. Loving blues and unmanageable greens distance themselves from each other. Unable to sit still Lawrence follows the camera. We see Lawrence as a young boy. Coal dust is on the table. He's reading his mother is sewing. Another camera pans in on H.D. She is talking to her father. He would like to say something to her. But she won't let him.

H.D. was married to Richard Aldington. Lawrence was married to Frieda Weekley (née Richthofen). H.D. and D. H. Lawrence met for the first time on August 14th, the day of the actual outbreak of World War One. H.D. said it was the only time she saw Lawrence clean-shaven.

War!

He found a coat to keep him warm. A trench to keep his feet dry. He wrote his mother that he was thinking a lot about her, and what he would do when he got home. He wanted a place of his own, but realized he wouldn't be able to afford it. He would like to have his old room back. He missed his bed. He doesn't tell his mother he is waiting for the order to go over the top. He'd been in no man's land before. He couldn't explain it but out there last night's dream is tomorrow's happening. He knew he'd killed some of the enemy. He didn't know why some men got it, and others didn't. His family had never been religious. He was sorry that he was a virgin and promised himself that he'd have a woman on his next leave.

He beat his wife and son and fucked his daughter. He was a hero in the war and received numerous medals. He was a quiet man who paid loving attention to his wife and son. To his daughter he was delicate and fatherly. He was a hero in the war and won numerous medals. He loved his wife but he beat her. He paid no attention to his son, and didn't even know he had a daughter. He was a hero in the war and won numerous medals.

Pause

Get rich. Be rich. Get rich. Be rich.

A charcoal drawing of Sigmund Freud by the artist Basil King.

Freud is seated on a chair. His body language is deceptive. He could be a lawyer, a businessman, a scientist who has spent his life accumulating knowledge, money. He is an old man. He has cancer. He will not give up smoking cigars. King has erased the lines he doesn't want. There is no shading, no shadows disturb the line. Nothing in the drawing tells us the Nazis are persecuting Jews. Freud lost a son who fought as a German soldier during the First World War. Even so as a Jew Freud has had to leave Vienna. He now lives in London, on the Heath. Where Lord Nelson and Lady Hamilton walked. Where Constable, Keats, highwaymen, and gypsies had lived. Where Rembrandt's great self-portrait, the one with the two mysterious circles, hangs in Kenwood House.

Pause

Freud says to H.D. during one of their sessions, you never lived with Pound or Lawrence. Will you live with me. Will you sit by me, sleep with me. Me, not the sorcerer you imagine me to be but me, the man who believes we know the size of our own souls.

I know you dislike yours. Your soul is large. You wish it wasn't. You wish that you weren't responsible for its needs. It needs your approval, your blessings. Be blessed, you have a large soul, use it and be the poet of all souls. If there was a Christ and he wanted to disarm the truculent of their desires, let him have his say. Me and Christ share something in common. His god haunts me.

The hero who found Dada in the dictionary struck deep. He beat his wife and son and he fucked his daughter. He was a hero in the war and received numerous medals. He was a quiet man who paid loving attention to his wife and son. To his daughter he was delicate and fatherly. He was a hero in the war and won numerous medals. He loved his wife but he beat her.

He paid no attention to his son, and didn't even know he had a daughter. He was a hero in the war and won numerous medals.

Pause

Fitz Hugh Lane never used a ruler. Not when he drew or when he painted. His legs had been crippled when he was young and he, like Toulouse Lautrec, had strong hands.

Draw the boat as if it were a horse galloping with a rider on its back. See the rider's pencil mark the shoreline. See the mast drawn as if it were the rider's back. Sea nature, go to sea. Draw your conclusions. Where is the vanishing point.

Fitz Hugh Lane, 1804-1865. John Frederick Kensett, 1816-1872. Lane and Kensett never got married. They loved the horizon line. Lane and Kensett's small marvels garnered many semi-precious stones. Opal, Topaz, Garnet and Amethyst stretch the horizon line's body clear across their canvases.

A woman crosses her legs, her long thigh is the Atlantic Ocean. A man crosses his legs, his long thigh is the Pacific Ocean. From the hip to the knee the landscape crosses the meridian, the subjective phrase "Mid Atlantic" Latitude 45 West, Longitude 30 North is never mentioned. But it has been said that when Lane and Kensett turned their paintings upside down the ocean always felt the sky moved too fast.

The pencil has not left the paper and curves around a woman's face. The lips will never be finished. She turned her head. We know she is smiling but at who will never know. The line continues to draw clouds.

Pause

A female astronaut and two male astronauts are to take a six-month exploratory flight into outer space. She has decided that she is going to fuck both men. She has decided that this is the best thing to do, the only thing to do. And what of love. What will she do if she falls in love. What will she do if one of the men falls in love with her.

To her right the Lion.
To her left the Tiger.

She is a Leopard. And when it is dark she has the Lion get on top of her. The Tiger roars and the lights come on and it is quiet again. The Tiger shivers when he and the Leopard are together. When she and the Tiger are together she whispers into his ear, and the Tiger hears.

> I see my Cactus brother.
> I see my Arizona, my Red skin.

At the end of six months the capsule lands. She is pale, Nordic. He is Black and comes from a large family. All of his sisters and brothers and his parents are suspicious. Coffee is served.

The Indian says nothing, he waits. He does not care how long it will take. She wishes her family were with her. No one asks her why didn't they come. She crosses her legs. She adjusts her jacket. Is careful not to check the time. The Black Lion roars. He knows that she does not love him. But he has become accustomed to being with her.

The Indian takes off all his clothes. The Lion's family sees the Tiger's stripes. The Lion takes off his clothes. She takes off her clothes. Lustful groans, blissful echoes bounce. When the lights go on she and the Indian are gone.

> Pause

Remember triangles, drawn with or without a ruler, right angles, windows, a house of concrete and brick. She types, he sleeps. He combs his hair, she brushes her teeth. Manners tilt the hat. She promotes the practical. He wants to be forthright.

A car stops and a woman gets out followed by a man. They climb the stairs and open a door. The room is bleak. The furniture old and used. The woman turns the lights on and takes off her coat, her hat, and her shoes. The man takes off his jacket and his tie. They are about to undress when they realize that they are in the wrong house.

> Pause

Dr. Williams wrote Louis Zukofsky and Zukofsky wrote back and told him not to despair. Not to give up. Williams lived in New Jersey and had a hard time keeping tabs on what was going on in New York City.

Dr. Williams and his wife visited Paris. It was a disaster. The Williams were not welcome. The doctor and his wife did not belong. They hadn't come to stay. Gertrude Stein, H.D., Bryher, all of Paris thought Williams was going back to America to become a provincial. Dr. Williams was rebuffed for being a small town doctor, a hick. For driving a car. For owning a home. For having children. For wanting to live in something other than a hotel room.

Dr. Williams was a Jew, a Latin, and an Anglo Saxon and his lines crossed as lines do in a drawing. Marsden Hartley said, *Williams is perhaps more people at once than anyone I've ever known – not vague persons but he's a small town of serious citizens in himself.*

1941. A man comes into Dr. Williams' waiting room. Sits down and reads a New York City paper. He's wearing a pin stripe suit, black socks, and black shoes. The shoes are expensive. His tie has a hint of gravy, but his white shirt is clean. He puts his hat on the empty chair next to him. Three women are waiting to see Dr. Williams. One of the women has her five-year-old son with her. The women think they know the man. Could it be Humphrey Bogart. He looks up from his paper and smiles. It's not Bogart's smile. It's the smile of a man who was brought up on a farm. Who left the farm without saying goodbye to his parents. It's the smile, not the clothes. It doesn't matter what he wears, he has always walked out on every woman he has known. Leaving one, sometimes two, children. It's a smile you remember because. The man smiles because he knows it is expected of him. He smiles and you smile back. He smiles and you see his teeth. They are even and look like they have been taken care of. The man brushes his teeth twice a day.

Except for the little boy who is banging his feet on his chair the waiting room is silent. The door to the doctor's office opens. A movie camera is wheeled out and stops.

Pause

1917. The French countryside. No Man's Land. One can feel Cézanne's little sensations along with all the accomplishments of the last half of the nineteenth century being crushed. Two mighty armies accommodate the industrial revolution's excesses. The First World War is being fought. Every soldier carries something that he doesn't need. An old cigar, one sock, a photograph of Master Chardin. Who in old age gave up oil painting for pastels. He said oil painting had become too difficult.

Old people take photographs of their children and grandchildren at Christmas and at Passover unwittingly recreating the Last Supper. It never occurs to them that one of the grandchildren will embrace an orthodoxy that is totally unacceptable to their parents and grandparents.

As a young man in Berlin Stieglitz has an affair with "Paula". Light and shadows bathe "Paula" as she sat at a table writing. Stieglitz photographed "Paula." "Paula" had been a peak experience. Stieglitz, "the Jew from Hoboken," as he was called by many of his detractors, came home. And after he returned to America he continued to send her money. O'Keeffe says Stieglitz was always photographing himself.

In 1913 Stieglitz buys Wassily Kandinsky's "Improvisation No. 27", 1912. The painting had been shown in the 1913 Armoury Show. Stieglitz said he could not bear the idea of it leaving America. That same year he was helping support and champion John Marin, Charles Demuth, Marsden Hartley, and the urban mystic Arthur Dove. Stieglitz asks O'Keeffe: If you could do anything you wanted for a whole year, what would you do. "I would paint." At the request of her uncle, Stieglitz's niece gave O'Keeffe her studio.

1917. Every day Stieglitz visits O'Keeffe. She says: the camera always stood near the wall. Twenty-three years her senior Stieglitz wants everyone to see his beautiful American, his Origin of the World sleeps with him. Alfred Stieglitz had never known a woman like Georgia O'Keeffe.

Stieglitz had already photographed "The Steerage" in 1907. And "The City of Ambition." New York, 1910. "Dark Iris." "White Rose." O'Keeffe will paint her own. In 1927 O'Keeffe paints "Radiator Building-Night, New York." "Dark Iris", "White Rose". O'Keeffe's patience never dances, it stands as still as a skyscraper. Even so her torso flowers. It blooms and everything that does not have to be said vows naked. Stieglitz loves her. And she is overwhelmed by a tempest that she did not know existed. She wants to have a child. She wants to be a mother.

Stieglitz wouldn't give her a child. It was one of the few things he wouldn't give her. She never forgave him. She moved to the desert.

Ansel Adams, D.H. Lawrence, Paul Strand, Marsden Hartley came and left the desert. O'Keeffe stayed and lived there without anyone. In 1931, Stieglitz takes a photograph of O'Keeffe. "A Portrait with Cow's Skull." O'Keeffe paints "Cow's Skull with Calico Roses." The skulls frightened Stieglitz. They may even have revolted his sensibilities. Like bread, the desert rises, revealing O'Keeffe's grief.

At the age of forty O'Keeffe undergoes two breast operations. Precision was her revenge.

As O'Keeffe gets older her body sinks into itself. Faith, not religion but a plastic faith, something that simplicity sees through, continually grows in her and she overcomes her jealousies and her contempt for those who couldn't do what she could do. She could get inside the flowers, skyscrapers, and skulls that she painted. Featureless, faceless, a mentor to her fears, she devoted herself to this image, this little woman whose torso became mother.

        Be Rich. Get Rich. Be Rich. Get Rich.

Mirror, mirror on the wall the daguerreotype is not just small. It is the essence of detail, a modern addition to the ancient miniature. Delacroix called it more than just a tracing of an object, but a mirror of one. For him the daguerreotype displayed details of the human body that often went unseen when the artist drew from a living model. The daguerreotype's gradations of light allowed the true surface qualities of the body to emerge, showing exactly their solidity or softness.

The Parisian critic Theophile Gautier said of the paintings on view at the 1861 Salon, "The daguerreotype which has neither been given credit nor medal, has nevertheless worked hard at this exhibition" and "spared much posing of the model."

None of this made it any easier for Vincent Van Gogh. A crying baby, a postman, a landscape. Everything Van Gogh drew and painted no matter what, even a jug, like the letters to his brother Theo, expose the core of his devotions. Van Gogh didn't express his feelings. He devoured them. He ate them as a Lion eats raw meat. This wild man wanted a wife and children. A home where he could cage his temperament. A safe house, a home and a family that would not be overwhelmed by his contradictions. It's a wonder that his work didn't become sentimental and trite.

Enter Pablo Picasso. Louder than a poem, hard as a hard on, Picasso smothers his canvases with – is it love to expose oneself? Picasso loved Goya, Delacroix, and Velázquez. Old master, dear masters it is you who absorb me, not me, you. Picasso grabbed what Van Gogh started and turned it into a flesh-eating fucking body that breeds with paint. He created a new creature. One that has a mobility that has never been seen before. His creatures are not hampered by convention. They wiggle, smirk, and show their genitals. They know that Picasso stole his children's toys and made sculptures out of them. But Picasso never found it acceptable to think of his works as one of his children.

        Pause

Theo sits next to his brother Vincent. They are sitting on a park bench. Behind them there is a path that follows a line of trees. Vincent is taller than his brother. Theo is better dressed. They are talking about their parents. Theo wants Vincent to visit them. Vincent is giving too many reasons why he shouldn't. Someone took a photo of this encounter. The photo is now lost. But before that someone drew the two brothers. But there was an accident. The man who drew the brothers had a child. No one knows how the child got hold of the drawing. The child drew over it with coloured pencils. Because there was so much admiration for the Van Gogh brothers the drawing was framed. It now hangs on a sitting room wall somewhere in Holland.

Pause

Dear Theo.
The sun compels me to stick candles in my hat, taste wax, and inhale the stars. Theo, Do you remember Hiroshige's moral restraint, his sharp edges and brilliant sense of colour. How he transformed me. Theo, did Hiroshige unwittingly teach me what Delacroix knew. "Feelings must not be expressed to the point of nausea."

Theo, do you remember my Yellow chair. My Red hair. Gauguin's Brown and Green chair. Theo, I know that I smell bad. I drink too much. I forget to take off my clothes at night. I've slept with my boots on. With a brush in my hand. With a pipe in my mouth. Theo, I'm not afraid of Rembrandt. I am of Cézanne. Before his brush touches the canvas, he meditates. Not his mountain, not the apples that he paints or his wife move without his permission. For him time is one continuous sensation. Thick paint, multiple flowers, it is impossible for me to praise my soul. I know nothing is personal. But what can I do, to me everything is a memory of Hiroshige's cloudburst. A blue object squeezed out of a tube of paint, an allotment of space, and traditional perspective vanishes into infinity.

IT'S A DAY IN A DAY OF MY CHILDHOOD'S DAY BOOK

I phoned Earl Heuer and asked him if he could remember a man with pale eyes, pale complexion, thin fingers and large feet. The man never said very much. The line between his lips held something spent maybe a secret. I can't remember his name. I don't remember what he taught.

Did Earl remember anyone who fits this description. Earl referred me to another old colleague Dan Andersone who was on our school Thomas Jefferson's review board. Dan couldn't help me. But both Earl and Dan said that I must have gone over to one of the other colleges possibly William James and seen someone who had more authority than either one of them.

I had gone to speak for John. He had a touch of brilliance that he squandered. Every semester for three years he took just about all the courses that were offered. Because he had never focused on any one subject he was never going to graduate. The administration was getting ready to expel him.

I wanted the board to give John another semester. What I wanted was time. If I could get John to focus and not just accrue more credits he would graduate.

I had John's folder. He was an "A" student. He would play two to three games of Go all at the same time. He played poker and he would come to the Pot Shop. His pots were zany and sensitive as were his drawings. These he would send to his grandmother and she would send him more money than he could spend. He sent his paintings home to his parents and they would send him money. John was handsome, sweet and a mess.

The colleague and I spent time going over John's credits and behaviour. At first he would not be persuaded but I continued and he began to show an interest and then he cut me short and said, "You went to Black Mountain College." "I did." "Then you must know Wes Huss." "Yes, he taught theatre," and before I could say more he looked at me and began to cry.

He said that he had been a conscientious objector in the Second World War and had been sent to a camp. The camp was horrible and they were treated badly. He said Wes held them together. Wes had them write plays, do pantomime, keep their bodies active.

This man never got over what had happened to him. He was unable to forget and the memory of it had become his tomb. I wanted to put my hand inside him and squeeze his heart.

> It's A Day in a Day
> Of my childhood's Day Book
> A room in the Museum of Modern Art
> With Rothko Kline
> de Kooning Lee Krasner
> And Pollock
> Seeing Monet watching Camille drift
> Down the banks of a river
> She's gone
> She's gone
> She's gone
> Monet's feet his elbows
> The torso that they both had
> Amongst the lilies
> The serpentine path breathes
> As the body breathes
> The body is paint
> Paint is the body
>
> PAINT
> What you see
> Paint
> What you don't see
> Paint
> I've painted houses
> But never a Water Lily
> Paint
> I've painted death
> But not as Monet painted it
> Did Franz Kline
> Ever get over Elizabeth's
> Madness
> Does anyone know someone
> Who has not known
> A vehicle without wheels
> A tree without branches
> A house without a roof

A frog with no legs
A person who is
Unable to function

I sit down in front of a Monet Water Lily
And an elderly man in his late seventies
Turns to me and says, The seats are very comfortable
But we haven't tried to get up
The woman next to him smiles
And I say I know what you mean
That's the hard part getting up
And then another woman
Who is sitting on the other side of me says
I don't know how they do it
They must know an awful lot
To give us so much
How do they do it and I said
A little Dab and sit back Bip Bop
A little Dab and a Bip Bop and sit back
She looked at me and said
You're pulling my leg
And she got up and walked away

      Pause

I drove all the time when we lived in western Michigan. Shopping for food, to the movies, to Chicago, to Detroit, to school. I was teaching at Thomas Jefferson in the Grand Valley State Colleges complex and we lived on Pennoyer Street in Grand Haven, Michigan. It was an hour's drive from my house to the school. I saw him building a porch on the side of a house. I stopped and asked him if he did work in Grand Haven. Our kitchen needed a new counter and some shelves. He gave me his phone number and that's how it began.

Joe Stoltzer believed America allowed him to do what he did best. Joe said he was free to be a farmer, a plumber, a carpenter, a builder, a husband, a father, and a wealthy man.

Joe Stoltzer's grandparents came over from Germany in the late 19th century. Arrived in New York and didn't like the city. They eventually settled in Western Michigan and converted. They became Catholics. Joe said that his grandparents were very proud that they had been Jews. So was Joe.

      Pause

She says: Her mother's family was on the last boat to leave Frankfurt. She says: forty miles outside of Frankfurt there is a small town where her father was born. Maybe a population of 2500 lived there at that time. She says: She, her sister and a cousin are planning a trip to Germany. They plan on going to Frankfurt. That is where her mother was born. She knows that Frankfurt was bombed extensively and that nothing that her mother knew as a girl remains. It's all been rebuilt but they plan on spending a few days there. She says: She knows that English will be spoken in the large towns but she is sure that in the countryside they will need an interpreter.

She Googled the small town where her father was born and found the mayor's email address. She told him who she was and gave him her father's name. He told her the town's historian traces her father's family as having lived in this same town since the 17th century. No one knows anything further back beyond her mother's grandparents. She says: She will visit a concentration camp because they are now museums. She says: The mayor has given her the names of two people who are able to translate for them when they go to Germany. One lives in Queens and the other lives in the Bronx.

She says: That her mother and father met in this country. She says: Her mother and father would take them to Lundy's on Brooklyn's waterfront and every time their mother would tell them that their father proposed to her in this restaurant. She says: We would roll our eyes but we never said anything because we loved them.

Pause

If Joe likes you his generosity is overwhelming. I come home and Martha shows me the Jerusalem artichokes that Joe dropped off on his way to seeing a client. He stops by and gives us dry wood. The wood has knots and he says people don't like the knots. He arrives with a truckload of coal. It burned beautifully in the fireplace. I can't remember but something is not quite right with the coal. He brings fruit, potatoes, and flowers. Joe would stop by in the early evening on his way home. He'd walk in the back door to the kitchen, pour himself a drink and join us wherever we were. He never had more than two drinks. He said we were more fun than going to the bar.

If there were two men cut from the same cloth Joe and Joel Oppenheimer were that. It was amazing. Joe Stoltzer looked like, talked like, and had the same gestures as Joel. Joel was a printer, a poet. His grandparents came from Germany and had stayed in New York and Joel had grown up in the Bronx, or was it Yonkers. We'd both been students at Black Mountain College. I'd babysat for his eldest son. And when our oldest daughter was born Joel and his brother came over to our apartment with a crib, a playpen, a high chair and all kinds of kid paraphernalia.

Pause

Joel introduced me to Samuel Greenberg's poetry. Greenberg was born in 1893 in Vienna. In 1900 he came with his parents, brothers, and sisters to New York. From 1881 to 1910, a million and a half Jews came to America. Most of them came to New York's Lower East Side.

Samuel's father Jacob was an artisan. He worked in gold and silver brocade, and at first they were fairly prosperous. The family lived on Suffolk, corner of Grand. Samuel went to Public School No.160 on Suffolk Street. He loved baseball, dime novels and until things began to go badly for his father he went to school and played in the streets.

He left school in the seventh grade and took a job in a luggage factory. He worked twelve hours a day. In his autobiography he wrote: "In the street of Suffolk, corner of Grand, we lived for ten years. The poverty and insult of life cannot find sufficient words on paper; it was a struggle for decency for which we were usually gifted, but which soon drew to a conclusion … We woke in a dreary cold web: sleeping cave of rats and cabbage, sawdust floor – smelling sulphur fumes in an empty musical tomb."

The first symptoms of tuberculosis appeared in 1913. He had already started to write. But it was in the hospitals until his death in 1917 that Greenberg did his writing. Seventeen notebooks of poetry, over 600 poems, prose, and pencil drawings, and a large, mixed collection of poems and prose on loose sheets, wrapping paper, backs of programmes, menus, and calendars.

In his *Hart Crane: The Life of An American Poet* (1937), Philip Horton describes Crane's excitement upon first reading Greenberg's work at Greenberg's friend William Murrell Fisher's house in Woodstock, New York, in 1923.

Crane copied a number of Greenberg's poems, made typescripts and was influenced by the work. Mr. Fisher kept the manuscripts until 1939 when James Laughlin published a pamphlet of twenty-two Samuel Greenberg poems, with critical and biographical commentary.

Joel gave me a copy of this pamphlet and I had it for more than ten years until I lent it to someone. I must have mentioned this to Andrew Crozier on one of our visits to his and Jean's house in Sussex, England. On May

19, 2006 I received a package from Andrew, a copy of *Poems by Samuel Greenberg: A Selection from the Manuscripts*, edited with an introduction by Harold Holden and Jack McNanis. Preface by Allen Tate. Copyright, 1947.

Pause

Greenberg was not the only person to cry God help me. Help me find a place to live where I can build a house of my own. Give me something that isn't filthy, crusted and coughing. Give me clothing. Give me grammar, a syntax that I can rely on. Greenberg was to say in his autobiography: I have rested from writing at the end of "dictation."

Nurse Bring Me Medicine

Nurse brings me medicine! Medicine?
For me! God, twenty years old!
Medicine? I'll leave it to thee!
The truth is a draught,
Fondly fought
To agree!

She left me. The tinkling glasses
Lent me her distance.
The hurried call I'll disdain forever!
She shook the pulse
Like Samson the vaults:
Well I never!

I'm still proud! Yes proud! —
Though charity is aiding me!
This future painter
Does not hinder
What is going on—or shall be!

Pause

And when you write a poem where do you start
At the bottom or at the top
Do you describe the object
The material that the object is made of
Can you put your hand inside the object
Is it human

Do you measure height and weight
Do you concern yourself with colour
The division of light
A field where daffodils grow

      Be Rich. Get Rich. Be Rich. Get Rich.

It's A Day in a Day
Of my childhood's Day Book
A room in the Whitney Museum
With Rothko Kline
de Kooning and Pollock
It's A Day in a Day
Of my childhood's Day Book

Seeing their paintings
For the second time in one week
Brought on a series
Of horizontal and vertical
Afterthoughts

I can love a teacher
More than my father
I can want what
A teacher did more
Than what
My father did
I can reach
What my father did
But what my teachers did
Is distanced by
What Marsden Hartley did
When he followed Cézanne
What Arshile Gorky did
When he followed Picasso
By alternatives
Consider a teacher's
Footsteps and when I
Put my feet into their footsteps
And measure what fits and does not fit
The external whereabouts
Is influenced by

When I admire
Someone else's bravery
Then I am not influenced
By them
I am an admirer
To say I am influenced
I have to become
As brave as the person
I admire

                        Pause

It was about 5:am and Dan Rice saw there was a light on in Kline's studio. Kline let him in. He'd painted all night and he was miserable. Dan turned all the lights on and "Torches Mauve" glowed and Kline said, "You've done it again Rice."

                        Pause

I knew a man in San Francisco. He'd been a priest he left his order and got married. I think he said there were children. He said one of the jobs that he had after he left the priesthood was working on a gambling boat that docked outside of Seattle. After seven or eight years of marriage he left his wife. I met him in Mike's Pool Hall. He was making his living as a quick sketch artist and he was good. He was well read and we'd talk and sometimes we'd get drunk. We went to the movies and saw Kirk Douglas playing Vincent Van Gogh and Anthony Quinn as Gauguin. He drew Douglas and Quinn and the man who played Theo and the postman. He drew the night scene the pool hall he drew the women the cornfields and he never stopped drawing the whole time the movie was playing.

In the movie Vincent says to Paul we will put all our money in this box that way we will always know how much we have to spend. When Martha and I moved in together she had a beautiful wooden box from Czechoslovakia that had belonged to her mother and I said let us use this box for all of our house money. The box broke long ago but to this day sitting on the counter is a box that holds our running money for the week.

It was months after Martha and I had moved in together we were walking down Market Street and I saw him. He was playing trombone for the Salvation Army. I said hello and introduced him to Martha. There wasn't too much to say and we said goodbye.

All poets talk too much, not enough, too much. Catch the line before it gets behind you. Catch it before it strangles you. Hangman I saw you first. I see you putting on your hood taking off your shirt. Hang man poet. Joel became a teacher and died of cancer. Joe Stoltzer was a farmer, a plumber, a carpenter, a builder, and a wealthy man.

Pause

Margo is tall and she is beautiful. She is taller than me. When she was a little girl she and her parents and an older brother and sister left Germany and came to Detroit. We went to the same school and I'd see her just about every day. I asked her if she would like to go to the movies and she said yes. We were going on fourteen and I didn't want to put my arm around her. I wanted to hold her hand. And when I took it she smiled. We started seeing each other after school. Get a coke, a milk shake. I still had a British accent and she asked me what it was like to be in England during the war. She asked me if I would like to come to her house for supper.

Margo told me that her father never stops talking about having to leave Germany. He was a German. His parents were German. And she said sometimes he cried. Margo said that if I came to supper I could expect to hear him say these things. She asked me are there people in England who hate Jews. I told her there are.

I shined my shoes put on a clean shirt and walked over to Margo's house. Margo's family asked me a lot of questions about England, about the war. Who were my parents and why didn't I live with them. I answered everything except I didn't tell them the truth about my parents. Margo's father didn't really say too much before and during the meal. But afterwards he became animated and began to talk in German. My Yiddish was a lot better then than it is today and I could understand that he was saying all the things that Margo said he would say. He was a tall man with dark hair. His wife was blonde. They were a handsome couple as were all their children. He was bruised. I could see the welts were not imaginary.

My father didn't know what to do after he came to this country in 1947. It was as if a piece of him disappeared and was never seen again. He would say to my mother, "You brought me to this country," and then, like Margo's father my father would name all the things that are wrong in America.

I didn't know then I loved Margo and maybe she loved me. We saw each other a few times after that evening but it didn't work any more. We were young and we were embarrassed. And neither one of us knew what to do.

PAINT
What you see
Paint
What you don't see
Paint
I've painted houses
But never a Water Lily
Paint
I've painted death
But not as Monet painted it
Did Franz Kline
Ever get over Elizabeth's
Madness
Does anyone know someone
Who has not known
A vehicle without wheels
A tree without branches
A house without a roof
A frog with no legs
A person who is
Unable to function

QUARTET

Nathaniel Tarn: Poet
Jacob Lawrence: Painter
J.G. Johnson: Collects European art
Robert Frank: Photographer

Four men each using different instruments find a way to migrate to something that is not his, a resource that documents possibility.

Ever since the first couple walked out of Africa there has been migration. Hear their feet the weight of their apprehensions is engraved into our behaviour. We want to be assured that it is safe to cross the street. We want to be assured that we are entitled and we will never have to change. "Everything changes but the will to change."

        Leave home. Meet strangers. And learn to draw.

Nathaniel Tarn

Avia

Consider
A homeless man
Is he at home
In the poem

At night the stars
Have legs and arms
Ancient eyes
Made Orange by Sunset
Consider Nathaniel Tarn's
Flooded World
If war is monstrous
Are the men and women
Who fight in it
Monsters

Consider
A homeless man

Is he at home
In the poem

    Pause

First there was Cézanne who said we could have intellect and sensation all at the same time. Then Picasso and Braque invented Cubism and announced that function was to be included into the aesthetic fabric of the twentieth century.

    Not in ideas but in things

Cubes

Charmed by
Chardin
Morandi's
Edges purr

No people
No agendas
No political manifestos
No master plan

    Pause

Dare we rejoice
Dare we have peace
Dare we
Dare we
Cover our eyes
Dare we have
What no one
Else has

Dare we untie
Alexander's knot
Dare we
Release
Arthur's
Excalibur
Dare we
Dare we
Shoulder

Evil
And
Cut
The heart

Dare we
Dare we fly
Dare we
Dare we command
What we
Dare
Dare we fly
The Secret Sky

        Pause

A little boy wants to be a man
He wants to kill but doesn't know what killing means
He wants to be tall
He doesn't know what it would be like to be tall
He doesn't know
Do you have to be tall before you can kill

        Pause

We were boys and we looked up at the sky and we watched dogfights and squadrons of aeroplanes going over to bomb Europe. But there is no way you can look up when you read Nathaniel Tarn's *Avia*. You have to fly with every man and every woman. No matter if they are your enemy or an ally. Nathaniel flies and if you are willing to impose yourself you (I) fly with him. War, the destruction of peace, and the multitude of reasons invented to sustain all of the criminal acts that are committed.

Some people stay
Some move
Some sit in a chair
Some carry a cross and
Some remember the dead and
Some before they die

Some before they die
Some drive by day
Some drive by night
Some drive with the lights on

Some drive with the lights off
Some with the windows closed
Some with the windows open

                Pause

Can you pilot a plane
Do you fly.– BAZ

Yes. – Nathaniel Tarn

Seized by
Ancient
Monuments
The Sun
Considers
The killers
Grief

Seized by
Rain
Seized by
A bird
The night
Has its first
Born
And is
Seized by
Light
A figure
Every one
Recognizes
But nobody
Knows

Seized by
Leaves
Seized by
Trees
Seized by
The Holocaust
Fathers
Hypocrisy

"We are at WAR"

Get Rich Be Rich Get Rich Be Rich

In *Avia – A poem of international air combat, 1939-1945* Nathaniel Tarn's research is overwhelming, restless. In *Avia* the sky becomes a battlefield. Where like all battlefields no one knows who is going to live and who is going to die. His meticulous mapping pinpointing flights over Britain, Malta, Pacific, Russia, and Europe are compulsions juxtaposed by detailed cool compassion for every man and woman who has flown and has dared to find a space for themselves and their airplane.

Pause

Nathaniel Tarn was a teacher, is an essayist, an anthropologist and a POET. Born in Paris. Educated in England, France and America. He immigrates to America in 1970. In *Avia* Tarn floods our ears determined that we follow the airmen who fought the Second World War. *Avia* is divided into ten sections and together they make a chorus; each section has its own structure sculpting features of every airman who uses the sky. And always present the morbid sensation of death circles every aircraft and down below there are towns and cities and the Atlantic and the Pacific oceans remind us "Things" are subject too.

> People
> Agendas
> Political manifestos
> Master plans
>
> Nathaniel Tarn says,
> "I was born into exile."
> I am not an orphan
> But I have
> No home
> No country
> The food I eat
> The liquid I drink
> I rely on them
> As I rely
> On my instruments
> To get me to my
> Destination

Birds do not live in the sky
No one lives in the sky
Imagine a bird's co-pilot
Blue Haze and BLUE MOON
Sunset
Why is the Mars sky red
Why are airplanes
Able to fly
The answer is not
In Tarn's poem
What is in Tarn's poem
Is men and women
Their imaginations
Their will to live
And willingness to die
For the time they spent
Preparing to die
Tend your machine
Know your enemy

I live
Because I know
I am going to die
Because my imagination
Has to die
Has to be flamed
By the will
To never
Repeat itself
I see constellations
Planets and moons
In the solar systems
I see dignity
Animal crackers
Emptiness

Jacob Lawrence

The Migration of the Negro

Get Rich. Be Rich. Get Rich. Be Rich.

Before Frederick Law Olmstead became a landscape architect he had a career as a journalist. He travelled for fourteen months in the South visiting plantations and observing the living and working conditions of the owners and the slaves.

From *Wikipedia* March 23, 2009:

> Frederick Law Olmstead was commissioned by the *New York Daily Times* (now *The New York Times*) to embark on an extensive research journey through the American South and Texas from 1852 to 1857. From the Texas trip, Olmsted wrote his narrative account published as *A Journey Through Texas* (1857). It was recognized as the work of an astute observer of the land and lifestyles of Texas. Olmsted believed that slavery was not only morally odious, but expensive and economically inefficient.
>
> Slavery in the United States began soon after English colonists first settled Virginia in 1607 and lasted as a legal institution until the passage of the Thirteenth Amendment to the United States Constitution in 1865.

Pause

I was angry when the police handcuffed me. Afraid they would beat me up and throw away the key. I am a Jew and I've been called names and I've had fights. But I can't begin to and won't pretend to imagine what it is like to be a slave subjected to an owner's whims and perversions.

Some people stay
Some move
Some sit in a chair
Some carry a cross and
Some remember the dead and
Some before they die

Some before they die
Some drive by day
Some drive by night

Some drive with the lights on
Some drive with the lights off
Some with the windows closed

Pause

Before Eudora Welty published a single one of her short stories, she had a one-woman show of her photographs. In the early to mid 1930s she photographed the rural poor of Mississippi. It was the time of the Great Depression and she was White young and privileged.

She recalled moving
"through the scene openly
and yet invisible because
I was part of it, born into
it, taken for granted."

Not in ideas but in things

2009. Because of the bad economy people are abandoning dogs and boats. Dogs are replaceable, boats are. But are they replaceable. Slaves weren't replaceable and because they weren't they were subjected to cruelties that would keep them in constant fear. Dogs, boats, and what about sweaters, vases, are they all to be thought of as castaways. Throw out your old sweater the broken vase the dog and the boat. Maybe not even the sweater that you wear and the vase that you use are they own-able.

You are
They are
We are Americans

Pause

From 1910-1970, approximately seven million African Americans migrated from the rural Southern United States, where blacks faced both poor economic opportunities and considerable political and social prejudice, to the industrial cities of the Northeast, Midwest and West where relatively well paid jobs were available. This phenomenon came to be known in the United States as its own Great Migration.

>The Black man shines
>The White man's shoes
>The shoes are Black
>The socks are Black

The skin is White
The baby is White
The woman is Black
The White uniform
The Black arm
The long White line
The Great Migration

1940-41 Jacob Lawrence paints *The Migration of the Negro*. 60 paintings tell the story of the African American's migration from the south during World War II. Thirty paintings. The odd numbers (1-59) are owned by the Philips in Washington D.C. The even numbers (2–60) are owned by The Museum of Modern Art.

Each painting is numbered and given a caption describing the particular event. The paintings are not large. All 60 paintings are 12x18 or 18x12. The casein tempera colours painted flat on a hard board enhance the content. Lawrence never forgets that he is painter. He doesn't preach and he isn't mean spirited in any of his paintings.

Other series painted by Lawrence: 1939-40 *The Life of Harriet Tubman* (31 panels). In 1941 *The Life of John Brown* (22 paintings). Followed in 1946-47 by *War* (14 panels). In 1967 he returns to Harriet Tubman and paints (17) paintings *Harriet and the Promised Land*. All the paintings are small. Lawrence never forgets that he is a painter. He doesn't preach and he isn't mean spirited in any of his paintings.

You are
They are
We are Americans

The sidewalk is covered with nails
Doors open and long arms
Holding hammers threaten
The world
Is playing chess
With Josef Albers
If it doesn't work
Begin again

Pause

1946. July 2-August 28: Lawrence teaches in the summer session at Black Mountain College in North Carolina at the invitation of Josef Albers.

Albers hires a private train car to transport the Lawrences to and from Ashville so they need not move to the "coloured" section of the train at the Mason-Dixon Line. The Lawrences never leave the school's campus during their ten-week stay.

J. G. Johnson

Not in ideas but in things

Martha and I are walking through galleries we had never seen before in the Philadelphia Museum. We turn a corner and BANG! Before us Roger van der Weyden's diptych "The Crucifixion, with the Virgin and Saint John the Evangelist Mourning." Both panels are topped with a band of Black. Under the Black band and behind the figures a bright Red background engages the pale figures of both panels. The left panel is the Virgin and Saint John the Evangelist mourning. And the right panel contains the Crucifixion.

This magnificent painting is a testament to van der Weyden's belief there was a Christ and he was mourned.

Black and Red, my first thought was, Stendhal, Ammi Philips, Rothko, *The Red Badge of Courage*. I clear my head and turn to Martha and say something about van Eyck.

A guard gets off of his stool and comes over to us. "Would you like to see the van Eyck." Yes, and he walks us into another room takes out a magnifying glass and gives it to me. "Saint Francis Receiving the Stigmata" is a 5x5 inch miniature. The brushwork corresponds to the immaculate work that the monks did for the *Book of Kells*. Van Eyck painted with an eyelash. Did van Eyck use his own eyelashes or did he use his assistant's.

The guard tells us he is not employed by the museum. He worked for the John G. Johnson estate and now that he is retired he is but one of the men who worked for the estate who now guard the Johnson Collection.

The guard continues to tell us about John G. Johnson.

In 1900 J.G. Johnson campaigns for female teachers to be paid the same as their male counterparts.

Some people stay
Some move

Some sit in a chair
Some carry a cross and
Some remember the dead and
Some before they die

Some before they die
Some drive by day
Some drive by night
Some drive with the lights on
Some drive with the lights off
Some with the windows closed

And like all short stories. A short story never ends.

John G. Johnson (1841-1917) was probably Philadelphia's greatest lawyer of the Guilded Age. At his death, the *New York Times* pronounced him the greatest lawyer in the English-speaking world. His clients included J.P. Morgan, Andrew Carnegie, Henry Clay Frick and the Pennsylvania Railroad, then the world's largest corporation two times over.

Johnson became a rich man but never attained the wealth of the men he worked for. And after having dinner with Frick and some other multi-millionaires he wrote a friend telling him that he had just dined with the "squillionaires".

And because he could not compete with their buying power he became something of a scholar he used the expertise and friendship of the art critic Roger Fry and the art historian Bernhard Berenson to buy the unexpected. The first time Berenson visited Johnson of all the hundreds of paintings he saw he found only three to be fakes. Mrs. Berenson was appalled when she saw paintings stacked in the bedroom, hallways, dining room and closets. Paintings surrounded Johnson. They were his love – his reasoning possessed the paintings, elated his day.

                Get Rich Be Rich Get Rich Be Rich

The son of a blacksmith he passed the entrance exam to Central High. A secondary Municipal school in Philadelphia that guaranteed boys of modest means opportunities then only affordable to wealthier boys who could afford college. Students were required to master draftsmanship in art classes that met for four hours weekly. It was there that he met and became a lifelong fried of A.B. Widener.

In his last two decades Johnson also amassed a world-class collection of some 1,300 paintings, all of them kept in his home on South Broad Street. This is where he wanted them to remain, and he said so in his will, which donated the entire collection to the citizens of Philadelphia. Much like Albert Barnes, Johnson directed that the home and the art were to be preserved just as they were. Unfortunately, as a prudent lawyer, Johnson left a small opening that allowed his will to be changed if some extraordinary unforeseen reason arose in the future.

After the Philadelphia Museum of Art's present neo-classical building opened in Fairmount in 1928, it found itself with acres of empty, fireproof gallery space on its hands. So its officials and lawyers launched a campaign to acquire Johnson's collection. By 1933 they came up with the necessary extraordinary reason to move the collection: They convinced Philadelphia's Orphans Court that the paintings were threatened because Johnson's home wasn't fireproof. The home was condemned and the Art Museum snatched the 1,300 paintings, in the process becoming a world-class museum without spending a cent on acquisitions. But the court insisted that the museum honour the remaining provisions of Johnson's will – namely, to keep the collection together, intact, as a tribute to his civic generosity and his astute eye. Flash forward to 1989. This time the Art Museum convinced the court to allow the Johnson collection to be broken up so that his paintings could be more effectively integrated into the museum's overall collection, allowing (as the museum's website puts it) "for a more unified presentation of European art between the 14th and the late-19th centuries."

Robert Frank

The Americans

The Best Years Of Our Lives (1946) a very overrated movie has one great camera shot. It's at the end of the movie and it's worth waiting for. Fred Derry (Dana Andrews) looks across the room at Peggy Stephenson (Teresa Wright). Fred loves Peggy and Peggy loves Fred. It's a great photograph. It was bleak in America. The Great Depression isn't over it's on both their faces.

Do you know you are in the photograph
Do you know you have your mouth open
Do you know your shirt was dirty
Do you know Robert Frank
Do you know Bob Dylan

Do you know Allen Ginsburg
Do you know Robert Creeley
Do you know Miles Davis
Do you know the Abstract Expressionists
Do you know they grew up in the Great Depression

You are
They are
We are Americans

Americans had fought the Germans and the Japanese. Many of those who fought were the children of immigrants. It was a year after the war and Americans wore drab clothes and were having a hard time finding their equilibrium. It was 1946. Coal dust covered the cities.

Teen-aged girls wore long skirts down to their ankles, lipstick and fluffy sweaters little or no skin showed. Some young men wore pegged pants a tie with a Windsor knot and a cardigan jacket. It was 1946. Coal dust covered the cities.

Pause

Ever since the first couple walked out of Africa there has been migration. Hear their feet the weight of their apprehensions is engraved into our behaviour. We want to be assured that it is safe to cross the street. We want to be assured that we are entitled and we will never have to change. "Nothing changes but the will to change."

Leave home. Meet strangers. And learn to draw.

A bar in West Virginia the woman behind the bar says she has Bud, Pabst and Greasy Dick. I ask for a Greasy Dick and sit down. The customers stare at me. Five minutes pass and a young man with a rifle comes in and shoots the fat young woman and the skinny young man who sit in a corner of the bar.

Language doesn't drive itself across the country, like love it needs a lover. Use a compass, navigate the documentation, North, South, East and West. Robert Frank kept his eyes open and sometimes he flinched. He didn't always like what he saw. It's there in every photograph that he takes he memorized the curve of a back the tilt of a head where the light comes from and when to sit down and when to leave. Some people stay – some move. Robert Frank's timing was impeccable. Click! He had a fast finger. Click! Some people stay – some move. Robert Frank's timing was impeccable.

Click! He had a fast finger. Click!

Faces with
Click!
Faces with thin lips
Faces
Faces with headaches
Click!
Faces with
Faces
Faces
Faces

    Not in ideas but in things

Robert Frank born in Zurich, Switzerland, 1924, comes to America in 1947. Robert Frank received a Guggenheim grant to travel across the United States and photograph its society in all strata. Starting in 1955 and for the next two years he took his family along with him for part of his road trips. Frank took 28,000 photographs documenting *The Americans*.

  The bone
  & meat
  Of past
  Suppers
  Support
  The root
  For another
  Day

      Pause

  Robert Frank doesn't ask
  Anyone's permission
  He invites himself
  Like Brueghel
  He channels the motif
  The long white line
  Between sour and sweet
  Between daddy long legs
  And what will they say
  About me if I don't
  Show up for work

You are
They are
We are Americans

                        Pause

"Trolley – New Orleans" is a terrific introduction to the book. Frank uses it for the cover. Two white adults, two white children and two black adults look out of separated windows. Only one adult is not looking at the photographer. It's a black woman sitting at the end of the trolley. She is interested in something else besides being photographed.

Robert Frank took 28,000 photographs on his trek across America. Eighty-five photographs are in *The Americans*. When I first looked through the book I saw a random choice of dissociated photographs. Not so. Frank is deliberate. His selection of photographs avoids making conclusions. It is a long poem. He captures the poor, the rich, the ignorant, the lonely poetry of a nation that can't understand whites and blacks separated by expectations their positions in the community and why are they so often fearful and miserable.

There are men and women who look at Frank and wish he would drop dead. There are those who don't give a hoot and there are the workers and the politicians. She stands behind a counter he whispers into another man's ear. The Jukebox is playing. Her belly is swollen. Is there enough food. A woman who wears a strapless gown and in her hand she has a cigarette that she uses to distract her victims. New York is not the South. You have to go to Hollywood to see a real blonde. And in Butte Montana if you want to join the Navy you'll have to wake up the recruiter. So be it. Cover your ears. Remember pick up your mail and go to the Drive-In. Have faith the field and the sky redeems salvation. Forgive the hotel in Miami where you sit and get rich and fat. During the daytime sleep in the park. And at night the great white line in the middle of the emptied highway sleeps.

        Be Rich Get Rich Be Rich Get Rich Be Rich

Philip Guston and Jackson Pollack were kicked out of high school for printing a subversive magazine. Not all but some angry young men become killers and a few grow up to become artists. There are always angry young men that are willing to face death daily.

                        Pause

St. Joseph, Missouri to California in 19 days or less.

1860
WANTED

YOUNG, SKINNY, WIRY FELLOWS

Not over eighteen. Must be expert riders, willing to risk death daily. Orphans preferred.

Wages $25 per week.

From April 1860 to October 1861 the Pony Express was the fastest way to get your message from the East to the West; and back again. The "*young, skinny, wiry fellows*" all had to weigh less than 125 lbs and had to cover the 1966 miles from St. Joseph, Missouri to Sacramento, California in ten days. Through every imaginable type of hardship they rode across the states of Kansas, Nebraska, Colorado, Wyoming, Utah, Nevada, and California. In October 1861 the telegraph wire was completed to the West Coast and the Pony Express was finished.

Some people stay
Some move
Some sit in a chair
Some carry a cross and
Some remember the dead and
Some before they die

Some before they die
Some drive by day
Some drive by night
Some drive with the lights on
Some drive with the lights off
Some with the windows closed
Some with the windows open

                          Pause

I knew a farmer in Celo North Carolina who told me about his dealings with a foreigner and I asked what country the man came from and he replied "the next county."

You are
They are
We are Americans

The Franks would arrive in a small town, where do they eat. Who should they talk to. Where do they stay the night.

All through the 1930s, during the Dust Bowl era, large numbers of farmers fleeing ecological disaster and the Great Depression migrated from the Great Plains and Southwest regions to California mostly along U.S. Route 66. More of the migrants were from Oklahoma than any other state, and a total of approximately 15% of the Oklahoma population left for California.

Robert Frank crossed the states of Kansas, Nebraska, Colorado, Wyoming, Utah, Nevada, and California. If he travelled alone or when he had his wife and two children with him Robert Frank was conspicuous.

He wore glasses
He didn't wear a tie
He didn't shine his shoes
He wore restless
He had poetry
He had prose
He had a beautiful wife

Pause

Till the End of Time released in 1946, the same year as *The Best Years of Our Lives*.

The story concentrates on three ex-marines: Bill Tabeshaw (Robert Mitchum), Perry Kincheloe (Bill Williams) and Cliff Harper (Guy Madison). Harper comes home from the war a troubled man. His mother and father are unable to listen to what their son has to say. They insist nothing has changed. Cliff meets Pat Ruscomb (Dorothy McGuire). She is a war widow distraught and lonely, she drinks too much. Cliff falls in love with Pat. He woos her she hesitates. He is tense she is in shock.

Tabeshaw endures one disappointment after another as he tries to buy his own ranch; and Kincheloe, rendered legless by the war, intends to spend the rest of his life wallowing in self-pity. All three men find a new lease of life when they engage in a cathartic barroom brawl against a bigoted group of self-styled patriots led by hate-spouting Ray Teal (forever typecast as a rabid racist during the post-war years). It was this climactic scene (outside of its Chopin-inspired theme song) that caused a lot of headaches for producer Dore Schary, screenwriter Allen Rivkin and director Edward Dmytryk during the House Un-American Activities hearings a few years later: what was accepted as pro-American in 1946 would soon be labelled "Pinko" by the anti-Red zealots. — Hal Erickson, *All Movie Guide*

> Pause

1947 was the year I came to America. I was two months shy of my twelfth birthday. I could not explain it but the sky was higher than the sky I knew in England and everything looked bigger, there was so much space. I saw a white man put his hand on a black man's back and I thought he was going to hang him. It doesn't matter what your upbringing is it is a shock to come to this country. It's a high and when you first arrive you hallucinate. Some immigrants become terrified and some become greedy. I couldn't believe there were foods that I'd never seen before. Everyone in my mother's family had a car and went to the movies once a week. Transplanted I put on my first long pants and memorized car grills. I learnt I must not spell a-e-r-o-p-l-a-n-e but I must spell a-i-r-p-l-a-n-e, and I was not to say whilst.

> Leave home. Meet strangers. And learn to draw.

DICTATION

A voice that is not your own tells you the draftsman Saul Steinberg's line exposes solace and challenges sentimentality. Sentimentality, maker of war, inventor of borders, shaman of greed, portrays itself as hope.

Oh Jew, you serve justice but it so rarely serves you.

January 10, 1963. Steinberg writes to his friend Aldo Buzzi: "I work my 2-3 hours a day, and looking at what I've done, I can see that I rid myself of terrors etc. by drawing them in a comic way – in the manner of savages – and so what I draw is part of a diary."

A diary not my diary
A diary. But it is my diary
The one I've never written
The one I'm about to write
The one that if I'd already
Written would I have to write

>Leave home. Meet strangers. And learn to draw.

Jury duty. I'm panelled. It's a civil case and I'm made foreman. The judge is an African American woman. She wears glasses, a black turtleneck and a string of pearls. The cornrows show off the shape of her face, and when she raises her arms and the sleeves of her judge's robes slip down, and you can see that lentigo covers both arms. The lawyer for the plaintiff is doing his first case. The lawyer for the corporation that's being sued is a seasoned warhorse.

And the stenographer, her large presence demands our, that is the jury's, attention. When we are closeted in the jury room all of us have something to say about her. She never looks at the jury, the judge or the lawyers. She wears cheap stretch pants and tops that expose her large breasts. Is she bored. Sometimes her face shows contempt. In her heart the judge, the lawyers, the plaintiff and the jury are all guilty. She rarely asks for anything to be repeated and I don't think she memorizes anything that she hears.

I was coming back from lunch and I saw her in the hallway. Is she divorced, maybe her husband is dead maybe if her husband is alive he too eats too much. Maybe she was never married. Everything that is precious to her is in her pocketbook. Cigarettes, cell phone, her lover. He never lies, never gives false witness. He knows that justice had failed her. That the soft bag that she holds under her arm is there to absolve her of her guilt. She feels guilty. She doesn't want to wear judge's robes or be a lawyer; she wants to be a Marine, a drill sergeant. She wants to be in charge and give dictation, not take it.

Be Rich. Get Rich. Be Rich. Get Rich.

Sitting on a stool at the counter of the Fifth Avenue Diner having a Spanish omelette they make great omelettes. Four stools to my left a young Marine, a lance corporal. The Marine's shoes shine, they glow. His back is like a broomstick. His uniform is pressed and his head is partially shaved. He wears a few medals. He wipes his knife and fork with his napkin before he begins to eat. He eats slowly, methodically, never dropping a crumb. He doesn't own the shoes, the shirt, the uniform, the underwear that he wears. It isn't Socialism. There is nothing altruistic about any of the armed services. All the services supply their enlisted men with food, clothing, medical care, and clean sheets. They follow orders and are dictated to by officers and the medieval rote of the drill sergeant. Memorize what I tell you. This is all you will ever have to know.

Memorize. Isn't that what all communities tell those who enlist. If you want to belong never forget it.

The Marine picks up a clean napkin and wipes his hands. Is about to pay when the waitress tells him that a gentleman sitting in the booth behind me wants to talk to him. He goes over to the booth. An old man shakes his hand. Tells the young Marine that he'd been a Marine in the Second World War. That he'd fought in the Pacific. He asks him how are they treating you. "They can be pretty brutal." The young Marine says there's a sergeant. Have you been out of the country. Yes, did a tour in Iraq. No. They told us we weren't going back. Well, good luck and take care of yourself. The two Marines saluted each other. The old man's wife kept her smile. She was proud of her husband. He was proud that he'd fought for his country.

The young Marine paid for his meal adjusted his hat and left the restaurant.

Sitting in the booth the old man looked a lot taller. He has a cane. And as the three of us were leaving the restaurant I held the door open. She smiled and he thanked me. I said, "You're welcome."

When we walk we carry frailty in our shoes
When we cut a piece of bread

We hold frailty in our hands
When we have contempt for humour
We do ourselves and everyone else an injustice

Will I ever stop waking up at night thinking about war, about dictators their first and only concern is self-protection.

Pause

Franz Kafka, you are different, something got to you, something struck you, maybe it only touched you but whatever it was, it was profound, and for the rest of your life your imagination was aroused replenished by a surreal ardour that compliments fantasy. You heard and you saw that purity is the curse of the twentieth century.

Kafka is learning Hebrew. He intends to go to Palestine.

Oh Jew, you serve justice but it so rarely serves you.

Kafka's gentility frightens his father. His father says he is a German. He ignores Kafka and smothers himself between Kafka's mother's breasts. She would have supported her son but she loves her husband more.

Kafka is sick
His chest is crowded
It heaves and coughs
The room is crowded
shadows
Talk to the crease
That he always wants
His pants to have
Kafka speaks to Steinberg
Steinberg knows where the entrances
And the exits are to every country
He has been in

In Vienna Kafka walks
Not always in a straight line
Imagine his contradictions
His social and religious beliefs
He was known to have fallen
Off his chair laughing as he read
One of his stories
To a group of his friends

Pause

Saul Steinberg had wanted to be an architect.

Steinberg leaves Romania, leaves Paris, leaves London. Who stays. Diane Arbus leaves her husband. Diane Arbus never stops. In her writing and her photographs she never stops telling what it is like to be Diane Arbus.

In a black and white photograph Diane Arbus has the tallest Jew in the world look down at his parents. He doesn't know who they are and they don't know who he is. A young man who is taller than the ceiling has to think about it. He's the tallest Jew in the world. There's not enough room in Israel for him to lie down and go to sleep. His feet are in Galilee, and his head is on a cross. He speaks in tongues. People think he is the Son of God. He tries to tell them that he isn't but no one understands what he is saying.

Build a city with towers that reproach the bigots before they have a chance to open their mouths. Is every Romanian a surrealist. Is every Jew who visits Israel a better Jew. A Diane Arbus twin a man-child who would be a woman makes overtures to a dog that has just had its nails clipped.

Steinberg went to Israel and he loved being surrounded by Jews. But he didn't stay.

What would have happened if Lot's wife hadn't looked back. What would have happened if they had gone to Israel. I can only speculate that the roots of all our imaginations begin with a desire to understand good and evil. Dear justice your scale is indifferent. You have no heart. Abstract forces, briefs that are on-going dictation, propel you.

There is so much to remember that the past is known to give incorrect information. Check it out. Not everything that is written is a lesson sifted through sand.

Pause

Kafka sees they are getting closer, closer. Best to look in the mirror and make sure of who you are. They will never tell you. They will tell you you are not you. You are a person who was but is no more. You are a person who is obscene, was obscene and is now obsolete, redundant. And as they pass you they don't even look at you. They don't see you. You are of no interest. You do not exist.

Kafka has no place, no house of his own, no woman that he is sure of. He is unsure of his body and he doesn't trust. Contemplation gives Kafka his humour. Yes, he laughs. No, he never cries. Yes, he likes to swim. Atlantic, Pacific – relative to justice the ocean is unbiased. It favours no one it condemns no one.

A diary not my diary.
A diary. But it is my diary.
The one I've never written.
The one I'm about to write.
The one that if I'd already
Written would I have to write.

> Leave home. Meet strangers. And learn to draw.

Saul Steinberg and his wife Hedda Sterne were at The Club last night. I got cold feet. I didn't know what to say to him. I didn't want to make myself conspicuous but I kept looking over. If he saw me he never let on. Steinberg had drawn a small mural in one of the corners of the Detroit Museum and I remember wondering how had he drawn it. It looked like one continuous line. Had he drawn it without stopping. And if he had how did he know where to go.

In those days things came at me faster than I could digest them. Arshile Gorky's work in *Art News* – I'd never seen a line like that before. His line was a line to remember. Alberto Giacometti was having a show. His figures looked as if they were walking across the floor of the museum. I didn't understand them. It wasn't until I read Beckett that I began to understand Giacometti.

> Pause

When we walk we carry frailty in our shoes
When we cut a piece of bread
We hold frailty in our hands
When we have contempt for humour
We do ourselves and everyone else an injustice

Will I ever stop waking up at night thinking about war, about dictators. Their first and only concern is self-protection.

A voice that is not your own tells you. There are people who hear voices other than their own. Who answer those voices and some of them have been known to take photographs.

DICTATION 55

Pause

The first time Jerry Shore got high was in our loft on Delancey Street. Jerry stood in front of the mirror and made faces at himself in the same way Rembrandt did when he drew himself for first time. Every thirty seconds Jerry made another face. Every other minute Jerry gave his body another shape. Jerry Shore came to New York to be a painter. I remember he said he wanted money. And he made it. With a painter's sense of space and a young man's hard-on Jerry made Pepsi, Revlon, and Maybelline ads and thirty-second and one-minute TV commercials I remember the Pepsi commercials, they were brilliant.

Jerry talked about the long hours in the editing room and how after days of being in the dark the crew would come out and go to Paris and spend money. Money. Jerry gave money to his parents and his brothers. He'd take six people to dinner. Three of the six want work, two want his bed, it was something to watch. When he was on the phone to his agent or his clients he was the boss. It was like being in the movies, and Jerry was the producer. He was organizing the lighting as he spoke. He saw the close-ups and the distance that he would have to have to keep it all organized. It was fast and competitive and Jerry thrived on it. I saw a lot of Jerry's black and white photographs. Naked whores in Brazil or Argentina. The two women are not ashamed of being photographed and Jerry wasn't ashamed of having photographed them. And then there are the Girl Scouts, boys and girls marching bands in the Mid-West, towels drying on a fence on Long Island. I can't remember anything that he did in colour. He'd shmear the camera lens so that there was a kind of shimmered muted tone to the photos. They were like the Jerry I'd first known, shy and hesitant.

David Glotzer, Basil King, and Harry Lewis in the late sixties and early seventies edited a magazine called *Mulch*. Jerry gave me some of these early black and white photographs for two of the covers.

Pause

We didn't see Jerry after we came back from Michigan in the mid-70s. The last I'd heard of Jerry was that he'd come back from Hollywood and that he was drinking. That his friends were making sure he had some work. So he wouldn't go hungry. That he was taking photographs just about every day was never mentioned. That things had changed and big money jobs were no longer available to Jerry doesn't explain to me why he drank. If all Jerry wanted was money he would have found another way to make it. Jerry didn't need drink to do his commercial jobs, for him that was easy. He drank so that he could do the work that was hard and not easily available.

For those who can use it booze opens a door to a thin almost invisible wall that has to be gotten through to get to the things that you need. I'm not interested in romanticizing booze. But I know Guston the painter, Spicer the poet, and Jerry the photographer used booze to succeed.

There are no people
In any of Jerry's photographs from the 1980s
All of Jerry's photographs are beautiful
Composed of colour space and light
They are paintings
Light and space surrounds the beaches
Counters and stools at the amusement parks
Of the Jersey Shore
In the New York City
Streets driveways back lots
Industrial buildings and houses
Always there is space and light
But there are no people

Jerry Shore grew up in Philadelphia. The painters George Catlin, Thomas Eakins and the poet H.D. lived in Philadelphia. Only Eakins stayed. I don't know how many American cities have a lot of Red walls. In *The New Yorker*, Adam Gopnik says that Shore seems to have carried a paint can of the red he liked with him; some inauspicious walls suddenly appear covered with it.

I didn't know that Jerry had died in 1994 at the age of fifty-nine until Mark Melnick was designing my book, *77 Beasts/Basil King's Beastiary*. He asked me if I knew of a photographer by the name of Jerry Shore. And he scanned a *New Yorker* column for me, "A Critic at Large, Jerry Shore's New York, and Ours," by Adam Gopnik.

Have you ever gotten lost
Did you see anything
You hadn't seen before
Did you like what you saw
Were you frightened
Did you start to walk fast
Take longer strides
Did you lose weight
Did you answer
All these questions

There's a bug crawling up a mound that sprouts a pyramid. Philip Guston's father keeps appearing from behind a brick wall. One-eyed Guston is surrounded by red paint. Guston eats a sandwich, smokes a cigarette. He hasn't shined his shoes in years. What is left on the canvas is about Philip's father's junkyard and has nothing to do with suicide.

Pause

The young lance corporal has become a sergeant and he's home on leave. He owns a car. He drives down to the Supreme Court Building on Adams Street in Brooklyn to meet his mother who is on a jury. His mother tells him she had lunch with the stenographer and she would like him to meet her. The stenographer has lost a lot of weight. She has changed. No more stretch pants, no more tops that expose her. Instead she is dressed appropriately. He likes her and he gets her cell phone number. They have dinner in an Italian restaurant and he drives her home to Staten Island. He has stopped the car in front of her house and she grabs his balls. What she doesn't show: she is angry. She says, "If you catch me give me a face, a body that is strong and able. Then when I breathe I will be the strange skinny girl with good legs who defies the knife and feeds the sharp edge of anger." He says to her my balls don't belong to me. Only this car belongs to me. I am a sergeant in the United States Marines and they own me. You have to know this before we go into the house.

IN THE FIELD WHERE DAFFODILS GROW

Mirror, mirror on the wall. In the field where Daffodils grow there is an abundance of Narcissus. Daisy chains are worn by all. Buttercups wind their way through a chorus singing a Sunday hymn. Marsden Hartley draws his genitals but decides not to paint them. Instead he paints a group of tall men. He loves these men. He has always loved men. He has sung himself to sleep knowing he will dream about men. A man's shoulders, his gait and his stride, the way he covers the ground with his shadow. Mirror, mirror on the wall. Marsden Hartley was unable to applaud himself for having sympathy for birds and fish. On land a narrow brush paints a Red shirt. Red roses, Red lobsters, tomatoes.

Harsh articles for a dish using everything that was left over from three previous meals. Mirror, mirror on the wall. Marsden Hartley is tall. It annoys him that he is always being told that he is photogenic. That his nose is Roman. That he postures. Mirror, mirror on the wall. Don't make the cloud too dark. Let the light show that a tall young man can have fun being alone. That his thighs are, as his lips are, human. Mirror, mirror on the wall. Remember Mount Katahdin. Remember that for Marsden Hartley, man is big. He is a hero, a mountain, a poetic combination of bather, wrestler and lumberjack. He said, "I want the whole body, the whole flesh, in painting." Painting isn't a race. There is no finish line. If it fails begin again. Mirror, mirror on the wall. Marsden Hartley was so poor that on his fifty-eighth birthday, January 4, 1935, in a "massacre of the innocents", he destroyed 100 paintings and drawings. He had no place to store them. It was imperative that he keep painting. It was imperative that the future be considered.

Mirror, mirror on the wall. Do not use literature to explain love. Marsden Hartley travelled, crossed bridges, met strangers, and learned to draw. Give him paint. He paints the sea, rocks. Fish on a plate, men, waves. Marsden Hartley said, "I love to paint."

Pause

Ezra Pound had met Hilda at a birthday party. Hilda was fifteen, and Pound and Williams were in college. She became Pound's girl. Williams may have had a crush on her but she frightened him. She never listened to him. She listened to Pound. Her courage and her erratic behaviour put

Williams and H.D. at odds with each other. Hilda Doolittle would hike up her skirts and run through the fields abandoning herself. In the field where Daffodils grow there is an abundance of Narcissus. Daisy chains are worn by all. Buttercups wind their way through a chorus singing a Sunday hymn. Let the light show that William Carlos Williams was introduced to Hilda Doolittle by Ezra Pound. She was tall. Taller than most of her contemporaries. Let the light show that a tall young girl's thighs are, as her lips are, human. Did Dr. Williams disapprove. It's possible. Let the light show that the great poet from New Jersey was complicated. He and his contemporary Charles Demuth threw caution to the wind and went on to claim for themselves a territory as vagrant as history, as varied as the paintings of Bruegal. In *In the American Grain* Williams makes Daniel Boone, George Washington, Aaron Burr initiate their own space as do the calligraphic characters on a Chinese scroll.

>Pause

>Whereas a drawing is always contemporary
>A short story never ends.
>Greek narcissus. French daffodils.
>Asphodel.
>Calligraphy is for lovers.

>Pause

H.D. looks across the room at a large painting hanging on a wall. She studies the painting.

>Mirror, mirror on the wall.
>Paintings stay alive because people look at them.
>And when they don't, they die.
>They die in museums, in private collections, in
>artists' studios. They die leaving an heir
>a hue of monochrome thoughts.
>I have died but I am not dead.
>I live on a wall in a house
>that is warm and comfortable.
>The people who live in this house
>pass me every day.
>They always make sure
>that I'm hung right.
>My edges are dusted
>my surface is clean.
>But they never stand back and look at me.

> I have travelled
> in group shows
> and been seen in countless museums.
> I am worth a lot of money.
> H.D. has brought me back to life
> and I thank her
> and hope the pleasure
> that I saw on her face
> will be repeated.

Pause

William Carlos Williams and H.D. cross the street. Williams is saying something that we do not hear. The Precisionists are pacifists; their arguments take place in manifestoes. A Precisionist painting has no traffic, no commerce, no people. Riff-raff and garbage are removed. Deceit and arrogance are removed. Our eyes behold muted operas, empty buildings. Where are the children. Their presence would demand an answer to a question that is being evaded. Where is nature. H.D. wonders why the lights are on. Who benefits from having the electricity on in a building that excludes people. The object benefits. The object doesn't need the disclosure of the painter's presence, his brush stroke or his emotions. No one need paint a painting. An object that is bathed in light and focused with utmost clarity and precision creates a state of "perfect consciousness," so said Charles Sheeler (1883-1965).

William Carlos Williams asks H.D. do you remember the drawing you did. Well, Charles Sheeler said about your drawing, "I just don't want to see any more than is absolutely necessary of the physical materials that go into a picture." Sheeler used photography as a standard to measure painting against. Sheeler's impersonal attitude disturbed Williams. He saw Sheeler becoming judgmental. But what was Williams to do. What were Williams and Sheeler to do. They both want to take H.D's arm and go around the corner with her. Before H.D. has a chance to speak, a large woman pushing a baby carriage comes around the corner.

Emily Carr pays no attention to H.D. or the two men. She is busy having a conversation with the occupants of the carriage: A monkey, some dogs, and some cats. Light became Emily Carr's oar. With it she navigated her family on their nightly constitutional.

Pale face, what gives us permission to do or not do what we want. Pigment. The colour of sex. The colour of choice. Beware, the tattoo is too permanent. Is it thick skin, thin skin, rough, or beautiful skin that makes the difference. Or does skin have absolutely nothing to do with giving ourselves permission to do what we want.

Emily Carr was to say: You have to meet everything half way. Everything but paint needs a handshake, a smile, a greeting of hello and goodbye. Everything but paint will meet you half way. But not paint. No. Paint lays its plastic body out, and I trust it.

I don't know if having your work ignored is good for you. I don't know if it makes you work harder; I don't know if it makes you more sad, more depressed, but I do know if you hadn't had to do something in your childhood that was almost heroic, you would never be able to tolerate being ignored. You would meet everything and everyone halfway, or change your mind and become domestic.

Born in 1871, died in 1945, Emily Carr lived a life overshadowed by something that frightened her. As a teenager, she recoiled from explanation or forgiveness, and presumed the world was against her. She didn't become a criminal, an enemy of the state; she became different. Her republic became her life, and she documented it. Not with people, but with totems, skies, dogs, cats, and a monkey.

Emily Carr painted trees with skins, not bark. Skins, the colour of sex, the colour of choice, the colour of her autobiography. Sitting in the forest of British Columbia, she asked herself, how can I put myself together. How can my many components become one, one with nature, one with the forest that both frightens and awes me.

Wood Interior 1932-35

Emily Carr

> Men whisper as they hunt
> they cover their tracks
>   with thistle
>   and a malice
>   towards Sappho
>   explains
>   the darkness
>
> Men whisper as they hunt
> they cover their tracks
>   with thistle

and a malice
towards Sappho
explains
the darkness

Men whisper as they hunt
they cover their tracks
   with thistle
and a malice
towards Sappho
explains
the darkness

A large and strong-willed woman, she has been to San Francisco, London, Paris, and New York. But always comes back to Vancouver, the root of displeasure, the root of her colour.

Above the fir trees, there is a land she has come to know as the sky of natural history. There in the sky, where everything is forward, and yesterday is tomorrow, colour finds a creation that is not style. Aunt Emily wanted a rainbow, a spectrum of fish that she could drop into the mist and spray the trees with.

Aunt Emily was to say: I don't go to anyone. I lie in bed alone. I dream alone. I eat alone. Art is grace. What would the critics have to say if the artists did not do their work? What law, what fairytale speaks to everyone? Hush, listen, see: the forest unloads its secrets. Sometimes, I use house paint and add gasoline to get fluidity. It dilutes the colour and loosens the forms, and the critics don't like this. They say my work has become disquieting and is losing its fascination. Well, I know when my heart pounds, and I don't need to meet anyone half way.

On some parts of my body the skin divides into thicknesses, from cheek to thigh, from ear to toe, and I feel, and I hurt, and I forget nothing. Memory – is it now fifty years or is it more than that, that I can remember. What I don't remember, I don't forget. A short story. An Indian tale. A beaver. A repeat. Come, monochrome, hue me. The art or process of producing such a picture depresses me and I am unable to give myself permission to enjoy what is rightfully mine.

Cedar. Pine. I am as durable as wood. Cedar. Pine. Your skin, your weathered skin, your coniferous skin, gently airs mine and renews it. Everything about you explains the glorious beauty of reproduction, the holiness and joy of it.

Pale face. Aunt Emily was never married. She never had a mate, someone to teach her the things that they knew. She was a wild card. She came to know. You have to meet everything half way. Everything but paint needs a handshake, a smile, a greeting of hello and goodbye. Everything but paint will meet you half way. But not paint. No. Paint lays its plastic body out, and I trust it.

I don't know if having your work ignored is good for you. I don't know if it makes you work harder; I don't know if it makes you more sad, more depressed, but I do know if you hadn't had to do something in your childhood that was almost heroic, you would never be able to tolerate being ignored.

You would meet everything and everyone halfway, or change your mind and become domestic.

Be Rich. Get Rich. Be Rich. Get Rich.

Let the light show the doctor instructs his patients. He tells them stories.

Pause

Giotto (1266/7-1337) when asked to supply proof of his artistic skill for the pope, complied by drawing a perfect circle with a single fluent movement.

Waslaw Nijinsky (1890-1950) and his sister understood that if they were to become modern choreographers they would have to be explicit.

Nijinsky's wife Romola reported that by 1918 Nijinsky had become fascinated with circles and arcs. She recalls his telling her, "The circle is the complete, the perfect movement. Everything is based on it – life, art." Nijinsky was planning a Renaissance ballet with circular choreography, curved scenery, and a rounded proscenium. His notation system was based in part on the circle, and his drawings, as he notes, often involved an eye shape formed by the joining of two arcs. Nijinsky seems to visualize a theatre designed to imitate the curve of the eye. With obsessive consistency, Nijinsky composed circles and arcs. The arcs seem to form eyes, and Nijinsky says they do: "I often draw one eye." Those "eyes" also look like fish, the sign of Christ. They also look like the female genitals, the thing that, in his conversion to Tolstoyanism, he had renounced.

Pause

Did Rembrandt know the story of Giotto's O when he painted his "Self Portrait with Two Circles" (1665-9).

The man who had once wanted to emulate Rubens stands right of centre, between two half circles. Gone are the dandy's clothes. The look of "I got ya!" Instead we see an old man who looks at us without hostility. His clothes are tattered, his posture sturdy; he apologizes for nothing. He is a painter. And he has painted his own portrait. Rembrandt believes that the two circles behind him are important. They circumvent his loneliness and he emerges as the Rembrandt we remember, a man alone, secure in his neutrality to all things hostile. Yes, the circles fill in the space and augment the background. They are as decorative as they are patient. Without them Rembrandt would never have been able to blur his hands and keep "Self Portrait with Two Circles" ambiguous.

> When next you draw. Please remember
> to say good morning,
> good evening will return the compliment.

> When next you paint. Please remember,
> to draw is to trust.

Pause

A mother puts her daughter to bed, reads, kisses the child's forehead, and leaves the bedroom door slightly ajar. The hall light brings philosophy into the room.

The daughter will not know until she is a grown woman that all the stories that her mother read to her were made up to frighten her. The mother did not want her child to grow up. She wanted her daughter to always be with her. The daughter's love of knowledge made that impossible.

Pause

Virginia Stephens, Leonard Woolfe, bless them. They marry when she is thirty. Three years after their marriage Virginia publishes her first novel, *The Voyage Out*. The novel had taken her seven years to write. Leonard is a meticulous man. Virginia is vivacious. She is electricity, she wants to be a mother. Leonard won't allow it. Alfred Stieglitz wouldn't let Georgia O'Keefe have a child and she never forgave him. Did Virginia forgive Leonard. Leonard doesn't want the responsibility of children. He has become the wife, the good wife Woolfe cares for Virginia. He tells her if it fails, begin again. He tells her the voices that she hears are not as important as she is. He tells her, Sing crunch! He will not leave her. He will not forfeit her trust. Because her older sister Vanessa stands when she paints, Virginia has to stand at a podium when she writes. The sisters compete for nursery rhythms, for stones. Sing crunch! They are sisters.

Vanessa had three children, two sons with her husband, Clive Bell, and a daughter with Duncan Grant. All the time Vanessa lived with Clive Bell he had male lovers. When Vanessa and Duncan Grant lived together Duncan Grant had male lovers. Vanessa and Roger Fry were lovers. After she suffered a serious miscarriage while on holiday in Turkey, it was Roger who nursed Vanessa, not Clive.

No one told Vanessa that she was important. No one told her that she too could find amazement. Vanessa served and partied, and when her son Julian was killed in the Spanish Civil War, she cried alone.

> Mother, I am hungry. I haven't eaten all day. It's cook's day off and no one will make me a sandwich.
>
> No one will feed me.
> No one no one knows
> I haven't taken
> a bath in four days. I haven't
> brushed my teeth. I haven't combed my hair.
> My bed isn't made. And my shoelaces
> are untied.

Vanessa had a lot to contend with. She always did. She had protected Virginia before Virginia's marriage to Leonard. No one told her if it fails, begin again. No one told Vanessa, "I support you."

Vanessa's woodcuts for the covers of her sister's books are thoughtful, delightful bits of domesticity, less hurried than her paintings. There's a charming flower pot for *The Common Reader*, a clock for *A Room of One's Own*. Vanessa had gone to art school and continued to be an art student till the day she died. There was always something else to do. She decorated her houses and painted views of the garden, coffee pots, empty bottles, armchairs. And there was always talk. Every day and every weekend there was talk. But no one supported Vanessa as Leonard Woolfe supported Virginia.

Bloomsbury buzzed as it created a gracious Bohemia, a style of living that is today, with contemporary variations, still in fashion. Bloomsbury baked their own breads, and Virginia was known for her bread. They made jams, bottled fruits, and they travelled. They painted their furniture and kept their household help to a minimum. With the exception of Leonard who was Jewish and was one of nine children, Bloomsbury came from privilege. Their families were socially established and moneyed. Virginia's great aunt was the photographer Julia Margaret Cameron. Lytton Strachey's family had helped Disraeli secure his seat in the Houses of Parliament. Clive Bell was the son of wealthy mine owners. Leonard's father went broke while Leonard was attending Cambridge.

In 1912, a year after Roger Fry had nursed Vanessa, he curated the now famous Post Impressionist show that featured Matisse, Picasso, and Cézanne. The English public, for the most part, ignored or mocked the show.

Cézanne's male and female figures meditate. Vanessa Bell, Duncan Grant, Roger Fry, and Dora Carrington admired Cézanne. Not one of them was able to absorb his inherent belief that violence precedes thinking.

Did Bloomsbury, that epicentre of social experimentation, forgive Leonard and Virginia for starting The Hogarth Press. The thing that was most important to all of Bloomsbury and its extended family was comfort. Hogarth Press had deadlines, responsibilities. Hogarth Press affected the lives of everyone in the immediate Bloomsbury group. Manuscripts were accepted or refused. Art was published or rejected. The press did not always do what Bloomsbury expected. Bloomsbury thrived on good food, an appreciation of writing, and painting. But comfort – comfort was essential. Not business.

And all the while, Paul Cézanne's little sensations go on kissing his maternal motif, space. The apples on the table become ripe and juicy and take on the appearance of a living atlas. Space swallows up the painter's arm. The painter cannot free himself. The arm is lost. Cadmiums that had never felt secure on their own now dance. The painter feels movement. Can it be that the arm is constructing "The Large Bathers." Can it be that all Cézanne's bathers have been recruited to do perverse things. They sleep with nature, they fuck with turmoil, they pose a problem. Cézanne's bathers wear no Armour. Their heads are not covered, their bodies are naked. They are philosophy's love of knowledge. As Cézanne was to write to a young artist, "Perception of the model and its realization are sometimes very long in coming…"

Close your eyes, breathe.

Cézanne intrudes. He is a rapist. He penetrates his totem. The totem cries mercy, but mercy does not come. With extended arms the totem's legs grow feet. Its hands hold a ball in the air that is then placed onto a neck. Eyes appear. Ears, nose, and mouth correlate the face. Devastation is complete. The mountain has a mate.

> No one
> can pronounce
> your Cat's name.
>
> Who paid
> for your
> Glasses.
>
> Who feeds
> the Cat.
>
> Who tithes.
>
> Who airs
> the androgynous
> Ocean
>
> Who
> climbs
> the Mountain.
>
> Who Asks
> but never
> Answers.
>
> Who vanishes.
>
> Who points.
>
> Who corrects.
>
> Who dismisses.

The creatures that sit in the trees are birds. Winged reptiles that remind us that we cannot fly. That we who paint can move. If not mountains, we can move ourselves and find an edge so sharp that just touching it bleeds the negative. When excavating the art of a thousand years past, the tablecloth mulches, the breast triumphs, and the edge uncurls.

"WE ARE HOME."

There is more.

Leave home, meet strangers, and learn to draw. Green will not always tolerate Blue. The sculptor Henry Moore owned a small Cézanne "Bather". The painter Jasper Johns owns a small Cézanne "Bather".

> A source
> as sturdy
> as an arch
> will always have
> an entrance
> and an exit.
> Close your eyes,
> breathe.
> If the sun shines,
> the snow will melt.
> She contemplates.
> She has the body.
> She clothes herself
> in Still Lifes.
> Before sleep
> She opens the door.
> She dismounts.
> Her libido rages.
> Her landscape
> refuses to walk
> behind what she knows
> does not exist.

SOLO

Stored in Robert Stroud's mind was the knowledge that betrayal is a crime. Fifty-four years in jail this self-taught untutored scientist breeds three hundred birds, writes two books on bird diseases and their cures, and writes a history of the penal system in America. Stroud was 18 years old when he killed a man who beat and raped his girlfriend. Robert Stroud turned himself in to the police and a harsh and perverse Judge who wanted to make a name for himself and "teach offenders a lesson" sentenced Stroud to twelve years imprisonment. Robert Stroud (1890-1963) quit school and left home at the age of 13. For four years he does odd jobs, stays out of jail, and grows to be 6' 3". When he is 17 he comes home to his abusive father and distraught mother. He leaves within the year and the rest is history.

The Bird Man of Alcatraz wrote two books on bird diseases and their cures and a history of the penal system in America. In prison he murders an abusive guard and stabs a fellow inmate for betraying him. All of his visiting privileges are revoked. Not even his family is permitted to see him. He marries, but he and his wife never live together. Because of the laws of Kansas, the authorities are unable to transfer him out of Leavenworth as his wife lives in the state. When his wife moves, he is transferred to Alcatraz, and his birds and all his equipment are taken away. Day after day he reads. Robinson Crusoe's loneliness cannot be imagined. Did Stroud count how many steps he took to get to the exercise yard and then back to his cell.

The distance between the artist and the criminal is but a hair's breadth apart. Write a poem, paint a painting, draw. Icarus is getting closer to the sun. His father King Daedelus warns him not to. But with each flight Icarus obsesses.

December 17, 1903, the Wright brothers fly for the first time.

May 20-21, 1927. Charles Augustus Lindbergh (Lucky Lindy) age 27 is a soloist. He flies his plane "The Spirit of St. Louis," from New York to Paris without accompaniment, he is alone. Tell Icarus to retrieve his feathers. Lindbergh doesn't want his coat. He would never wear it. He would never let his heart melt. He wants purity, a race without blemish.

Tell them Birdman, passion endures. Stroud is also doing solo, he's in solitary confinement. He too has a destination, sanity, he must keep it. If he doesn't he will slip away and never be seen or heard of again. Birdman, tell them, tell them about kindness, tell them justice comes first. Tell them you've heard the telling.

Birds

The young of any feathered
Vertebrate or, later, of
Any animal; any member
Of a class of warm-blooded
Vertebrates, distinguished
From all other animals
By the body being more
Or less completely
Covered with feathers

Someone by the name of Bill
Is covered with feathers

Free, free at last, hold on to justice. Hold on. Stroud paces like a caged Tiger. He knifes an inmate (stool pigeon) for telling the guards that he stole some food. Please Sir, can I have some more. Who in their right minds can deny the question with a negative answer. Tell them, Gruenwald. Christ suffered because he was in pain. He was hungry and tortured by the nails in his body. Tell them, Birdman. Tell them, Charlie Parker, Uccello sings. Tell them, we birds flock into Stroud's cell. Who else can bring the sun into his cell but we birds. Bitterness is a disease, as volatile as cancer. Who else but the artist can understand the anti-social behaviour of an angry man.

Pause

George Catlin spent only a few years in what he considered "real Indian country." The rest of his life was devoted to promoting, repainting, and trying to sell his collection, his Indian Gallery.

Be Rich. Get Rich. Be Rich. Get Rich.

Catlin wanted the American government to buy his Indian Gallery; he wanted their patronage. He never gave up trying. Letters to Congress, to well-heeled, well-placed men, petition after petition, Washington politicians, European royalty, millionaires. Everyone refused.

Catlin's wife and son died in Europe. He sent his three girls home to the United States. He stayed, convinced that what he had chronicled was important. He said he wasn't after fame or fortune. He said he wanted to save, "how they lived, how they dressed, how they worshipped ... in the uncivilized regions of their uninvaded country." It was, "a vast country of green fields, where the men are all red."

> Pause

Catlin painted Indians. Native Americans.
Thousands of years ago they came from
a cold climate. They adjusted, before we
did, before the horse came, before the
Jesuits came; there was religion. Faith.
No man can create a universe that compromises
nature. The sky speaks. Braves, horses, squaws,
their children and the bears drink the same water. Buffalo hunts,
war dances, prairie fires, and Indians pursuing Indians. American
history.

Here comes the train. It is on time.
The conductor doesn't want you to spit
on the floor. It annoys the other passengers.
Here comes the steamboat. Slavery has
already taken its toll. Gold is discovered.
Wealth for some. Hardware for most.

George Catlin (1796-1872) went to
law school, passed the bar, but never
practiced. Something else besides the
practical seemed to precede his drive.
He thought he made plans, he didn't.
He became a painter. He painted miniatures
and portraits. Then he dropped portrait painting.

Catlin had to work fast. He wasn't
the only one. Delacroix's brush was
in and out of the Harem.

"Women of Algiers" 1834 – Eugene Delacroix

Gentle women you sit
you pose in contradictions
your bodies step over the silent
carpet. Only Red speaks. Olive.
White. Yellow. Red. Red, pale

soft thighs decorate the
cabinet, the Eunuch's Black skin.

Be Rich. Get Rich. Be Rich. Get Rich.

Delacroix never got married, never had children. By the time he was 45, most of his family had died. For three summers he visited George Sands and Frederick Chopin in Sands' country house and was treated by them as a member of the family.

The tale is told of how Delacroix, seeking to give emphasis to a yellow drapery, decides to go to the Louvre to see how Rubens would manage it. The cabs in Paris at that time were painted canary yellow, and Delacroix noticed that the cab standing in wait for him cast a violet shadow in the sunlight. This was the knowledge he sought; he paid the cabman and returned to work.

Eugene Delacroix (1798-1865) was fascinated with anything that was wild. In the zoo at the Jardin des Plantes, Delacroix draws two panthers showing the basic skin and bones that underlie the fur. In 1846 Delacroix watches a troupe of Ojibwa Indians dancing with war whoops and drums. The Ojibwa have been brought from Iowa to tour Europe by the American painter and ethnologist George Catlin. Delacroix sketches the event as it occurred, seeing in these American Indians the same classical dignity that excited him so much in the native Moroccans. Later he designs a poster, since lost, to help Catlin publicize the Ojibwas on their European tour.

Pause

It is 1850 and Eugene Delacroix takes a photograph of a young woman's back. Delacroix is one of the first painters to use photographs as a model.

The young woman cannot read and she doesn't know how to write her name. Men have promised her that they will teach her. But so far no one has. There are times when she is afraid of the men she poses for. So far no man has hurt her or demanded anything of her that she has been unable to give.

Her mother is always telling her that she should please the men she poses for. Her mother thinks that all artists are rich. The artist she lived with bought her a new hat, a dress, shoes and an umbrella. Then he told her he didn't want to see her anymore. She went home to her mother. Her mother and all of her mother's friends envied her; they had never been given new clothes.

Her brother said he was going to America. But instead he went to Canada, or where was it. She doesn't know. He never came back. Her brother was always kind to her. He was older and she thought he knew everything. He knew how to read and write. He said he would teach her what he knew. He never did.

She has acquired the pose of indifference. Surrounded by people that she neither loves or hates, she wants to live alone. She wants a cat, and she doesn't want the cat to go hungry. She hopes that she will never have children. She wants to take a train and not get lost. She wants to be able to read the newspaper.

Pause

Catlin knew there were Americans in and out of the government who wanted the Indians annihilated. The Indians weren't white, and they were not Christians; their only value was their land.

Catlin wanted the impossible. He wanted his contemporaries to change their policies, their minds. He wasn't greedy. Why were they. Couldn't they see their greed. It pained him, got under his skin … and he'd begin again. Another letter, another proposal. He wanted the Indians to remain on their lands. He wanted them to pray, and wash, and eat the way they had always done.

After thirty-two years in Europe Catlin and his Indian Gallery had become inseparable. His brother Francis finds him in 1870 doing what he always did, painting and writing letters. It is time for him to come home. At 72 Catlin is deaf and living in a cheap hotel in Brussels. He is still hunting for a patron.

Every day he goes down stairs to the cafe and eats steak and potatoes. He never digresses. He'd ask himself, why do I, year after year go on doing what I do. He thought he should know, but know what. He'd known self-hate. Every artist has known that. Why! And each time he asked why he would make another painting, another cartoon. He completed hundreds of them. They were all done from memory.

He came home to his three daughters, their husbands, and their children. He never forgot that the Plains Indians made their clothes and their tepees from buffalo hides. Catlin hadn't romantised this or made a Utopia of how the Indians lived. He had painted the Indians' forbearance, their love for the bear, deer, and porcupine that they hunted, ate, and worshipped. Catlin never forgot the Indians and he never forgot America's light.

Recall the Sparrow drinking next to the Cardinal, the silent Gold Fish, the three arguing Crows. Tell them, Birdman, Mozart loved the voice.

Remember the miniatures that they all wanted, the prints Akbar commissioned. Remember Rauschenberg's white paintings, the ones he wouldn't paint on, the organic metamorphosis, the passion he endured. Tell them, Birdman, America's light is never easy. If you pretend, you fail. If you want rewards, you are disappointed. I insist light abstracts the simplest things. Then beware, beware of pity. You have no one to compete with; you are alone. The competition among painters is always intense.

Pause

Catlin had no control over what might happen to his Indian Gallery. It could die of neglect, fatigue, be burned in a fire. Catlin thought of his Gallery and his cartoons as living things. As living things they could die of starvation. Be caught in a famine. Be forgotten as the Indians were being forgotten. Catlin taught himself not to be bitter, not to hate, not to sentimentalize his position. He had to be sure that he and his work were part of history.

Everyone needs something to look forward to. Catlin looked for the sale of his Indian Gallery. Catlin never completed the sale. After he died, his daughters were unsuccessful too. Mrs. Joseph Harrison, Jr. wife of the man who had taken possession of Catlin's Gallery after he'd paid off Catlin's debts in London – she, in 1879, made a gift of the original George Catlin Indian Gallery to the Smithsonian in Washington D.C.

Pause

A nineteen-year-old blonde with long legs, a short black skirt, and a white blouse looks at the George Catlin painting, "A Pretty Girl, Mandan" (1832) in the National Gallery of Art, Washington, D.C. She looks at the jewellery and the embroidery on the girl's buckskin dress. She sees white streaks in the girl's hair. The streaks are hereditary. This anomaly seems to have affected one in ten of the Mandans. The women were very proud of their white streaks and some grew their hair over their knees.

The young woman leans over the yellow cord that keeps the crowd from getting too close to the paintings. She reads that the girl was twelve years old when Catlin painted her. Twelve, she says to herself, twelve. She remembers when she was twelve. She looks down at her feet. She is wearing sandals. She moves her toes and shakes her head, twelve, her short blonde hair. She must let it grow.

She and her mother and father are in Washington for a vacation. One year of college and she still doesn't know what she wants. She is a conservative young woman. When she considers marriage she thinks about the young man she last slept with. Had he gone home and said anything to his parents. She was on top of him, when he hadn't asked her. She doesn't know why she wanted to come to Washington.

Her parents indulged all their children. They had taken them camping. The family had two tents. One for the parents and one for the children. Later, the son and the two daughters each had their own tent. They gathered wood and cooked their meals on a fire. The parents taught the two girls and the boy to swim and fish. They hiked in the woods that had once been occupied by the Indians. They found arrowheads, mushrooms, and sometimes heard bears.

The young woman loves the woods. She feels that the dampness and the smells protected her. She wasn't adopted. But she's never sure. She looks at the Indian girl's appearance, the colour of her skin, her buckskin dress.

> She wants to erase
> the Indian's portrait
> and replace it with her
> blonde hair. She will wear
> a string of pearls. Her nose
> is not too long. Ear rings,
> an expensive blouse. Her eyes
> are blue. She will wear a suit.
> Her teeth are clean. The skirt
> will be just above her knees.
> She will wear stockings and
> her shoes will have small heels.
> She wants a
> "correct likeness."

Pause

In the early 1950s in Helena, Montana, I knew a painter. I can't remember his name. What I do remember is that he was hired to paint a number of dioramas for a local museum. Again, I can't remember if the museum was in Helena or Bozeman. He painted winter scenes. One had buffaloes, the other birds and wolves. He made wonderful whites, made distances as far as the eye can see. The mountains, the leafless trees were bare. The birds and the wolves were hungry.

When some members of the board of directors saw these dioramas they were shocked, appalled, hurt. They called in another local painter who painted over the whites with pinks and purple-blues. Safety was restored.

A HUNDRED AND ONE BEASTS

Franz Kline put his bathrobe on and tied a butcher's apron around his waist. As he'd done many times before Franz smiled and chuckled to himself and painted all night. Having spent a lot of time alone he knew who his friends were.

In the private life of a painting
I have a memory of the purple thistle
Growing by the side of the road
Rubbing the side of my leg
In the private life of a painting
Every colour is a colour antiqued by untried memory
In the private life of a painting
The ego challenges every line every edge
That comes from outside
Cranach Beckman Franz Kline Ad Rheinhart
In their paintings Barney Newman's blacks strut
As if he were a coat of many colours

Pause

Gilles wears satin
He is never alone
Watteau's Gilles
Is he a she
Describe Narcissus
Define hermaphrodite
Black the sensor
White the incorporate
Incorporates the antique
If Franz Kline were to
Incorporate the antique
He would have to
Begin without colour

Pause

Gilles wears satin
He is never alone
Watteau's Gilles
Is he a she
Describe Narcissus
Define hermaphrodite
Alongside a little
Model train his father
Had carved
A book of Max Beckman's
Paintings displayed
On Kline's mantle piece
Sometimes alongside
A little model train
His father had carved
In the closet
Nijinsky's portrait
Colours not yet absorbed
Interpretations
Black White
The Zen master

                      Pause

When I carved frames at Dain & Schiff there was so much work that Chuck and I couldn't handle it. A young man was hired he came from the Black Forest in Germany. Every day before lunch he would carve a fork and a knife and eat his lunch with them. Then he would throw them into the dustbin.

It was Sunday and their mother had made a picnic and they had gathered all the paraphernalia and packed it into the car and the car wouldn't start. And it was hot. Mother unpacked the car. Connected the hose. Watered the car down and then turned the hose on herself and her children. Then they ate the picnic and took photographs of each other.

                      Pause

Diane Arbus's photographs
Virginia Woolfe's writing
Sylvia Plath's poetry
She could have been a spy
She could have been a saint
She witnessed cruelty

White sails black ties
Women wear black

She is married to a man
She does not enjoy fucking
He is married to her because
She has been given to him
She can never remember his name
He can never remember her name
They do not own a mirror
They do not know their children
At mealtime no one says
Slavery has to be abolished

                Get rich. Be rich. Get rich. Be rich.

It is raining soldiers are getting wet
Wounds begin to fester in no man's land
No one can be sure have we lost
Have we won the soldier who
Wrote home told his family
The enemy has been shooting birds
All morning feathers have been floating
In our camp men have been sticking
Feathers into their caps
This morning the Captain read psalms
We all want to go home

                          Pause

Before moving to Camden N.J.
Walt Whitman lived in Washington, D.C.
During the Civil War Whitman visited
And nursed the wounded Whitman brought
Fruit paper pencils tobacco and books
He always comes washed and cleanly clothed

                          Pause

Walt, you wrote letters to my wife. She is a tall woman. I always liked it that we could look each other in the eye. She, like you, knows how to nurse pain. I wonder if she will keep my letters. I wonder if she will read them to the children when they are older.

Pause

Walt! I remember you told us the first time you saw the President you were in New York City. I also remember how overcome you were with his appearance when you saw him again in Washington.

Walt! I want to write prose long lines with no commas or full stops. Let this period be meaningful. I want my wife and children to know that my time has not been compromised. I wanted to fight for the Union. I was brought up, as the President was, by a father who detested slavery. You told me that the Whitmans had owned slaves.

It isn't the first time a soldier has died in Whitman's arms. Whitman the Shaman, master of prose, describes the new recruits marching into Washington D.C. They are clean-shaven their blue uniforms sparkle. No man is ugly. No man is out of step.

Pause

Whitman brings a cake to the hospital. He divides it into eight equal pieces. Eight soldiers eat. Another eight do not. Whitman sharpens his pencil. Another soldier dies.

Whitman reports. Men being brought back from the prisoner of war camp, Andersonville, are starving. Most of them can't walk and have to be carried off the boat. Whitman describes the horrors of the camp and the traumas the prisoners endured. Documentation reveals that the South inflicted cruel, inhumane treatment on their prisoners. Documentation shows that both North and South were known to show mercy to each other's wounded. Documentation shows that families were divided, brother killed brother. Other documents reveal Andrew Johnson and George Armstrong Custer were retrogrades. Neither one of them had any understanding of "Union" as Lincoln defined it. Andrew Johnson belittled the ex-slaves and subverted their freedoms. George Armstrong Custer wasn't satisfied that the American Indians' lands were being taken away from them; he wanted genocide.

We paint from memory
But experience gives
Us our background
Background: the sum of
One's experience re-invented
And made conspicuous
Brings the disparate together

Pause

1945. James Cagney sees Audie Murphy, the most decorated soldier of World War II, on the cover of *Life* magazine and invites him to Hollywood. Cagney started his career in show business just after World War I. A fellow employee at Wanamaker's told him a troupe of vaudevillians were auditioning singers and dancers, and paying $35 a week. Cagney auditioned, and although he could neither sing or dance, he got the job.

James Cagney was born in the Yorkville section of Manhattan, New York. His father was a bartender and amateur boxer. As a youth, Cagney had a fine reputation as a fighter.

James Cagney, an intuitive actor, a master of improvisation, could change his personae from gangster to clown. However superficial, violent, brutal or downright nasty his characters are, he gives them an understanding that cannot be faked.

Why did Cagney invite Murphy to Hollywood. What did Cagney see in Audie Murphy's photograph. "A touch of the gutter" ambition. He knew that Murphy was a hero. Did Cagney know that Cagney was a hero. Who defines the actor, the hero who paints his self portrait and can say, "I have become who I want to be."

James Cagney retires from movie making in 1961. With his wife, Frances (Bill) Willard Cagney, he moves to his 800-acre ranch in Duchess County, New York. On his ranch he swims, paints, plays tennis and writes poetry.

The Cagneys adopted two children, Cathleen (Casey) and James Junior. They had married in 1921 and remained together until his death.

Get rich. Be rich. Get rich. Be rich.

I'd written my father and asked him for some money I needed to get a job, get a new shirt, or get the old ones cleaned. He wrote instructions: wash your shirt, and before it is dry, paying special attention to the collar, cuffs and front of the shirt, rub the shirt over a bare light bulb. The shirt will become presentable. Before you go to sleep, put your pants between newspapers and put them under the mattress. Your pants will get a crease and look pressed.

Painting isn't a race.
There is no finish line.

In 1929 Philip Guston (along with Jackson Pollock) was expelled from Manual Arts High School in Los Angeles for disorderly behaviour and for drawing cartoons ridiculing the academic programme.

Born Philip Goldstein in Montreal, Canada, Philip Guston moves with his family to Los Angeles in 1919. When Philip is very young, his father commits suicide.

Pause

Ever been in jail
Ever been blue
Ever been poor
Ever been rich
Ever been in the desert
Ever had breakfast with a desert rat
Ever hitchhiked from the desert to L.A.
Ever sat in a bar and seen somebody get shot
Ever seen a man walk on water
Ever seen a Spider crawl up the wall
Ever seen a Spider crawl down the wall
Ever seen a square ball
Ever seen Krazy Kat
Ever seen George Herriman
Ever seen George Herriman with his hat off
Ever seen Raymond Chandler
Ever seen Raymond Chandler without his gloves
Ever seen Philip Guston without a cigarette

Guston knows he shouldn't smoke in bed
Philip Guston wants a comic strip of his own
He knows Van Gogh slept with his boots on
Guston paints boots (Socialist symbol)
A coat without buttons
One-eye mountains of empty cans
The arroyo of empty bottles
Coloured oversized fish discarded sardines
Only the cigarette gives comfort
Father I haven't any room
To store your belongings
Father you use me
I am running out of paint

A mound of red pigment dries on the newspapers covering a small table in Guston's studio. Guston buys cheap pigment and dries out the excess oil, saving himself the hassle of going to the art supply store with little money.

Pause

It was a Sunday morning Martha and I were in Washington D.C. the streets were empty all the stores were closed and we were looking for a drug store. I spotted what looked like a small bundle of folded money on the sidewalk. I scooped up the money and put it in my pocket. We walked on turned a corner and there was a drug store and it was open. When we got back to our room in the hotel I counted five one hundred dollar bills. We weren't sure if the bills were real so we decided to hold on to them. When we got back to Brooklyn I took the bills to the bank. The teller counted one, two, three, four, five and deposited them to our account.

That evening our daughter Hetty called. She was living in Montreal at that time. Dad do you have any money. I'm completing my course in Labanotation and I need $300 to graduate. I told Hetty how we had found $500 on the sidewalk in Washington D.C. I mailed her a cheque for $300 the next morning.

PART II

A boy stands next to his mother holding some flowers in his hand. He does not move. She does not move: they are posing for a photograph.

Pause

He is an American cowboy. He sits on his horse rolling a cigarette with one hand. He has lived outdoors most of his life. He knows the wild flowers, their fragrance and their colours. He knows that his mother is cutting apples. She will bake his father a pie. At night in bed his parents talk. The father tells his wife that he still has the photograph that was taken of the two of them by an itinerate photographer. He remembers the two of them didn't like posing. They had to be still and not move for what seemed like eternity. He remembers his son was always picking flowers, wild flowers that he would bring home. She doesn't say a word. Jackson Pollock's mother has been reading Walt Whitman. He's the poet who held strangers in his arms as they lay dying. He's the poet who wrote about Lincoln's assassination. He's the poet who had his portrait painted by Thomas Eakins.

Get rich. Be rich. Get rich. Be rich.

Mothers take your children
Into the house
Wash them and feed them
France wants its citizens
To be orderly
Rousseau never patronizes
The women he paints
On an orange tablecloth
In the middle of the jungle
She arches her back
She is asked will you marry me
And after the Tiger gets a job
They meet to decide
Who is to pay the rent

Pause

Max Beckman cannot be anything but personal. When he moves to Amsterdam he turns Rembrandt's self-portraits to face the wall so that he can reinvent himself. "Self Portrait in Tuxedo," 1927, "Self Portrait in Tails," 1937, and "Self Portrait in Black," 1944.

Pause

Max Beckman is the third child of a prosperous merchant. His brother Richard is ten when he is born, and his sister is fifteen. His mother comes from a wealthy farming family. Max Beckman is ten when his father dies. As a youth he is rebellious. As an adult Germany could not live up to his expectations. Wagner romanticizes Germany's Gothic sweetness, and Hitler's posturing sours Beckman's dignity. Max Beckman never cried. "I do not cry, for I despise tears and consider them to be a sign of slavery."

Beckman's Black lines thrust themselves between Columbine. Columbine is a big woman with large arms and large shoulders. She smokes, and in her left hand she holds a pink clown's hat with red circles. She sits on top of a round blue table. Her huge legs are spread open. A Carnival Mask covers her eyes. Cranach's offspring has grown weary of posing naked. Columbine wears a black slip, blue and yellow markings cover her torso. Her naked thighs show a violet background, the closed door, yellow under her knees. The Beckmans are childless. No one crawls on the floor, wakes them up at night. No one interferes with them when they are alone.

Pause

The room is always too small
The ceiling is too low
No one opens a window
Beckman suffers from claustrophobia
And the floor where is the floor
Beckman smokes cigarettes
He draws fish and eats
With his friends
Max Beckman wants Germany to be as strong and as
Beautiful as
Lucas Cranach the Elder's
Black backgrounds
Beckman wishes his wife were with him
He wishes that she could see
Henri Rousseau's paintings
He wishes Cranach could see Rousseau's paintings
Cranach had a very profitable workshop
Owned a bookstore and other businesses
He painted Martin Luther's wife
Luther's mother and father
He was godfather to Luther's first born
Beckman tells the poet
Entrapment comes with what I draw

Pause

Pound didn't follow his own instructions. He threw away everything that he had in London and joined the Axis powers. Their lengthy diatribe against the intellect dismissed Klee, Ernst, Beckman, and many other artists. Degenerates. Paul Klee played the violin. His father, a professional musician, wanted Paul to follow. Klee fought him, became a painter, and played his violin when he wanted to. Max Ernst's parents were Catholics. Ernst became a secularist, a surrealist, and a great sculptor. Beckman translated the Grimm Brothers' Fairy Tales and Greek Mythology into paint.

We paint from memory
But experience gives
Us our background
Background: the sum of
One's experience re-invented
And made conspicuous
Brings the disparate together

Pause

Not always straight
Not always connected
In Washington D.C.
Lincoln sits in torment
Martin Luther King and Malcolm X
Shame the founding fathers

Abraham Lincoln was willing to submit to one humiliation after another in order, as he put it, "to preserve the Union." When Lincoln stopped compromising he realized that the Union if it is to survive, slavery has to be abolished.

Pause

Beckman, Klee, and Ernst never expected their beloved Germany to turn on them. Neither did Einstein, Freud, Schoenberg, Weil, and Wolpe. They all escaped before they were gassed or cremated.

Pause

Diane Arbus's photographs
Virginia Woolfe's writing
Sylvia Plath's poetry
She could have been a spy
She could have been a saint
She witnessed cruelty
White sails black ties
Women wear black

She does not enjoy fucking
He is married to her because
She has been given to him
She can never remember his name
He can never remember her name
They do not own a mirror
They do not know their children
At mealtime no one says
Slavery has to be abolished

Get rich. Be rich. Get rich. Be rich.

In *The Heads of the Town*, Jack Spicer sits on a bar stool next to the painter Francis Bacon. Bacon is using his Swiss knife to peel the rind off a Lemon.

Spicer says, "It's my Lemon." Bacon replies. The camera can focus on brutality, but it cannot protect you from it. The lemon is real. "We are meat."

                        Pause

George Herriman's Ignatz and Krazy Kat tell us if you've never spent time in the desert, you will never understand what makes America different from Europe.

                        Pause

The Indian walked on the land before he had a horse. He faced the grotesque and recognized it for what it is. His gods say stop, withdraw and stop fighting. The white man's god is mean-spirited. It refuses to accept our gods. The white man calls us names, bad names. Because he wants our land he slaughters the buffalo and eats the fish that we eat, and then he calls us heathens. Chief Joseph was to say. "From this day forward I fight no more."

Oh, Magic Workshop, I remember waking up. I had all of my clothes on. Jack Spicer had all of his clothes on. We were on his bed. And the bed was surrounded by hundreds of empty beer bottles. I don't know how we had avoided the bottles getting to the bed. Not one bottle had been knocked over. And I don't know how we made it out of the room. Oh, Magic Workshop, Jacks sits in a bar as if it were his living room.

Francis Bacon takes off his clothes.
Francis Bacon dyes his hair green.
Francis Bacon loves a petty thief.
Oh, Magic Workshop, Joe Dunn
became a *White Rabbit*. John Ryan
has one eye. Burt Lancaster
is an Apache, and Robert Duncan
grows side-burns. Ebbe, dear Ebbe,
is not the tallest man in the world.
Tom Field swims the Pacific all the
way to Japan and brings back a tea pot,
as big as Max Ernst's Elephant.
Ron marries Sue. Dora marries Russell.
Basil moves in with Martha, and draws
playing cards. Lo, the line comes from
outside. The line depicts one side of
a nose, one eye and one ear. The cheek
bone and lips curve under the chin to
the neck. One shoulder, one breast,

a solitary forearm. In a deck of cards
the Jack (the Prince) is drawn in profile.

Pause

H.D. never stopped believing in Pound, his *Cantos*, his poetry. Writing her poetry was harder. She became a patient of Freud, she travelled, visited Egypt, starred in silent experimental movies, and worried about not having enough money. Sometime in the 1950s on one of her trips to America Bryher had a conversation with Harold Doolittle, H.D's brother. She learned to her surprise that H.D. was a wealthy woman in her own right. Together with Bryher's 1940s settlement on her and brother Harold's investments of the family's money on Wall Street, H.D. was worth two million dollars. Still she worried about not having enough.

But for a few short return visits to America the poet H.D's maturity was lived in Europe. When she came home she came home to die. The painter Emily Carr had lived in San Francisco, London, Paris, and New York. But always came back to Victoria, the root of displeasure, the root of her colour, Canada. Except for a few short visits to England the photographer Evelyn Cameron spent her maturity in Montana and there she died.

Pause

Before Gilles Before Kline
Before Diane Arbus Before Virginia Woolfe
Before Philip Guston Before Jackson Pollock

Before Pound broke off the engagement
Before D.H. Lawrence grew a beard
Before Ezra Pound left for Italy
Before there was a war
Before William Carlos Williams
Before there was slavery
Before there was a war
Before the forgotten
Before the dead
Before there were bombs
Before there was a war
Before there was a war

IN THE MOVIES

In the movies I found chalk
In the movies I found fish skins
In the movies I found family photos

DNA proves
family relationships
Rembrandt
Einstein
the family tree
the secret is secular
grandmother Rose
never was familiar
with the art of flower
arranging. Another grand
mother always shows her
teeth when she cooks.

In the movies I found chalk
In the movies I found fish skins
In the movies I found family photos

DNA proves
Family relationships
Chaucer
Audubon
the family tree
the secret is secular
Uncle Lew had been gassed
In the First World War.
He repaired watches and
Loved to play cards.
Another uncle wanted romance
a radio show of his own.

In the movies I found chalk
In the movies I found fish skins
In the movies I found family photos
DNA proves
Family relationships

Zapata
Tazio Nuvolaro
the family tree
the secret is secular
My mother's brother stowed
way to this country from England
on board a ship wearing pressed
white pants. My grandfather hid
soldiers who were AWOL. Cousin Johnny
became a judge. Cousin Geoffrey
became a liver man. Cousin Naomi died.

BLACK JACK

A Queen sits next to an Ace.

He married the Queen. He didn't want to. She made him. They were always together. That they didn't trust one another never occurred to any one who knew them. She was always beautifully dressed. He either wore all red or all black clothes. He wasn't tall and he wasn't short and he hated tattoos. Her eyes were beautiful so she never wore jewellery. They had agreed love infuriates. Can we be friends?

BLACK JACK

The day the slave saw one of her children sold was the day Jazz prevented her from killing her other children. Call her boxer. Call her feet. Call her Mother-fucker. A big white wall with pink stripes and orange polka dots with eyes and teeth and a neck that elongates the shoulders has been scored, burnished, and refurbished. Oh, cotton tail. Uncle Remus tells you what you want to hear.

> Pause

> Get rich. Be rich. Get rich. Be rich.

> Pause

RED and WHITE

The Frobisher expedition to Southern Baffin Island in 1577 abducted three Eskimos. John White chronicles "Eskimo Woman with Baby". Was "Man Seen From Behind" the father?

John White may have begun as a limner, a self-taught itinerant artist. He may have been a member of the Painters & Stainers Company of London. He may have been, he could have been. It's not known; there were so many John Whites. But whoever our John White was, he had some abilities, some training, and knowledge of reading and writing. And he was adventurous. An Elizabethan. Like Shakespeare, he wasn't highborn. Our John White was quick and alert enough to get Walter Raleigh's attention before Raleigh's knighthood by the Queen in January 1585.

What little is known of the man named John White is confined to 1584-1593. It can be deduced that he was in a reconnaissance expedition of the Carolina Outer Banks in 1584: He drew the villages of Pomeiooc and Secoton. "Indian Women," "Indians Dancing Round a Circle of Posts," "Man and Woman Eating." Raleigh appointed White governor of Virginia in 1587. In August, White sees his granddaughter, Virginia Dare, christened.

Unwillingly White leaves the colony and returns to England to obtain supplies. Preparations against the Spanish Armada stop his return to the colony. White finally reaches the colony again in August 1590: "We let fall our grapnel neere the shore & sounded with trumpet a call & afterwards many familiar English tunes, of song and calls to them friendly, but we had no answer."

With this description of his last voyage, and the efforts to locate the Lost Colony, the last White is heard of is 1593. In a letter dated February 4, he accepted the fact that the settlers, including his kith and kin, were beyond human help.

John White's watercolours outline in clear sharp detail … "all strange birds, beastes, fishes, and plantes, hearbes, trees, and fruictes … also the figures & shapes of men and women in their apparel as also their manner of weapons, in every place as ye shall find them different."

White wants more Europeans to follow. He tells them they shouldn't be afraid. He shows them the Pictish men and women of Scotland were more heathen, wilder, more warlike. The Indians tattooed their bodies, but, look, they don't keep human skulls as trophies – or do they. If there was intrigue, it's not seen. Was it hidden from White.
John White was able to say he crossed the ocean and saw things that few other men had. But don't expect White's watercolours to do what they cannot do. White didn't make art. He was a reporter who gave the royal purse back in England a description of the natives.

Pause

In the movie *The Invasion of the Body Snatchers*, 1956, remade in 1978 as *The Pod People*, a California town is infiltrated by pods from outer space that replicate and replace the natives.

        Get rich. Be rich. Get rich. Be rich.

        Pause

        Get rich. Be rich. Get rich. Be rich.

        Pause

In the movies I found chalk
In the movies I found fish skins
In the movies I found eyes

Leonardo's
smile
Rita Hayworth's
shoulders
Durer's
hands
de Kooning's
women

Van Eyck said,
I was present.

        Pause

BLACK WALLS

Bill Traylor

He didn't know how to read. He didn't know how to write. He had been born a slave. People eat, someone drinks. The one-legged man has a woman. She has a dog that hates cats. MEOW, black Jesus needs a bath. Black skin, ebony. Oh, how we whites envy black skin.

Bill Traylor married, had children, and became a sharecropper on the very plantation where he'd been born a slave. At eighty-two he leaves the plantation and moves to Montgomery, Alabama. Nobody knows if Bill Traylor ever drew before the age eighty-two. He said, "It came to me." Bill Traylor's behaviour challenges the belief that one must practice, practice,

practice. I think that Bill Traylor had for eighty-two years practiced an innate form of calligraphy. He has no animosity. Grown men ride horses and carry guns. Men, women, birds, cats, horses, snakes and the pig think the turtle is funny. Using the hard surface of a cardboard he replaces the fields with a question, what do I look like.

I wonder, did the cave painters practice. We have no evidence that they did. We know young Basquiat was eighteen when the door opened and everything flooded in. Cy Twombly wasn't much older. Egon Schiele never erased his ecstasies. Leonardo never erased his compulsions.

In Bill Traylor's drawings whips are never in evidence. Grass never seems important. Men, women, animals and beasts are freely positioned on the page. Bill Traylor's designs make no grandiose claims. His empowerment lives in a negative space where he practices without preaching. Do not call him child-like. He never erases. Uneducated, unschooled, Bill Traylor the artist asks the question, what do I look like. And the answer is his legacy.

Pause

Get rich. Be rich. Get rich. Be rich.

WHITE WALLS

Cy Twombly

> Every day Billy scratched
> on the wall of his house
> where he lived and when
> all the walls and floors
> and ceilings had been covered
> he bought paper and crayons
> and paint and when the house
> in which he lived was full of
> paper he moved and started
> all over again and when his
> neighbours realized that Billy
> Boy was going to come into
> their houses and cover their
> walls they called the patron
> saint of painters St. Luke and
> he came and put his hand on
> Billy's shoulder and told him
> about vernacular and how what

> once was thrown away was now
> valued and how he Billy could
> demonstrate that trivia can
> make a perfect picture and
> that he Billy could become
> his own object and live in
> the world as a beautiful song

>> Pause

He wants more than anyone can give him. He isn't selfish when he turns off the lights and scribbles. Lo, the line comes from outside and draws on the imperfect. A child who has been trying to write her name gets frustrated. Signs and unattached vowels keep marking up the paper. The child doesn't know it but Cy Twombly knows calligraphy is for lovers.

> Greece, Rome, and a failed
> aristocracy. Bumble-
> bumble bee bumble bee
> history is my mother
> she feeds me
> Southern hospitality.
> Poussin went to Rome. What an
> un-Whitman like thing to do.
> Criss-cross I met Adonis
> Venus and Apollo. I met
> Mars and defined the
> red blue untitled.

Tomboy scribbles and the grass grows. The South has been deprived. It never was original. Its sons and daughters wanted Athens. They wanted Jefferson to do everything for them.

He wanted to hide his slaves. Gilbert Stuart painted Jefferson. He was six foot-three with red hair. It was hard for him to hide. Martha's great-great grandmother married Dr. Chancellor and they lived in a house that is right across from the University of Virginia. Tomboy scribbles and the grass grows.

COLOURS

Criss-cross
Criss-cross
I know where I'm going.

Pousson went to Rome. What an
un-Whitman like thing to do.
Criss-cross I met Adonis
Venus and Apollo. I met
Mars and defined the
red blue untitled.

Criss-cross USA
Criss-cross the Ancient World.
Criss-cross Charlottesville.

> Pause

In the movie, *The Invasion of the Body Snatchers* 1956, remade in 1978 as *The Pod People*, a California town is infiltrated by pods from outer space that replicate and replace the natives.

> Get rich. Be rich. Get rich. Be rich.

> Pause

In the movies I found chalk
In the movies I found fish skins
In the movies I found history

History is my mother
she feeds me
boiled potatoes
cod-liver oil
drippings and a
cup of what is
called Bovril.

Marmite Chaucer
D.H. Lawrence
William Carlos Williams
swing low
sweet Traylor

Twombly never could
erase culture
and yesterday he
had no time for
the Fourth of July.

America your days are numbered.

You squander
your wealth
and ignore
your children

Pause

Dear Dora and Tom,

I hope you are both well and enjoying Spring.

Last Sunday we went to the Botanic Gardens and then to the Brooklyn Museum and saw Basquiat's show. I wish you had been with us. The show is divided into two floors. The 5th floor has his early work. WOW! What a start. It takes your breath away.

Basquiat's language is the language of a fighter. He became Joe Louis and I think it shocked him. Erase, no, there isn't enough time. Basquiat's rage accomplishes everything in the first round. I haven't read any of the essays in the catalogue. But the reviews I read compare him to Rimbaud. Basquiat is not a visionary. He has no new world. Far from it. His world is a heavy now and it weighs on his chest. I wondered how did he breathe. Certainly he didn't sleep. So the drugs. What else could he do. Basquiat's painted outpourings are in no way a direct consequence of Rimbaud's visions but I think if it were not for us knowing Rimbaud's insights, his poetic disseminations, his air to speak the truth, Basquiat's monologues would be unrecognizable to us.

The narrative that was targeted by Jasper Johns transposes the Zen of Archery into a workable common idiom. Johns' language questions his own refinement. Basquiat trusts his heroes. He questions society and the culture that produces it. He questions culture and the society that produces it.

Things begin to change. You can see it on the 4th floor. He is reinventing himself. He is becoming a writer. He seduces the canvas, the word, and the page. He fucks without caution. Nothing is personal until it hurts. Art can't take the hurt away. But try and make art without hurting.

I never forget that Picasso and Rimbaud are colonials. This attitude has to be considered. Picasso tried to obliterate African sculpture. If he had had his way we would never have known where "The Women of Avignon" had come from. African sculpture would have disappeared just as all the slave owners hoped their slaves would never be seen.

> Pause

> Miles Davis
> feeds
> the high
> that C's
> me through
> the Delta.

> Charlie Parker
> can't cross
> the street
> when the
> light is
> green.

> Step and
> Fetch It
> ate
> Eggs.

> The Black
> policeman
> never shoots
> till he

> sees the
> whites
> of their
> eyes.

> Pause

Bless Bill Traylor, Twombly, and Basquiat. I love their courage, their remake of things that have already been told. They tell us in no uncertain terms where they and what they speak about come from. Bless Bill Traylor, Twombly, and Basquiat. They are honest. Not all of us are.

SHORT STORIES

Antoine Watteau came from Belgium, he settled in Paris, and died of consumption at the age of thirty-seven. He loved the theatre, the minuet. Watteau painted gardens, actors, skies without rain, courtiers. We see them acting, playing. He shows us a silken torso, nature's anomaly. Experience the gestures of a feather, Pan's territory. Nature's anomaly. Sing "La Vie en Rose."

Pause

I knew a woman who sang in French with her back towards the audience. She wore a knitted cap and a pale blue coat and held her handbag on her right arm. She was sixty-five or maybe seventy. In her left hand, she held the mike. Martha and I heard her in a restaurant one New Year's Day. She sang "La Vie en Rose." In her handbag she carried what all migrants carry – the past. She will not face the future. She sings "La Vie en Rose." Her voice does not betray her; she hides under her coat a path to where brambles, thorns, and uncultivated grasses lie. Her experience has made her angry and she wants to empty the museums of their artefacts, strip their walls, wash their floors, and return all the stolen properties.

Pause

There was an old man who sold potatoes in the Essex Street Market in the early 1960s. He never smiled. He might have been born in Europe; he might have been born in America. His long face looked like a potato. El Greco elongated the flesh. El Greco might have been born in Greece and he might have been born a Jew.

I first painted "The Potato Man" in 1970. In the 1970s, I smoked three packs a day. In the 1970s, Soutine and Giorgione shook their heads when I told them that the old man had no teeth and that his eyes, small and grey and watery, hadn't always been that way. When he was a little boy, his big generous ears covered the sides of his face. Later, when he played ball, did he play ball. I painted him in 1988 as "Herman the Ballplayer" – as a ballplayer who wore his uniform as a judge or cleric wear their robes. By the 1980s, I was giving the canvas more than one or two sizings. By the 1980s I had stopped smoking.

My potato man never played piano. He accepted the fact that the potato originated in America. In 1995 I did another painting of him.

The Moon had me tread lightly on the path behind the trees. There brambles, thorns, and uncultivated grasses say what the young Essenes said as they trekked into the desert to cleanse themselves, "There shall be no more lies." But I have to say, this is not my experience, El Greco might have read the Cabbala and he might have adopted the occult; he might have believed the words of the Essenes: "God will deliver Israel. He will refine for Himself the human frame by rooting out the spirit of falsehood from the bounds of the flesh." The distance between El Greco and Watteau is measured in experience. Black Mountain. Oranges. "La Vie en Rose." Watteau invented French painting.

       Get rich. Be rich. Get rich. Be rich.

Liberty show me your breast. Show me justice. Show me "Tempest" – Giorgione's farewell to his loved ones.

       Pause

The ballplayers were on the field warming up. As they exercised they performed a Martha Graham dance. It was then that I saw Martha Graham, with her arms raised out in front of her. She was stretching her back, and had her left leg extended behind her. She was looking fierce. She turned to Nijinsky who was leaping as he had done many times before. He put his hand on Merce Cunningham, Viola Farber, and Ralph Lemon. The stadium was slowly filling up. Japanese tap dancers and students with fans were slowly filling the stadium.

The Pitcher turns to first base, checks third, looks at the catcher, turns. Beethoven wrote into his Pastoral, "Democracy is yet to come." The runner returns to first base. Nerves twitch, who will falter. The Pitcher. The runners. Or the man at the plate. The Pitcher stretches, kicks his leg and releases the ball. Beethoven wrote into his Pastoral, "Democracy is yet to come." Liberty showing one breast sails down the avenue and strikes. The batter having swung and missed steps away from the plate. Following the avenue that has been made by avoiding justice the batter recovers his dignity and returns to the plate.

The Pitcher raises his arms. I draw a left leg. The batter looks around the field. Pastoral, French painting began with Watteau. Pastoral, the Pitcher's arms are above his head. Pastoral, the city between the trees is an avenue where I strut my art. The Pitcher does not look at the batter I draw a right leg. The Pitcher's body is coiled I draw his back. The Pitcher releases his intentions, I draw his face, the Pitcher is trying not to think, not yet, he will wait. He must control himself, and the batter, and every player positioned on the field.

Sixth inning, no outs with a man on third the Pitcher's team is winning 6-4. The Pitcher reads the catcher's sign. He waves his head, turns to third base, and looks at the runner. The third baseman looks like a bullfrog squatting over the base. The Pitcher leans over and takes another sign. First base, third base, an avenue stretches before him. He sees three people sitting having lunch in the middle of the avenue. A second woman in a shift stands in a pool toying with the water. Behind her the avenue continues for an indefinite length.

> Get rich. Be rich. Get rich. Be rich.

"Luncheon on the Grass," 1863

An engraving after Raphael's "Judgment of Paris" encouraged Manet to use the same arrangement for his three central figures. Like Giorgione and Titian, Manet lived in a city. Manet in Paris and Giorgione and Titian in Venice. Manet's painting has two men clothed and seated. The third member of the trio is a naked woman. She holds her right hand on her chin; her right elbow rests on her right knee. A mature woman, she is no "Olympia," she services no one. Is someone taking a photograph of her. It's hard to tell because she looks out and we are forced to look at her. Her white body, her intelligent face, her knowing eyes. Oh, darling, you, like Bizet's Carmen, know purity is the curse of the twentieth century.

Why would any woman go out to the countryside and sit naked with two men who are fully clothed. Why would two men who are fully clothed sit and talk to each other when there is a naked woman between them. Is it because they have finished eating their picnic. And what of the other woman who has some clothes on. She's standing in a pool of water. There is a boat, and you can see by its oars that it might have been used a few hours ago. It's peaceful now. But is it. There's a plot to all of this. Watteau taught the French to be cheeky and always have good table manners.

Bizet's Carmen would consider all of this a waste of time. Sitting naked with two men who are talking about things that she is not concerned about. Carmen wants to be paid attention to. She takes what she wants and gives in return everything that she has. She wants results.

There's a mystery novel quality to all of this. We can guess one of the outcomes. The women will put on their clothes and they will clean up the remains of the picnic, and they will all go home.

But what if there is another plot. The woman in Manet's painting is looking at Edgar Allan Poe. He knows she likes being photographed. He's seen prints of her that Nadar has taken. He knows that she is unknown to her own time. When she crosses the street she is seen as a monster. She is gorgeous. She is a woman who faces the future. She is a modern woman. She can read and write and she is not afraid to go home alone. She knows Poe grieves, that he asks questions that he can't answer. She would love him if he would have her, but she knows Bizet committed suicide because the opera, *Carmen*, failed.

Pause

We came home and put down our bags and opened up the house and went into the garden and sat in the green chairs that surround the green table. The grass needed cutting and some of the potted plants needed water. Except for an unusual number of crows screaming, everything seemed the same. Martha commented maybe this was the year of the crows, and we went inside to unpack.

The phone rang and Martha answered it. It was the young woman with the baby, who lives on the top floor of Carol's house. She and her baby look like a medieval mother and child. She is a small woman and her baby looks large. Family photos. There is one of my mother holding me. We are smiling and I look large, my mother also being a small woman, we have taken on the appearance of an icon. The young woman on the phone said there was a crow with its leg caught in our old watering can. The crow was hanging Tarot-like by one leg. It was the Hanged Man, and it was fighting to get loose. I had no intention of touching it. The young woman said that she had been watching the crows all day, that the crow that couldn't fly had been stumbling around the gardens, getting through the cracks in the fences. She thought it was a young bird because the other crows were larger, and they had been diving at the cats to keep them out of the gardens or from walking on the tops of the fences.

We went out to dinner, and when we returned it was dark. The next morning, the crow was hunched next to the wall, with its head between its legs. I decided again to leave it alone. Hours later, I saw the crow flapping around and I thought it was getting better and would fly away. But it didn't. Again, it began to stumble over the plants and go from garden to garden. I said, "It will die overnight," but it didn't. And the next morning, I chased the crow with long stick into the garden next door and boarded up the cracks with stones. We went out. When we came back that afternoon, the crow was in our garden again, stumbling over the lilies and crushing the impatiens. I again chased the crow, this time up against a fence and there I crushed it. I killed it. It was the third day, and I killed it.

There are no photographs of this unholy happening, where a young mother witnessed what she thought were parents trying to protect their young. I didn't document my thoughts. But I know I didn't want to kill the crow. I wanted something else, something else to happen, something Dada-like to objectify, to detach me. I wanted the crows in the trees to surprise me. I wanted patience. I wanted to wake up and say I had been dreaming. But instead.

PSALMS

Hart Crane wrote in 1929: "For unless poetry can absorb the machine, i.e., *acclimatize* it as naturally and casually as trees, cattle, galleons, castles, and all other human associations of the past, then poetry has failed of its full contemporary function."

"Trees become bushes, barns toys, cows turn into rabbits, as we climb, I live only in the moment in this strange, unmortal space, crowded with beauty, pierced with danger."
— from Charles Lindbergh's
description of his first airplane flight in 1922.

In 1928, Elsie Driggs paints "Aeroplane". The year before, she painted "Cabbage" and "Pittsburgh".

Elsie Driggs was born in 1898 in a farmhouse in Hartford, Connecticut. But her family lived in an apartment on Central Park West. Her father was an engineer; her mother spent her early pregnancy attending lectures at the Metropolitan Museum of Art hoping her child would be an artist.

Elsie Driggs' father woke her up to see the spectacular light of Pittsburgh factories as they passed in the train from Sharon, Pennsylvania to New York. When she grew up and returned to Pittsburgh, steel-producing methods had changed. The spectacular night-light was no longer visible, so she made pencil drawings of "the great velvet forms" of the Jones & Laughlin mills and used them to paint her "Pittsburgh".

Elsie Driggs

I saw a photograph of Elsie Driggs when she was an old lady sitting in front of a fireplace smiling and talking to a young woman who was asking a lot of questions.

"Pittsburgh"
"Cabbage"
"Aeroplane"

She told the young woman that in 1924 she was advised to sign her paintings "Driggs" – no first name – so there would be no indication that the artist is a woman. She didn't take the advice. She didn't need to ask anyone's permission to drive a car, paint an "Aeroplane" or enlarge a "Cabbage". She had left the pilot's seat empty in "Aeroplane" so that she could fly it. Elsie Driggs told the young woman she had learned to live with machines, trees, and the flowers that she grew.

She told the young woman that she had married a painter that they had had a daughter that she did not feel incomplete.

> She told the young woman
> "Pittsburgh" gives me
> Immaculate spaces
> Delirious verbiage
> Precise lines
> "Aeroplane" transcends
> Taking off my shoes
> Stockings my dress
> And my underwear
> I am the flyer
> I am in control
> I pass through
> A Blue sky
> Yellow Jackets
> Supper and eating
> Cooked cabbage I think of
> My husband and the windows
> We left open last night
> I think of my daughter
> And "the great velvet forms"
> Immaculate spaces,
> Delirious verbiage
> Precise lines
> Taking off my shoes
> Stockings my dress
> And my underwear
> I am the flyer
> I am in control
> Take off my shoes
> Stockings, my dress
> And my underwear
> I am the flyer
> I pass through a Blue sky
> Yellow Jackets
> Supper and eating

> Cooked cabbage
> I think of my husband
> The windows we left open last night
> I think of my daughter
> And "the great velvet forms"

Pause

Psalms, cruel or otherwise reflective every year Martha orders new bulbs for the garden. One year we had Black and White tulips and the squirrels ate every one of the Black tulips and didn't touch the White ones. Martha never again ordered Black and White tulips.

> A family sits down
> To Sunday dinner
> The son tells his father
> He is leaving home
> He will not tell his family
> Where he is going
> He will not follow
> In his father's footsteps

Pause

My daughter Mallory is married to a Thai. They have two children. My daughter Hetty is married to a WASP, and they have two adopted daughters. One is a Wasp and the other daughter is African American, Italian, Native American and Czech. My wife Martha is a WASP and I am a Jew. When we collect together at the table we sit down to eat and we all talk at the same time. My daughters are no longer children. Their children are my grandchildren and when they ask me for the time I have to remember that it is their future that they are concerned about.

> Artefacts sometimes wild
> Often Blue know
> What Thursday will bring
> By Friday the Anemone
> Has lost its voice
> And whispers Lily
> Please I need you
> The Rose insists
> It is more important
> Than the Daisy
> Splash!

True tales
The law is not equal to the
Demands put upon it

Get rich. Be rich. Get rich. Be rich.

Mary Cassatt watches her niece being given a bath and remembers lunch at Monet's house and how appalled she was with Cézanne's table manners. Later that afternoon she was taking a walk in the garden and Cézanne was sitting on a bench. He said hello and invited her to sit down and they had a lengthy talk. When she got back to the house she told Degas that Cézanne was one of the most intelligent men she had ever talked to. Degas never married, he had no children. He was suspicious of all women and Mary Cassatt loves him for his reserve.

Mary Cassatt visits the Louvre.

1880 Degas shows us the back of a slim self-assured young woman leaning on her umbrella. Her hands are gloved. But I can see her torso and the shape of her thighs. Degas shrouds her face from our view. Is she blushing, is he.

Oh, naked lady leaning on your umbrella Degas told you his mother was born in America. You left Philadelphia for Paris. Thomas Eakins stayed. H.D. left for London and Pound reminded her that she should "Make it New" but as he said this to her he forgot to purge his own vernacular of one of the oldest of prejudices, anti-Semitism. So did Cézanne even though he loved Pissarro. Who was a Jew.

Oh, naked lady leaning on your umbrella Pound wanted change and his vanity got the better of him. He used anti-Semitism to blackmail the western world to do his bidding as did Mussolini and Hitler. But Pound was not a Mussolini or a Hitler he was a poet. *The Cantos* like *The Book of Psalms* continue to vibrate ethos. Pound told Paul Blackburn when Blackburn visited him after the war, "I made a mistake. I should have stayed in London. I had everything."

Oh, naked lady leaning on your umbrella
You were a precursor
Degas dancers
Renoir's nudes
Monet's Clusters
You told Philadelphia
Buy French Impressionism

Employ their spacious light
Psalms Psalms
The past excited Pound
And he went to the archives
The Troubadours
Venice Vivaldi
"Make it New"
Our family is a new family
Drive a car
Fly an "Aeroplane"
Elsie Driggs painted
Enlarged "Cabbages"
Spacious psalms
Flew Hart Crane's flag
Psalms Psalms
H.D. heard the burden of the Nile
Helen by definition could be her sister
Her spacious psalm
Dovetailed
Mary Cassatt
H.D. Elsie Driggs
Lindbergh Hart Crane
Ezra Pound
Exercised
Psalms Psalms
It is 4pm
The rain has stopped
And the sky has found
a new light
Myth should have flooded in
But
Obedience caution
Slow to activate to evolve
Some things never connect
The tempered tongue

THE TRUSTING CHILD

Leonardo di ser Piero da Vinci born the illegitimate son of a notary, Piero da Vinci, and a peasant woman, Caterina, at Vinci in the region of Florence. Much of his earlier working life was spent in Milan. He later worked in Rome, Bologna and Venice and spent his last years in France, in a home awarded him by François I of France.

When Leonardo left Italy to become court decorator for François I, he took "The Mona Lisa" with him, possibly unfinished. Why didn't he finish the painting. What was it that he was trying to find. Vasari tells us that Mona Lisa was Lisa Gherardini, the wife of Francesco del Giocondo. Is Lisa a mystery or is Leonardo a mystery.

Leonardo had no heirs, and the painting remained in France. It became part of the royal collection. There it might have languished unknown had not history being the accumulation of charged events flipped a card.

The Revolution turned the Louvre, formerly a palace, into a public art gallery. Suddenly "The Mona Lisa" found herself owned by the French state and housed in one of the most famous museums in the world. Writers began to circle around her.

"We feel perturbed in her presence," wrote the novelist and critic, Theophile Gautier, "by her aura of superiority."

Later George Sand listed Mona Lisa's drawbacks and detected an undertone of cold malice in her smile.

>Leave home. Meet strangers and learn to draw.

I know men who have asked me, tell me about my father. You knew him. Tell me what you remember. Was he attractive was he reliable did he smile was he likeable did he have a presence. Did you like him. I was a baby when he died. My mother tells me but there are never enough bricks, enough nails to complete the house and the roof remains unattached. And when it rains the unanswered questions get soaked. There are the boys who came from Germany, the Philippines, Latvia, Sweden, Japan and China who have to begin again.

They came with their mothers and sisters. They are the casualties of war, revolution and illegitimacy. Mothers lost husbands, lost lovers. Children lost fathers. One boy remembers. Another boy was too young to remember. They all ache. They ask was I ever a son. Was I ever a lover. She was a woman in love. She was a woman in need. She couldn't raise the children by herself. She was in need of a ladder. She climbed up and when she came down she came down to America and married an American. She was a very practical woman.

Five of the six mothers of boys I knew married American servicemen. The lonely men took off their uniforms. Their stiff cocks gave the women a little fear. The brides didn't know how they would be received. Would they be trusted. What will they have to prove to their in-laws to the American neighbours will they be thought of as conniving foreigners. Take a bath and keep yourself clean. Smell good. And when you cook caramelize the onions it's one of the kindest things you can do for your pain.

Pause

The metaphor for trust is plumb a weight indicating direction a line that plummets and becomes plum, a father, a stepfather a true or a false guardian. He loves his wife. He tolerates your mother. Is he jealous of your mother is he jealous of you. He corrects everybody's table manners. He eats with his mouth open. And then remembers to straighten his back and unbutton his coat, uses his knife and fork, and smiles.

Leave home. Meet strangers and learn to draw.

Vasari doesn't tell us that Leonardo's father Piero took the baby Leonardo from his mother. His mother married and moved to another town. Leonardo's father married and in total, Leonardo had seventeen half brothers and sisters. But at age 5 Leonardo was sent to stay with his grandfather Vinci. With the move, he officially became part of his father's family, although he was never given the status of heir.

Vasari tells us that when Leonardo was 14, Ser Piero apprenticed him under Andrea Del Verrochio in his workshop at Florence, where he learned various skills for the next seven to eight years.

Vasari doesn't tell us that on July 9, 1504, Leonardo received notice of the death of his father. Through the contrivances of his half brothers and sisters, he was deprived of any inheritance. The death of a beloved uncle also resulted in a fight over inheritance, but this time Leonardo beat out his scheming siblings and wound up with use of the uncle's land and money.

Pause

The artist tells the inventor and the engineer
If I didn't draw as well as I do
Your job would be twice as hard as it is
And the visionary said to the philosopher
My understanding of mathematics
Gives you equations that demand logic
Be bold and trust each other
Be bold you are as I am you
You who charge me with disruptions
Sit and eat at my table
I am as you are as I am you
You are many as I am one who is many
Conflict and disruption sit at our table
I sleep and I eat with you with you
With you I dissect the forbidden

Arise solo flight solo cadaver
Arise alchemy and be my mechanical wings
Arise
The self is a portrait a metaphor
For trust is plumb a weight indicating direction
A line that plummets and becomes plum
a father, a stepfather a true or a false guardian
He loves his wife
He tolerates your mother
Is he jealous of your mother is he jealous of you
He corrects everybody's table manners
He eats with his mouth open
He remembers he is obligated to set an example
He unbuttons his coat straightens his back
And smiles

Vasari tells us that Leonardo was unstable but what Vasari doesn't tell is conflict and disruption sat at Leonardo's table. Leonardo was a very brave man he had to be if he was to prevail. Being not one man but many Leonardo had to work hard to fulfil all of his necessities. It's no wonder he wasn't able to finish everything that he started.

When I think of "The Mona Lisa" I think of Nat King Cole singing her name. I think that she was a man that da Vinci loved. He was beautiful and he could when he wanted to assume the features of a woman. When I think of Mona Lisa I think of Nat King Cole singing her name. I think of Leonardo singing her name.

When I think of Mona Lisa I think of Nat King Cole singing her name. She is Leonardo. He is beautiful. He knows that he is beautiful. He also knows that he gives Lisa Gherardini, the wife of Francesco del Giocondo, his autobiography.

Pause

Why is Raphael thought of as more important than Gruenwald. Why are Manet and Degas more important than Munch and Ensor. Is it because the Northern Art acknowledges that there are demons and they have power and can be ugly and distorted when the South is forever attempting a smile, a Mona Lisa a dispassionate icon never says why she (he) is threatening. When you first see Picasso's "Les Demoiselles d'Avignon" she may look distorted and ugly. But look again her moves are calculated when she pulls back the curtain she welcomes the Italian masters. And they in response recognize a sister a woman who knows spontaneity has its own calculations.

The same can be said of Matisse and his wondrous experiments with colour and abstraction. He was born in the northern part of France and every winter he went to Nice for the sun and the warmth so he wouldn't have to tolerate Paris in the winter. His paintings pay homage to the facial expressions that brighten the eyes curves the corners of the mouth and depending on the intent show affection, pleasure, irony and derision.

Matisse wasn't the first artist to stick his fingers in the paint and like honey he rearranged and made his own colour wheel. Black became a noun a predator an intuitive device that could be placed in any room on anyone's face an eye a space is asked to take its clothes off. Men are given violins a suit and tie. Some women the ones that aren't given hats are asked to take off their clothes. Her breasts are clean as is her torso. She is exotic. But her sister isn't she frowns and purses her lips. She is Paris and Paris reminds Matisse the north can be cold, it can be bitter, it can be without a smile.

She clicks the camera. And what you see is an elderly man with a greying beard and thinning hair. I smile I frown I wish she hadn't taken the photograph and I'm pleased that she wanted to.

On television she is portrayed by a medium, he is a mentalist, a castle and a liar. She may look like the neighbours but she has something they don't she has dreams insights that can foretell the unexplainable. She is a muse who can live in a male's body she is an outsider who is acceptable to the establishment. The mentalist isn't an FBI agent but he can work and be vouched for by a real agent a woman who may be in love with him. He channels her as he does the suspects who throw smokescreens in front of him. Lie and you will be detected. These men and women aren't Sherlock Holmes. Hercule Poirot. Sam Spade. Philip Marlowe. Those are the old private eyes the men the police don't want to trust but at times have to call on for help. Our new character on television has the intuitive powers and instincts of an artist. Does this mean the corporations have infiltrated the artist and what we are viewing is a replay. Or are we seeing the beginnings of something new the metamorphosis of the culture's truly secular believers.

Get Rich. Be Rich. Get Rich. Be Rich.

"The Mona Lisa" was discovered missing on Monday, August 21, 1911 yet no one contacted the police because workers at the museum assumed that the painting had been taken to the in-house studio to be photographed for marketing purposes. It wasn't until the next day that the alarm bells went off.

"The Mona Lisa" was nowhere to be found. Police interviewed as many people as they could who might have any information concerning the lost masterpiece. Rumours circulated. The Germans took it to embarrass the French, a pervert took it, is it for sale. However, no one was able to provide any clues as to what had become of it.

Eight days after the painting was stolen the Louvre opened up its doors and thousands of people were lining up. There had never been a wait to enter the Louvre before. They came to see a blank wall with four empty pegs. One of the people known to have stood in line to see the blank wall was Franz Kafka and it is possible that he telegraphed Arthur Dove the American abstractionist and told him to come to Paris. Apollinaire and Dove were both born in 1880 the same year *La Gioconda* was successfully performed in its third and final version on March 28, 1880. And who knows what two, three surrealists will do given the chance to turn things upside-down. Sensation, propaganda fits all sizes.

Pause

Poet, art critic, editor and unintended recipient of stolen goods, Apollinaire had befriended Géry Piéret, a young artist, whom he had employed as his secretary. He had known about his earlier thefts, and when Piéret arrived at his flat with a Phoenician statue, he had placed the item on his mantelpiece.

When "The Mona Lisa" was stolen, Apollinaire was sure that Piéret had made off with it as well. He gave the Phoenician piece back, along with all the francs he had, and told Piéret that a long vacation outside the reach of the French police would be an excellent idea.

This Piéret did, but not before he sold the sculpture to a newspaper and wrote the letter bragging about his theft. Then he did something else that dragged Apollinaire into the mess.

Piéret wrote from Frankfurt confessing to the theft of three items and trying to exonerate Apollinaire, he quoted Apollinaire as saying, "My dear friend, You'd better go immediately. I don't share your opinions and I'm sorry I invited you to stay with me now that I believe in your crime."

With Piéret out of the country, the police began to focus on Apollinaire. He knew exactly who Piéret had sold the other two pieces to. Buried in the back of a cupboard at Picasso's Boulevard de Clichy apartment were two figures – a small, powerfully built stone man and a woman carved by ancient Spaniards during the Bronze Age. The bottom of each piece bore the stamp "Property of the Louvre Museum." Picasso had used them when he painted "Les Demoiselles d'Avignon."

She clicks the camera. And what you see is an elderly man with a greying beard and thinning hair. I smile I frown I wish she hadn't taken the photograph and I'm pleased that she wanted to.

Pause

There is no photograph, no movie of Apollinaire and Picasso concocting elaborate scenarios to mislead the police. First, they made plans to flee the country. Next, they would destroy the incriminating evidence. They would pack the stolen art in a suitcase and drop it in the Seine.

On the night of September 5, at midnight, painter and poet went out to dispose of their contraband. The distance from Montmartre to the Seine is three miles. Because they were afraid of attracting attention they walked. Never mind they were lugging a large suitcase. Skirting the Right Bank Apollinaire bent at a downward angle and Picasso reached up. Toting their old scuffed suitcase, they were too mismatched in size, and so they took turns.

They stopped, looked over their shoulders, imagined that they heard whispers, footsteps. Electricity was coming slowly to the City of Lights. In the shadows cast by the uncertain gas flames, they imagined policemen flattened against tree trunks and crouched on the riverbank. They were two frightened young men who knowing what they were doing was wrong were ashamed.

Two hours later they returned to the studio, trudging up the steep hill of Montmartre, puffing, breathless, exhausted and still carrying the suitcase and its contents.

Pause

Gardens. A forest where the trees are so numerous it is hard to walk and impossible for a person on a horse to see where he is going. The trusting child has no choice but to follow. The child is spliced to the parents. The parents do not always remember they have a child. They are looking for a clearing a place where they can build a home. They intend to breed. Muck the stable and he will be a great stud and win races. Muck the mare and she will breed her own. Muck the persona there is no ending to a short story.

Pause

On September 7, 1911, the police arrested and jailed Apollinaire on suspicion of stealing "The Mona Lisa." Apollinaire then implicated his friend Pablo Picasso, who was also brought in for questioning. Both men were released.

Nineteen days after "The Mona Lisa" disappeared the police paid a visit to Boulevard de Clichy. Picasso, who liked to sleep until noon, was roused at 7a.m. by a persistent knocking at the door. A groggy Fernande, a see-through dressing gown wrapped around her naked body, opened the door.

The detective read a summons from the safety of the doorway, ordering Picasso to appear before the examining magistrate for questioning.

If the detective had searched Picasso's studio, he would have found incriminating evidence. But instead, he remained at the door, while Picasso dressed in his favourite red and white polka-dot cotton shirt and an elegant silk tie that clashed violently. He was shaking so uncontrollably that Fernande had to button the shirt for him.

He was taken by bus from Pigalle to the Palais de Justice. No police vehicle was available. The government would not pay the taxi fare for an alleged criminal. Picasso would never again take the bus that went from Pigalle to Halle aux Vins.

Apollinaire and Picasso faced each other across the courtroom. Picasso in his polka-dot shirt and clashing tie was a gesture of bravado that appeared more pathetic than defiant. They contradicted themselves and each other, each accusing the other of bringing the stolen statues to the newspaper.

Now Judge Drioux fixed on the painter. Picasso swore he knew nothing whatever about L'Affaire des Statuettes. He did not know the primitive Iberian heads were stolen goods, and he did not even know Apollinaire. Like Simon Peter when asked, "Do you know this man" Picasso replied: "I have never seen him before."

"Why does Picasso say he does not know me. I thought Picasso was my friend. Picasso is a great man.

"He says: he has never seen me before. But I know because he feels he is superior to it he steals from African art and perjures himself. Does Picasso feel superior to me."

Pause

By incorporating Iberian statues and African sculpture into European composition and scenery when he painted the "Les Demoiselles d'Avignon" Picasso may have unintentionally struck a blow against purity. We don't have to be surrealists to understand the consequences.

Did Hitler understand the Industrial Revolution mixed the races, that it made bringing disparate things together possible. Did knowing this make him more insistent that there was only one solution and that was racial purity.

Pause

Apollinaire's mother was Polish. And as Apollinaire said the French believed all the Poles were Jews. Max Jacob converted and became a Catholic but the Nazis killed him anyway. I'm not sure what they would have done to Apollinaire. Would he have left the country or would he have stayed as Picasso did. Picasso never forgot that he lied about knowing his good friend Apollinaire. I know he said he would not leave France and lose another country. But my gut tells me this was his way of saying, I'm sorry.

Pause

Ah Giotto we all have angels living in our chest. They breathe in rhythm with our disruptions. Our lack of mercy sometimes takes refuge in the pleasure of someone else's skin. Matisse was married and there were a daughter and two sons. Matisse practiced and perpetuated domesticity as the wildest. He was a husband, a lover, a father who when separated from the family would write each one a letter every night and every day he would follow the same pattern, he worked.

Matisse didn't trust Apollinaire he thought he was a huckster. Matisse's relationship with Picasso began very badly. Paris wanted Picasso and cubism. Picasso didn't need Matisse and his crazy structures his jolting colours and his apparent need of the middle class until everyone who painted was painting cubism and Picasso saw the handwriting on the wall and he knew he could lose his legitimacy so he turned and acknowledged Matisse as a colleague. Matisse accepted Picasso's friendship and in time they became confidants.

The metaphor for trust is plumb a weight indicating direction a line that plummets and becomes plum, a father, a stepfather a true or a false guardian. He loves his wife. He tolerates your mother. Is he jealous of your mother is he jealous of you. He corrects everybody's table manners. He eats with his mouth open. And then remembers to straighten his back and unbutton his coat, uses his knife and fork, and smiles.

It's not surreal it's a coincidence I'd written the above before my friend Lynn St. John sent me *Matisse The Master: A Life of Henri Matisse The Conquest of Colour, 1909–1954*, by Hilary Spurling. He didn't know I was writing "The Trusting Child" and I hadn't thought of Matisse. But halfway into the book there is a quote by Matisse's oldest grandson about "Back IV," 1929-30: "You will find there the whole life of Henri Matisse: an extraordinary equilibrium returning always to the plumb line."

I trust the paranoid who understands that what we live is fragile and subject to changes that cannot always be predicted, that what is turned upside-down is being watched by someone who is competing with you for the prize you both want. That the surreal is an antidote an understanding, that paranoia is a tool a division and it is with division I divide. Trees and motorboats, jazz and the clouds that weather altruism remind me that there are men and women who share their generosity. They are not selfless. On the contrary they want and because they want they care. One such man was Apollinaire. He wasn't naïve and he wasn't a cynic I think he thought everyone he knew believed. Didn't they want what he wanted. He wanted to express his delights his fears and his anguish in a poetry that was relieved of tired and worn out phrases. He wanted painting to be something that was seen and could be seen again as an edge, a motif that presents you with a gift. Take it, it is yours and the child who trusts.

> Pause

She clicks the camera. And what you see is an elderly man with a greying beard and thinning hair. I smile I frown I wish she hadn't taken the photograph and I'm pleased that she wanted to.

> Pause

Apollinaire denied knowing anything about "The Mona Lisa" theft, but he was charged with complicity to steal and sent to the notorious Santé prison.

Later, he wrote:
Before entering my cell
They made me strip to the skin
I hear a sinister wail
Guillaume what have you become

Apollinaire was in prison for five days before police concluded that he really didn't have anything to do with the theft, and he was released. Picasso was questioned, but never arrested.

Later, Apollinaire would call it "strange, incredible, tragic and amusing all at once" that he was the only person arrested in France for the theft of "The Mona Lisa."

> Pause

Being accused
Arrested and jailed
Broke his heart
A broken heart no matter
How fast or slow blood flows
A broken heart
How do you repair
A broken heart

Apollinaire became a French citizen and joined to fight in the Great War. In 1916, he received a serious shrapnel wound to the temple. During this period he coined the word surrealism in the programme notes for Jean Cocteau and Erik Satie's ballet *Parade*, first performed on May 18, 1917. He also published an artistic manifesto, *L'Esprit nouveau et les poètes* and championed the Marquis de Sade, whose works were for a long time obscure. He called him, "The freest spirit that ever existed."

Two years after being wounded Apollinaire died at age 38, a victim of the 1918 Spanish flu pandemic. He was interred in the Père Lachaise Cemetery, Paris.

Pause

Two years would pass before "The Mona Lisa" would be recovered. A former Louvre worker, an Italian named Vincenzo Peruggia, was arrested in Italy after trying to sell the work to an art dealer. In the eyes of Italians, the theft made him a patriot, and "The Mona Lisa" was exhibited throughout the country before it was returned to the Louvre. Today it is exhibited behind reinforced glass.

WINDOWS

Two young women ride the same subway train. One is Asian. The other woman is Arabic. The young Asian woman is reading a book. She is beautiful; the calligraphy she reads is beautiful. The young Arab woman is reading a book. She is beautiful; the calligraphy she reads is beautiful. Lo, calligraphy is for lovers.

> blue   brown
> green   yellow
>
> Maybe the migrant understands
> when it is favourable
> and when it is unfavourable
> to rise like bread
> like sand in the desert
> calligraphy is for lovers

Pause

1940. Leicester Square. Henry Moore draws Eros before he is taken away for safekeeping. H.D. mails Nike a photo of her daughter saying: "I give her to you. My parents never believed anything Pound said. But I did. I still do. My father said, 'Mr. Pound, I don't say there was anything wrong *this time*. I will not forbid you the house, but I will ask you not to come so often.'"

H.D.'s grandparents, her mother's parents, lived next door to H.D.'s mother and father in Bethlehem, Pennsylvania. The two households shared a garden between them and young Hilda Doolittle thought of her grandparents as her other mother and father. H.D.'s father was professor of mathematics and astronomy at Lehigh University. When Hilda was nine years old her father became Flower Professor of Astronomy and founding director of the Flower Observatory at the University of Pennsylvania. The family moved to the Philadelphia suburb of Upper Darby. "Everything revolved around him," wrote H.D. "Everything but the household chores."

> Maybe it was Philadelphia
> Maybe it was her mother
> and father she was
> their only daughter
> H.D. had two brothers

and one half brother
Maybe it was because
she left Philadelphia
for London England and
Ezra Pound – Pound didn't
marry her – she stayed
And in the British Museum
She sipped tea, ate biscuits
And found Helen of Egypt

Maybe it was London
And not Philadelphia
Maybe it was Bryher
Maybe it was Freud
Maybe it was Helen
There was a Helen
before there was a war

In 1942 H.D. visits Benjamin West. He wasn't home, and the housekeeper didn't know when he would return. H.D. wants Mr. West to tell her about her ancestor, Mrs. William Henry (née Mary Ann Wood)

Benjamin West began his painting career as an untrained "plain painter," something bordering on itinerant, a folk artist. H.D's Moravian great-great-great grandparents befriended the young Quaker Benjamin West who in 1755 at the age of sixteen painted a portrait of Mrs. William Henry (née Mary Ann Wood) 1734-1799.

Benjamin West wasn't interested in the plain painters' "correct likenesses." He wanted the Enlightenment Rousseau's savage parable, Europe's soft lawns and documented histories. West the estranged Quaker thrived on flattery and the decorative arts. George the III had lost his Eden. Thirteen states had fought England and won their independence. The King wanted heroics, and West the ex-Quaker was his man. He seems to have had no trouble painting yards of canvas depicting war, Greek myths, and American Indians signing treaties with Europeans.

The King was impatient. Size replaced humility. Greed replaced the future. West's early paintings have no resemblance to the highly polished works that led him to become, after Joshua Reynolds's death, president of the Royal Academy in London.

Be Rich. Get Rich. Be Rich. Get Rich.

America's light is never easy. If you pretend, you fail. If you want rewards, you are disappointed. I insist light abstracts the simplest things. Then beware, beware of pity, you have no one to compete with, you are alone. The competition between artists is always intense.

Frederic Church and Calvert Vaux agreed with Olmstead's methods. Civilize nature. Brute force erects hills, collects pastures, moves rocks, blue jays, and streams. Church's large house *Oleana* sits on top of a hill. Olmstead landscaped Church's hill and all of his property.

Martha and I live in a four-story brick house three and a half blocks from Prospect Park, the Library, and the Botanical Garden. In the park a black cat sits on Daffodil Hill. Its green eyes complement the grass and a stone walk that contains the names of famous people who were born in Brooklyn.

> Frederick Law Olmstead
> The great American impressionist
> Built parks in Boston Massachusetts
> Louisville Kentucky
> Central Park New York
> Belle Isle Detroit
> Mount Royal Montreal

> At *Oleana*
> Windows, carpets,
> the Persian Crescent.
> Hats, little hats.
> Ones that fit
> his wife.
> Ones that
> fit his children.
> Frederic Church
> is a wealthy man.

Church looked out of the window across the Hudson River and saw Thomas Cole's house and studio. Frederic Church had been Thomas Cole's student.

> Born in England.
> Thomas Cole (1801-1848)

Founder of The Hudson River School
had begun as an engraver.

Cole wants allegory.
Symbols that do not
tarnish the past.

The Bowery,
the bowery,
the dancing bower,
sites our contempt
for the things
we do not own.

Not all outsiders migrate. Some stay home.

But a painting that hangs crooked is a humiliation.

Frederic Church (1826-1900) retreats to the exotic, coloured windows, glazes converse with the natives, the Victorian gentleman painted panoramas, Niagara Falls, South American mountains, views of the Andes.

Pause

>Two young women
>are arguing.
>They are
>buying
>a loft.
>
>Which one
>Will buy
>the left
>side.
>Which one
>Will buy
>The right
>side

Pause

Analee Newman understands what separates the two of us as we sleep together. She has her side of the bed, as I have mine. I have my pillow, and she has hers. We respect each other. The size of our bed never changes. But my paintings vary. Some are 7'x18" and some have been wrought out of emotions that are a few inches wide.

> Look at the eyes. White initiates White. Brown initiates the humble beginnings of a land that has not yet initiated Green. Windows, glass. Windows, mirrors, ice, and the water we drink.

> Be Rich. Get Rich. Be Rich. Get Rich.

A woman sits on a large chair holding a child. To the right of the woman there is an open window. In front of the mother and child there are men dressed in ornate robes. Black and white marble floors sparkle in the daylight. Each man kneels on one knee. The sky moves in conjunction with the mountains that are directly behind the town. The artist's left hand draws very sharp thin lines. The river begins to flow around the town. To the left of the woman the artist draws two rooms. We see servants and the furniture that they are polishing. The child that sits on the mother's lap is fat. The artist's pencil shades the child's thighs. The child doesn't seem to have any interest in the mother's exposed breast. She turns her face but she looks at no one. Her nose is too small. Her lips are full. The artist considers the mother's neck her most beautiful feature. The artist says the drawing is unfinished.

Pause

> Whereas a drawing is always contemporary
> No one can finish a short story.
> A short story never ends. A short story remembers what the photograph has forgotten. Whereas a drawing is always contemporary. Painting isn't a race. There is no finish line. The clock ticks twenty four hours a day. Whereas a drawing is always contemporary. A short story remembers what the photograph has forgotten.

Pause

A man and a woman are about to be married. Some have speculated that there are other reasons for the man and the woman to be in the room. So be it. Jan van Eyck wrote on the back wall over the convex mirror in "The Arnolfini Wedding Portrait," "Jan van Eyck was here (present) in 1434." Separated from the symbols of prayer and work van Eyck signs his name. From Giotto to Rembrandt. From Watteau to Soutine. To the present. Artists sign their work.

It's said that Jan van Eyck is one of the two figures in the mirror. The mirror reflects the entire room, of which the painting shows a part. The mirror is a wonderful miniature. It shows all the structural elements of the room. Between the two windows can be seen the framework and supports which hold up the crossbeam and on which the joists and planks of the ceiling rest. So, while the painting shows only one window, the mirror shows the second, which sheds light on the bride and groom.

Pause

Dan Flavin's pristine unorthodox use of fluorescent lighting controls all the material abundance that is conspicuous in van Eyck. Precious stones and knight's armour become saturated with light, decorative light. A feeling of well-being drugs the Virgin and she is quietly removed along with all the furniture that has accompanied the religious dogma of the church. A single light bulb can be dangerous. It can drive you mad. It can keep you awake all night and dismantle your senses. Light, decorative light, dismantled the frame, and the conception of painting, as Flavin understood it, ceased to exist. That was a responsibility that Flavin understood. He was willing to accept that his inventive light that decorated the walls, floors and ceilings produced a product that emulates nothing but beautiful light.

From Jan van Eyck to Dan Flavin, to invent a situation that appears perfect, artists have used artificial light. Dan Flavin's light, like van Eyck's, assumes that there are no contradictions. There is no dirt, no action. No absurd situations interfere with the flawless technique. Van Eyck and Flavin meticulously work their themes, creating a craft that dispenses with vulgarity. Van Eyck knew the courts' intrigues and manipulations. Looking through a door he could see into the next room. And there would be angles, maybe right angles. But most certainly there would be depth. Van Eyck transcribed this depth into clean space, leaving the figures and the objects in his paintings with a room of their own.

Van Eyck, known as Jan of Bruges, tells us just enough about himself in his self-portrait for us to be intrigued. He wears a flaming red turban, which we see filling the canvas above his face. By doing this, he doesn't have to tell us how tall he is. He has a long nose. His thin lips insist that he likes his privacy. His eyebrows are the only hint that the colour of his hair might be blond. He looks into the mirror. Damn it, van Eyck's red turban is on fire. I'm having a nightmare. The window is open and I'm fighting metaphor. Everything van Eyck paints has some symbolic meaning. It's maddening: shoes, dogs, and an orange from the Portuguese woman, a candle. They're unmovable. Debts, they don't exist. Jesus, you presented the state with a proposition the state found unacceptable. Will you ever be forgiven for throwing out the moneylenders.

Pause

I met a woman who asked me what I did. I said, "I'm an artist." She said that she had painted and that her family was in the art business. Her parents and her brother owned a frame shop. They sold prints and art supplies. When a customer asked for a print that they didn't have in stock, for instance flying geese, a sunset or a clown, they'd get the customer to give them the size and colours they wanted. Then a member of the family would paint the picture. She said they made a great living.

Pause

Everyone in Bruges knew we were Americans, they just knew. In Bruges, Martha and I sat at a table in front of a statue of Jan van Eyck. The waiter gave us an inflated check and I had to go inside the café and take care of it. Jan of Bruges dominated the square we sat in, as he had dominated the town of Bruges. Three brickyards had supplied the wealthy town with materials for its cathedral and secular buildings. The bricks of Bruges, someone whispers. The competition amongst painters is always intense.

> Hubert and Jan
> van Eyck
> had a sister
> and we know
> she painted.
>
> I've already told you
> their sister Margareta
> painted. Have I told
> you she never married,
> had children,
> paid a bill,
> grew a potato.
>
> Paint was under
> her finger nails
> between her fingers.
> Starlings, Grass.
> The bricks of Bruges.
> The family paints
> diamonds, pearls.

Blue eyes.
The long nose.
The narrow
lips.
Ears.
Eyes.
A
neck
capped
with
fur.

The family
never
wanted
to
lose.

Because Martha and I
have not lost
our daughters
have witnessed
in colour what for
us had been
Black and White
  espalier
   the past weighs
   against the garden wall.

The clematis flowers
  the foxglove braves
  the city's pavements.
  Dogs dramatize their
  owners' inefficiencies.
  No one rests.

In Ghent
waffles
are served.

The fork
is in the
left hand.

> The knife
> is in the
> right hand.
>
> Decorum
> feeds.
> The van Eycks
> and the Kings

> Pause

It is said that Paolo Uccello (the bird) was in love with perspective, that he loved his artistic problems more than he loved his wife. Paolo, Paolo, come to bed, his wife would call. Uccello lights a candle, walks up the stairs, and when he reaches the top of the stairs, he says to himself, yes, my bird is a mystery. But perspective is a battleground of unending fields. Between each tree, there is a triangle, St. George and the Dragon cannot be deceived.

Within the limited space of a chess board Paolo Uccello moves triangles and muscles up and down the grid. He could have compromised his emotions. He could have fallen in love with his own image and become Narcissus. This he did not do. What he did do was paint desire into the faces of "The Dublin Madonna and Child."

> Get rich. Be rich. Get rich. Be rich.

Every night he knew when she would be undressing. He sat at the window waiting for her. She must have known that he was there. She slowly undressed, deliberately pausing when she bent to take off her stockings. He watched her pale and pink body become naked. It was a ritual that they both participated in.

> Look at her eyes
> White initiates White
> Brown initiates the humble beginnings
> Of a land that has not yet initiated Green
> Windows glass water
> Windows mirrors
> The water we drink
> Look at her eyes
> White initiates White
>
> The passengers read
> Eat apples drink coffee

Others sit by the windows
Trees grass the countryside
Is as vital as the city
The train picks up speed
Close up one square
Open up another
Window

Be Rich. Get Rich. Be Rich. Get Rich.

When I saw the blue house on Pennoyer Street in Grand Haven, Michigan, I wanted it. The house looked as if a child had drawn it. One big window, a door, three steps and a peaked roof above that door outlined the front of the first floor. Two windows on the second floor looked out onto the street, and two windows, second floor rear, looked out into the garden.

The streets never had too many people walking on them, they all drove. When our neighbours wanted to visit their friends, they drove even if it was just three houses over in either direction.

My blue house on Pennoyer Street. I would have loved to roll my blue house with its generous windows, good fireplace, simple large rooms and ample staircase to Rhode Island. To where Gilbert Stuart was born and the fish are always fresh.

America is big. It's so big something is always left out. A person, families, a whole state disappears and is never heard from. Change your name. Change your religion. Grow a beard. Shave it off. The silent movies followed the gold rush. Oh, wilderness, this odd combination consolidates a dream. Instant gratification became part of our heritage. Everyone who comes to America is given one more chance.

Get rich. Be rich. Get rich. Be rich.

Nancy, Paul Metcalf's wife, is making breakfast. The breakfast nook walls are covered with old postcards, photos, on the table soft porn the pink tits are salt and pepper shakers. Outside the croquet wickets are still in place. A car pulls up next to the barn, and a tall man with a grey beard gets out of the car. Nancy gets a cup. She's going to cook bacon, eggs, toast, and coffee.

In high school cheerleaders compete for fame. They want big houses, clothes. Other girls want Hollywood. She wants the camera to makes her nose and her ears look smaller. He's too short but he has large shoulders. They embrace, and it's the scenery that becomes important.

Paul Metcalf (1917-1999) is the great-grandson of Herman Melville.

Herman Melville was the father of Paul Metcalf's grandmother. She would never know her father's contradictions would become part of her grandson's imagination. That by writing *Genoa* Metcalf opened the front door to his family's vanities the chairs are old but the carpets are clean. The Boston Red Sox are playing on TV. The phone rings. Paul answers. Nancy comes out of the house and says, Americans love fame. There is a Hall of Fame for Rock Music, for Country Music, for Baseball, Golfers and Wall Street Traders.

In Metcalf's book *Genoa* (1965), Michael's brother Carl goes mad, and Metcalf informs us, Americans tell stories, sometimes – bad stories.

Pause

Cheerleaders in high school compete for fame. They want big houses, clothes. Other girls want Hollywood. Other girls want babies. A croquet set and a kitchen. Breakfast. Some people have nothing but coffee for breakfast. Others eat a huge meal.

Get rich. Be rich. Get rich. Be rich.

I read that Dorothea Rockburne's maths teacher in Quebec was seven feet tall. But I read it wrong. It wasn't Dorothea; it was Klaus Kertess, one of her dealers, who has a seven foot tall terrifying maths teacher who would lean over him and say, "Kertess, rabbits can multiply. Why can't you."

Dorothea was eighteen or nineteen when she left Montreal for Black Mountain College. Max Dehn was Dorothea's maths teacher, one of the tutors at Black Mountain. And if I remember correctly he wasn't terrifying. Dorothea loves Max. Max taught Dorothea loyalty and not to fear her passions. But Dorothea isn't a mathematician she's a painter. And it is in her paintings that she melds craft to scholarship and the organic pursuit of the intellect. It's in her paintings that she equates the variations, manners and feelings and the delicious curves in nature. Oh, Renaissance! Oh, bare wall. I can see Dorothea standing next to Charles Olson's six feet-eight inches. Dorothea is not a big woman. She's blushing. He was always giving her *the eye*.

Pause

Paul Christensen in *Wikipedia*, November 29, 2008: Charles Olson's Life and Career:

Ishmael was Olson's ideal observer, a figure more interested in the life around him than in himself. Olson is at pains to demonstrate Ishmael's close scrutiny of life, achieved through disinterested curiosity. The body of work following Call Me Ishmael *was Olson's attempt to apply Ishmael's selfless attention to poetry, essays, a few plays, and his long poem,* The Maximus Poem, *on which he spent the better part of his writing life.*

In class Olson was a marvel holding a little piece of chalk in his large hand he'd turn his eyes. Would Ahab get the better of him and would he never see Gloucester again. Then as if Ishmael were beside him he would as he had as a young man pursue Melville's offspring. He knocked on Paul Metcalf's grandmother's door, Melville's daughter. He knocked on Paul's mother's door Melville's granddaughter. She had never known her grandfather. And her mother hated her father. Never mind, Olson wanted information that pertained. Process became a passion a declaration of intent that never wavered. He pursued those of us who were in class for information and by so doing he taught us how to use windows.

14 EYES – DESIRE

To begin: Paul Blackburn had close friendships with Joel Oppenheimer and Robert Creeley, and for a brief time in the 1950s he was the New York distributor of *Black Mountain Review*. Pound was Paul's mentor. It was at Pound's suggestion that Paul embraced the Troubadours. Paul wrote and visited Pound in St. Elizabeth's; he also visited Pound in Italy after his release. Pound wasn't talking to anybody. But he spoke to Paul and told him he had made a mistake and that he was sorry for it.

Pause

I was a student at Black Mountain College visiting New York City. It was either 1953 or '54 and Joel Oppenheimer took me to meet Paul Blackburn. Paul was still living with his first wife Willy (Winifred Grey). I can't remember where they lived or a thing that was said. Willy sat glaring at the three of us the whole time Joel and I were there. And I don't think I saw Paul again until I returned from San Francisco to the city in 1959. In 1961 Martha and I moved to 2nd Avenue. The apartment building was between 3rd and 4th Streets and at that time Paul and his second wife Sara were living on 7th Street, two doors down from McSorley's Tavern. Between readings, McSorley's, 2nd Avenue and my studio, which was on Delancey Street, I'd see Paul three to four times a week.

Paul Blackburn would meet me on 2nd Avenue, cowboy hat, eyeglasses, a pint of brandy, a smile, a giggle. When you went on a picnic with him he'd know the names of the wildflowers. When you walked through midtown, he'd know the bars and I would know that this walk would be re-lived in pictorial detail in his journal.

Pause

Back in the spring of 1970 Paul was considering the teaching job at Cortland. We sat in his apartment for hours going over the pros and cons. Either way he wanted his decision to be a practical one. If he took the job he and his new young family, Joan Miller and their infant Carlos, would have some security. It would also mean they would have to leave the city. Paul was freelancing as a proof-reader at the time.

Paul constantly organized readings, recorded the readings and promoted the poets, and sometimes promoted painters but never himself. He was the itinerant, the man who was always working for something other than himself. This changed when he got to Cortland. After he started teaching and before his cancer was diagnosed I visited Paul and Joan. It was the happiest, the steadiest I ever saw him. We talked about the drawings I was doing for his translations of *Peire Vidal*.

> "Peire Vidal (c. 1175-1205) was from Toulouse, the son of a furrier, and Paul says he sang better than any man in the world. He also says Vidal was one of the maddest fellows that ever lived, for he believed as truth whatever he wanted or whatever happened to please him.
>
> "Because [Paul Blackburn, 1926-1971] had the gifts and desire, he *became* one and all of them, as with genius and learning he gave their poems his own voice and new life in a new language."
> – George Economou, from his 1972 introduction to Paul's *Peire Vidal*.

Pause

For Paul, Joan, and their baby Carlos a showering a flux of well-being carried Cavalcanti and Dante up the stairs. It was a time of change, of soft edges and of students, a faculty that was not hostile. The house wasn't large but it was pleasant, and it had a back yard.

Paul said, "Draw me on a horse." And after a number of attempts I stopped. I'd begin and it would go well and then I'd cry. The horse became the vehicle that was taking him away. I was being selfish but I couldn't do it. In fact I wasn't able to complete the drawings that are in the book until after his death.

The troubadour cried "Mercy, mercy" but mercy does not come.

Pause

First the Poem
Then, the Theory

Paul was a weed lover.

We need Paul Blackburn. On the subway to Coney Island he thrives on reading Pound aloud. Splash! Catch a fish but it isn't a Codfish it doesn't have a name but it is a fish.

And it said
you think you can
take advantage of me
well you can but it
won't get you anything
more than what you've
taken. Because what you
think you want is not
what I've got to give.
What I've got to give is weeds. Weeds insist they grow amongst the needy, amongst the preferred, the upstanding, the beautiful, and the prosperous. Weeds, grass, clover between grasses, triptychs that reach out and condemn child abuse.

Pause

White on white, on white. Do you appreciate the Unicorn Tapestry? Paul did. By the fence surrounding the milk-white unicorn, there are carnations and a butterfly. What appears to be blood on the unicorn's body is juice dripping from pomegranates in the tree above. A wild orchid, a lily, and a small green frog fertilize a faith that marriage is lasting.

That his first two marriages had failed daunted him.

Pause

Paul was abused by his maternal grandmother; she whipped him. That Paul was able to keep his sense of wonder still amazes me.

If you knew the day you were born that your life was temporary would you be brave and want to live knowing no matter what you did the outcome would be the same? It's a question that can never be answered because no matter what you answer if you are alive you are responsible and if you chose immediate death I have identified the cause of your demise.

For example, Charles Bukowski was a scorched man. Bukowski's father's beatings literally beat the poetry out of him. He survived by telling and writing stories that are true social commentaries. And that's why they are so popular. But his poems are not poems. They are stories, narratives with an intended conclusion. It's not that he is a coward, far from it. But Bukowski knows he must not get too far inside of himself; it's too dangerous. He is no fool, he knows that poetry opens the seal and you can never be too sure once that seal is removed that what you find will protect you.

Pause

Paul's poems like change in his pocket are creatures of his invention, they gesture, "There is more." Paul had an aversion to aristocracy and I think that if this isn't understood we miss understanding how Paul connected his contradictions. Be it the Troubadours and their ladies or Lorca whose love of men initiates his ardour, language hurled itself against Paul's thighs and he reacted. As a thief breathes before committing the robbery Paul steals from the men that he translates. What else is a poet to do but respond to other poets their visions. As Martha King said: "Paul wants his meat," and as he pursues it history became meat's equivalent. History lives as a new face and a new body amongst us as Paul climbs the six flights of stairs to Gilbert Sorrentino's apartment on Tompkins's Square.

In a review for *Parnassus* (Spring-Summer 1976), poet Gilbert Sorrentino argues that *The Journals* represents a pinnacle, not a relaxation, of Blackburn's art: "That the poems seem often the thought of a moment, a brilliant or witty or dark response to still-smoking news, is the result of his carefully invented and released voice, a voice that we hear singing, virtuoso."

Be Rich. Get Rich. Be Rich. Get Rich.

"Stuart Errol Ungar (September 8, 1953-November 22, 1998) was a professional poker and gin rummy player, considered to be the best in history at both games. He is the only three-time winner of the World Series of Poker Main Event tournament. He is also the only person to win Amarillo Slim's Super Bowl of Poker three times, the world's second most prestigious poker title during its time."

Pause

Stuey Ungar was born to Jewish parents and raised on Manhattan's Lower East Side. His father, Isadore ("Ido") Ungar, was a loan shark who ran a bar/social club that doubled as a gambling establishment, exposing Stuey to gambling at a young age. Stuey began playing tournament gin at 9 or 10 and quickly made a name for himself.

In 1968, Ido died of a heart attack in his mistress's arms. With his mother virtually incapacitated by illness, Stuey drifted around the New York gambling scene until age 18, when he was befriended by Victor Romano, alleged Genovese family member. Romano, whose memory was so sharp he learned to recite the spelling and definition of every word in the dictionary during his jail time, shared the same interest in calculating gambling odds that Stuey did. The two became so close that Romano acted as a father figure.

Stuey Ungar was infamous for routinely criticizing aloud the play of opponents he felt were beneath him. However, his relationship with Romano gave him protection from various gamblers who did not take Stuey's crass attitude and assassin-like playing style kindly.

By age 14, he was regularly playing and beating the best players in New York. At 15, he dropped out of school when a big time bookie staked him to a gin rummy tournament. Stuey won the $10,000 first prize without even losing a hand, a record still held in the card rooms of New York City. A week later, after giving his parents $1,000, he lost the rest on horses at Aqueduct. It was a sign of things to come.

> Feed Me – I am starving
>
> Feed Me – I am frightened
>
> Feed Me –
>
> Feed Me

Stuey moved to Miami and in 1976 he reached Las Vegas. He won enormous sums of money and lost them betting on the horses and sports events. Somehow he found the money to enter a $50,000 tournament. His bravado got the better of him and on the last two hands he forecast the losing player's cards – correctly. This was another bad career move as it meant other players feared his skills. As a result, he could no longer find any games outside the tournaments.

It wasn't long before he decided to try his luck at blackjack. One night at Caesar's Palace he won $83,000 but the manager stopped the play. Stuey retaliated by correctly forecasting the last 18 cards left in the single-deck shoe. That was the beginning of the end for single deck blackjack tables. They were removed from Caesar's and later from other casinos, and Stuey's picture was posted in the security rooms of dozens of casinos.

> Pause

By 1990 Stuey was addicted to drugs.

In 1997, 16 years after his first win, he made his final tournament appearance. He needed the help of a friend to pay his entry fee. Fittingly just as he won in his first try he also won in his last, taking home the $1 million first prize. Two months later, after paying off gambling debts and suffering heavy losses on horse and sports wagers, Stuey was broke again.

>Feed Me – I am starving

>Feed Me – I am frightened

>Feed Me –

>Feed Me

>Pause

On November 22nd, 1998, in a cheap downtown hotel in Las Vegas he was dead. The Clark County Coroner's office ruled Stuey's death accidental based on the results of toxicology tests that showed a mixture of narcotics and painkillers triggered a heart condition that killed him. Clark County Coroner Ron Flud said, "The heart condition developed over a period of time. The attack was brought on by his life-style."

From the time he was a little boy the seal was broken. Numbers, figures, money didn't interest him. He wasn't interested in accumulating wealth, power. Marriage, children, a home he thought he wanted – but he didn't. Love, like owning a house and paying your bills, confused him. Numbers, a deck of cards with the joker discarded mines the face cards and the four aces, Black Jack, 21. You have reached your majority and now it's your turn to deal.

No visible contradictions ride the multiples. Rain, thunder and lightning, a patch of yellow, a ghost carpets paradise. The house of cards forfeits the truth.

Once you start the purpose is not to stop either the despair or the thrill of winning.

>Like a severed
>weed
>the weather renounces
>what was once omitted
>was once
>illegal
>now frames

oblivion
a math known to all
needs more than
what has been taken
psalms psalms desire

Pause

Knock, knock. It was 1968. I opened the studio door. There was Paul, cowboy hat, eyeglasses, a pint of brandy, a smile, and that giggle that always seemed to have come from the bottom of his bowels. He didn't say anything. He took one look at the painting I was working on. It was an arch, an important image for me. Said something under his breath and left. Some time later there was another knock. It was Paul. He handed me a large envelope that contained a photograph of another arch that looked just like the arch I was painting. The Zabriski Arch is at Bard College and Paul had taken the photograph on one of his visits to Robert Kelly. My painting is lost. But I have Paul's photograph. It hangs on a wall in our living room.

I also have another photograph. In this one Joan Miller stands on a wall with her left hand on Paul Blackburn's shoulder. He stands on the ground next to her. They both look at the camera.

By the fence surrounding the milk-white unicorn, there are carnations and a butterfly. What appears to be blood on the unicorn's body is juice dripping from pomegranates in the tree above. A wild orchid, a lily, and a small green frog fertilize a faith that marriage is lasting. That his first two marriages had failed daunted him. Paul was not a man given to excuses, white on white, on white. Do you appreciate the Unicorn Tapestry?

Pause

The Joker has sat by my side for so many years that I can't remember the first time he sat down next to me. He has told me that he was the last surviving card of the Tarot, that he had sat at the feet of Charles VI of France, and that in 1392 the king had ordered the first three games of cards, the first known Tarots, to be painted in the West. He told me that King René's sister Maria married Charles VI of France in 1404. He tells me of Margaret of Anjou, King René's daughter – how at the age of 16 she married King Henry VI of England. He was weak-minded and was unable to protect her – and how Margaret lost crown and possessions in the changing fortunes of the Wars of the Roses. In 1471, near Tewkesbury, the Lancasters were decisively beaten. Margaret lost her son and her husband. She then spent five years in the Tower, only to be sold by Edward IV to Louis XI, to whom she had to cede the legacy of her father, King René, as a show of gratitude for her liberation. And the Joker tells me this as he gossips with diplomacy and humour.

The King of Sicily and Duke of Anjou (1409-1480) was called Good King René. He fought by the side of Joan of Arc, and when he was defeated at the Battle of Bulignéville, Duke Philip took him prisoner and incarcerated him in his fortress at Dijon. It was said that at Dijon René became the pupil of the Dutch painter Jan van Eyck. Van Eyck could have been his master, could have taught the king colour and design. This extraordinary man, King of Sicily, Duke of Anjou, muted his colours, and wrote his autobiography.

No one knows for certain if René of Anjou painted the illuminations for his *Book of Love*. But we do know he was an aesthete who spared nothing for his pleasures and self-satisfactions.

The night scene in the *Book of Love*'s portfolio is amazing; the artist, whoever he or she was (Hubert and Jan van Eyck had a sister and we know she painted) those figures in the night I have never seen equalled.

No one knows and the mystery continues because not all medieval miniatures were painted by monks. Most miniatures were painted by itinerant craftsmen. The limner would draw in the motif. Then the colourist would follow with his apprentices. The gold leafier and his apprentices worked. It took many stages and many craftspeople to complete one miniature. Every one of these people would send a poster ahead of their arrival, giving the town the dates and times that they would be available. Sometimes they stayed for two days and other times they would stay for more than a week. It depended on how much work was available. This process was continued by itinerant artists all the way through the nineteenth century.

Pause

After Paul died I went back to the photograph – to Joan's stance and the delicacy of her left hand, her face and the complement her clothes gave her body. In the photo, Joan is young. Paul is older. But doesn't look that much older. His beret, turtleneck, khaki pants and shirt cover him like a uniform.

I painted Joan partially clothed. Having been exposed to sickness and death for the second time in her young life (her father had died earlier), nothing complements her body. Her left hand remains delicate, her face shows hurt and anger, a bitchiness. When Paul lay dying he asked for poems to be read to him. The great painter Turner as he lay dying asked for a crayon.

White on white. The empty canvas rewards those who have patience. But the machine is impatient. Oil not desire moves the machine.

Paul is dead. But the photograph of Paul and Joan isn't. From it I translated what I knew of them. Joan said she knew that look on her face and she didn't like it. And why should she. She is with Paul and he is dead – and she has become a body traversed. Will she change the painting. Will she paint "Joan and Paul". Will she smile and wear clothes. Will the fence disappear and in its place will there be buildings, romance, a rainbow. A Paul who is alive. A Paul who reads his poem aloud.

Pause

Excerpted from: *The Journals*: May, 1971

Carl is not coming to the reading. He has paper to correct. Marcia is not coming to the reading. She has a new baby. Joan is not coming to the reading. Carlos T. wants to play with the new baby & won't sleep. Walter is not coming to the reading because he thinks Carl will be there, besides, Diane arrived today for a visit, and she was at the reading in Milwaukee yesterday. Gerth is not coming to the reading because he's behind time as usual and thinks 9 o'clock is too late. It's my reading. I take Marcia's mother to the reading. A pleasant surprise, Mary and Ed are at the reading. No one else records it. I read until 10.30. It's a good reading.

Pause

Paul said poetry never failed him and he told me before he died that I had a long poem to write.

Pause

If Paul wanted a woman it was inconceivable to him that she wouldn't want him. And if she didn't he was crushed. This was all part of Paul's insistence, his belief that everything should be available.

No. He isn't going to burn your house down, break plates, smash windows or scream at your children. He might phone you, and read you a poem. He might stop you on the street, and read you a poem. He might take the A train and say this to the passengers:

"On the matter of song: I believe there must be a return toward the musical structure of poetry, just as there must be, for certain people at least, a return to warmth within a relationship."

The air that fills our lungs exposes us to the origins of our dilemmas. Paul heralded these daily fragments. He never dismissed them. He would have understood why I painted Joan partially clothed. Having been exposed to sickness and death for the second time in her young life (her father had died earlier), nothing complements her body. Her left hand remains delicate, her face shows hurt and anger, a bitchiness. Paul is dead. As friendly as we were with each other I know very little about him. He had secrets. Paul's lawyer didn't know and Joan didn't know but after he died it was discovered he had money in a Swiss bank.

Paul is smiling. He just got a letter.
Paul is smiling. He is drinking brandy.
Paul is smiling. He's just bought himself a new cowboy hat.
Paul is smiling. He is carrying a bunch of flowers.
Paul is smiling. He's smoking a Picayune.
Paul is smiling. He's just read a new poem.

Will Joan smile and wear clothes. Will the fence disappear and in its place will there be buildings, romance, a rainbow. A Paul who is alive. A Paul who reads his poems aloud.

To be precise, Paul deferred to precision as an act of generosity. He wanted to deplete jealousy of its powers. Wanted poetry to be not only in the bookstores. He wanted greed annihilated.

CLOUDS

In the early 1960s, John Manning asked me if I'd like to team up with him on a contract to paint and hang signs for the Big Apple, a chain of supermarkets. Most of the markets were outside of Manhattan, on Long Island. We'd arrive before the store closed for the night with templates, wooden letters, big cardboard apples with aisle numbers on them, our brushes, and a large nondescript bag filled with crumpled paper. We dragged this bag as if it were heavy. The stores usually closed at 9p.m. and the manager would let us out the next morning at 7a.m. The freezers had peculiar music – low, demanding – they were as if from another planet, and John and I were disturbed by them. Chickens, pigs, and cows. It was painting by numbers. We had templates, instructions, and premixed colours. We applied all this to the white walls. Then we'd take a break and decide what meats and canned goods we were going to put into the now empty bag.

One night we painted a huge basket of eggs with three different whites which we distributed Albers-like. Some eggs came forward some went back. About a week later, we got a call. The manager of the store was getting complaints from customers who said when they looked at that basket of eggs they got dizzy. The manager didn't know what was wrong – but we'd better fix it fast. One coat of white and safety was restored.

Get Rich. Be rich. Get rich. Be rich.

"It's always the same work that's so hard and uncertain," John Abbott McNeil Whistler wrote Fantin LaTour. "I am so slow," said the man who signed his paintings with a butterfly. "I am so slow. To know what to paint, and then to paint it."

Bryher's father, Sir John Ellerman, called her Dolly. Annie Winifred Ellerman 1894-1983 named herself Bryher, her favourite island in the Scillies, a group of islands 28 miles west-south-west of Land's End. Bryher's father was a poor young man when he was given his start by Sir Frederick Leyland, a prosperous Liverpool ship owner who was a patron of John Abbott McNeil Whistler. John Ellerman became a millionaire. When Sir John died in 1933 he was described as the wealthiest man in England second only to the King.

Bryher met H.D. in 1918. Bryher was short, intense, looked Jewish, and disliked herself for being a woman. She wanted to take over her father's empire. He told her women were not welcome in the male dominated clubs or allowed to sit in on their business transactions. "Outsiders" such as women would be forced into a losing game.

Bryher's mother and father were not married when she was born. In fact they didn't marry until her brother John was born, fifteen years later. Bryher knew that if she wanted respectability she would have to get married.

Bryher worshiped H.D. Even though active sex between the two of them seems to have cooled early in their relationship, Bryher's life-long devotion to H.D. never wavered. H.D. would become exasperated with Bryher. She had tantrums. At times she become impossible to live with. H.D. would write her friends letters condemning Bryher. But then, as it is in so many relationships, neither one left. Bryher wanted H.D.'s approval and H.D. wanted Bryher to be around. Bryher applauded and steadied H.D.

Lo, the line comes from outside, and the surreal knocks. It knocks for those who hear it, and it knocks for those who are unaware that we are related to clouds.

Robert McAlmon's father, a poor Presbyterian minister on the Minnesota border, had eight children. McAlmon's childhood was bleak and abusive. He left home early and after a semester at the University of Southern California he drifted to New York City.

To say he drifted describes something that is incorrect. McAlmon had a purpose. He rode the rails, hitched, and worked at odd jobs: dishwasher, possible tomato picker. He was looking for someone to talk to, someone who had ideas, literary ideas. People who were not criminals. He wasn't interested in going to prison.

McAlmon's *Distinguished Air*, a collection of stories about homosexuals, lesbians, transvestites, drug addicts, and alcoholics, was fiction. McAlmon wrote it after he and Marsden Hartley visited post-war Berlin. William Carlos Williams later claimed, "*Distinguished Air* heads the list of (McAlmon's) own writing. It is a brilliant piece of work, unfortunately all but unpublishable because of the material."

Marsden Hartley introduced Robert McAlmon to William Carlos Williams in Greenwich Village. McAlmon was a cowboy, he was self-taught, and when he wasn't defensive he could be thoughtful and caring. Williams was always the immigrant, the outsider. He was always uncomfortable with himself. They took to each other immediately. McAlmon and Williams started the magazine *Contact* together.

H.D. wrote Williams that she and Bryher were coming to New York. Williams introduced McAlmon to them. McAlmon was earning a dollar an hour as a model at Cooper Union when he was introduced to H.D. and Bryher. It was Bryher's first visit to America. Bryher had never met anyone like McAlmon. She told him that she wanted to be a boy. He told her about his boyhood, the beatings, humiliation, and bad food. He told her that to survive he had done things that he was not proud of.

Bryher was twenty-six, McAlmon was twenty-five. She was serious about everything she did. She couldn't separate herself from her family. She was dependant, especially on H.D.'s good opinion. McAlmon, the itinerant, was street wise. He wanted to teach Bryher, instruct her, he wanted her to have fun. He also wanted something he could never have. He wanted to love her. Did he want to have sex with her. Bryher and McAlmon were married at the City Hall in New York City on February 14, 1921, St. Valentine's Day.

Two years later, Sir John Ellerman gave McAlmon £14,000 for his publishing ventures. Between 1922 and 1930 Contact Publishing Press published "the Bunch" as McAlmon called them. They were mostly unknown: William Carlos Williams, H.D., Djuna Barnes, Bryher, Mina Loy, Ernest Hemingway, Gertrude Stein, Ezra Pound, Nathaniel West, and Robert McAlmon.

In Paris Bryher paid for everything. She gave James Joyce $150 a month while he was writing *Ulysses*. Robert McAlmon was one of Joyce's most ardent supporters. He typed much of the first draft of *Ulysses*. His marriage was supposed to be one of convenience. Bryher would have the marriage ring, and McAlmon's name. He would be secure financially. It didn't work. McAlmon wanted more. He wasn't happy, he wanted more. He cared for her and it hurt his pride that she didn't want him. He began to drink. They divorced in 1927.

> Maybe it was Buffalo Bill.
> Maybe it was Dante.
> Maybe it was Beatrice.
> Maybe it was London.
> Maybe it was Detroit.

The surreal knocks. It's 1949. Kenneth McPherson and Bryher's silent 1930 movie *Borderline* is being shown in the auditorium of a mid-western museum. Three fourteen-year-old boys are in the audience of maybe fifteen people. The month before they had been with almost the same audience when Hans Richter had spoken before showing his movie, *Dreams That Money Can Buy*.

They have never heard of Arthur Rimbaud, William Carlos Williams, H.D., or Bryher. The boys do not know that H.D. is a poet or that Bryher is a millionaire and a Lesbian. Their heads are shaved. They wear blue jeans, red suspenders, and engineering boots. The boys are art students.

The boys dream of fucking women who will never quarrel or clash with them. They are virgins and they want a classless society. The movie *Borderline* is as puzzling and new to them as was Matisse's "Dance" and Picasso's "Les Demoiselles d'Avignon." The violence, the distortions in all three works disturbs and exhilarates their young libidos. They leave the museum wanting more.

Get rich. Be rich. Get rich. Be rich.

Can you find a brush stroke a hair out of place. The master never had any trouble painting texture. Jean-Auguste Ingres painted Madame Moitessier and what he thought was her profile reflected in the mirror. But the woman in the mirror is not Madame Moitessier. Ingres did not paint the same woman when he painted the woman in the mirror. The woman in the mirror, the one whose back we see, the woman no one mentions, is nameless. She looks nothing like Madame Moitessier. She's the woman the Cubists painted. She is a modern woman. When she turns her back on us, she will have her own reasons for doing so. We know her. She went to the movies with us last night. She sat watching the movie with her right hand propped up against her chin, and afterwards she said she wanted to go home, alone.

Madame Moitessier's right hand is propped up against her face. She sits facing us. A beautifully glazed surface picks up every tassel, every minute fold in her dress. Her eyes are like a highly fired vase. She stares at us. We cannot get close enough to her. Her soft body cannot be harmed. She is Empire.

Ingres painted two paintings on one canvas. Madame Moitessier is an autocrat. The woman in the mirror is a romantic. Is she listening to a manifesto. Is she a Socialist. She is listening to nothing. She strokes Ingres's unconscious and says to her children: Boots are as important as trees. People are important. Bread is important. The woman, the one Ingres painted in the mirror, is a modern woman. When she turns her back on us, she will have her own reasons for doing so. We know her.

In defiance of myth science reveals some mysteries. What Titian so capably did in old age by blurring his edges, Impressionism turned upside down with vibrant colours that could be manufactured in a factory.

Impressionism, Socialism, and Communism, boots as important as trees juxtaposed a social and aesthetic walk through the park. A tube of paint and the steam engine competed for importance. With this new vocabulary Ibsen, Henry James, and D.H. Lawrence used language, not paint, to assault beauty. He wore her hat and she wore his. He rarely wore a skirt. But she wore pants. A man paints his nails. A woman changes her shoes. Who is going to take the garbage out.

A Story

It was a year or two before the war ended. I was nine years old and every two to three weeks for a period of a few months my mother took me to the dentist. Teeth were extracted. I had to be fitted for a retainer that I would wear at night when I went to bed. After each visit to the dental clinic we would treat ourselves to lunch at Gamages. Bangers and mash, fish and chips. Then we would tour the store. I remember a large display of cricket bats. And it was at Gamages that we bought me a Green Riley. Unfortunately I wasn't able to bring the bike with me when we moved to America. In Detroit I got a Schwinn bicycle. It never measured up to the Green Riley.

Gamages – From *Wikipedia*, the free encyclopaedia, Nov. 13, 2008:

> Gamages was a department store at 116-128 Holborn in Central London founded by Mr. A. W. Gamage. It closed in 1972, but prior to that had been unusual inasmuch as its premises were away from the main Oxford Street shopping area, being on the edge of the City of London at Holborn.
>
> Arthur Walter Gamage was the son of a Herefordshire farmer who was apprenticed to a London draper in St. Paul's churchyard. In 1878, at the age of 21 and having saved £40 (equivalent to £2,500 today) he decided to set up his own shop, in partnership with Frank Spain. Between them they raised the £88 necessary to lease and refit a small watch repair shop in Holborn. The owner assured them that a hosiery shop would do well in the area. The frontage was no more than five feet and above it Gamage hung his motto "Tall Oaks from Little Acorns Grow."
>
> The partners lived in the back room of the shop and allowed themselves no more than fourteen shillings a week for their living expenses. Gamage insisted on selling everything cheaper than anywhere else and gradually crowds began to visit the shop, even though the area was "unfashionable." By the end of the first year

trading had grown to £1,632. In 1881, Gamage bought Spain out and began to expand the premises by buying the small properties that surrounded his original shop until, by the end of the decade, most of the block between Leather Lane and Hatton Garden was in his hands.

Because of the piecemeal expansion, his Department Store ended up as a maze of rooms, steps, passages and ramps which Gamage now called the People's Popular Emporium. Children and adults alike experienced something of an adventure as they wandered through the warren in search of bargains. It offered a very wide selection of goods, including haberdashery, furniture, sporting goods, gardening supplies and utensils, camping equipment and clothing.

Gamage went on to become the official supplier of uniforms to the Boy Scout movement and continued to expand. A large zoological department and a toy department were joined by a motor department where one could purchase a motor car and all the equipment required for running it. One of the largest departments was that devoted to pedal bicycles and motorcycles. Gamage died in 1930 and tradition has it that he lay in state in the cycle department with a guard of honour made up of members of his staff.

The Holborn premises closed in March 1972 and disappeared in the massive redevelopment scheme which now occupies the site. The frontage on Holborn that was Gamages is now occupied by a W H Smith stationery store.

As my cousins Renee and Berthold in England wrote me when I asked them for the location and correct spelling for Gamages, "We all regret Gamages demise, it was a landmark and a joy for kids of all ages."

Get rich. Be rich. Get rich. Be rich.

Jean-Siméon Chardin (1699-1779) – no, no one ever saw him paint. Did he purr.

Chardin, Mondrian – no one ever saw them paint. Did they purr. Morandi's edges purr.

Mondrian's edges challenge Chardin's labour.

The revolution has taken place
The monarch has been deposed
Mondrian's palette balances blacks
Reds blues and yellows
Colours that symbolize
Royalty in the face cards
Mondrian strips these colours
Of their pedigree
Green is never used

The King and his family are in the fields
Working with the farmers and their families
Every male wears Red
Every female wears Blue
And all the children wear Yellow
Black is for Sundays
But no one pays attention
To the farmer who tells them
The future is suspect

Pause

Chardin, Mondrian – no one ever saw them paint. Did they use their thumbs. Did they purr. Morandi's edges purr. If domesticity is the wildest, defy class and have sex. Chardin was the first to teach that fruit and dead animals could be suspect, and he never painted them with the living.

Chardin painted "The House of Cards" twice in 1737. Both times he used the same table and the same boy and possibly the same deck of cards.

The boy contemplates his future. If he doesn't make a mistake, if he can keep his body still and his left hand from shaking, he will do honour to his class. The boy is old enough to know what his father does for a living. And what of the boy's mother the mistress of the house. In the private life of a painting, the mother and her children do what they do every day. So does Chardin. He paints. The boy's father, Jean Jacques Lenoir, is a successful cabinet-maker and furniture dealer. Chardin's maternal grandfather and his uncle are manufacturers of tennis racquets.

Pause

Europe is the museum
America is the attic

Old man that I am
But not old enough
To be old
Requires
Children
Bring to America
A Celtic witch
A Roman penis
A Danish braid
Circumvent the coast
Go inland
Toothbrush
Hair combs
A column
From
The British
Museum
Celtic witch
Roman penis
Danish braid
Circumvent the coast
Go inland
Old man that I am
But not old enough
To be old
Requires
Children
Hide in the attic
Loose change
Statues
Bicycle wheels
Toy trains
Aunt Lori's
Leg
Uncle Slim's
Passport
He never went
Anywhere
But up
And down
Stairs
Old man that I am
But not old enough
To be old

Sailed the Ocean
Went to all
The museums
Except the ones
In Denmark
Cousin Malcolm
Went to Wales
And saw
What Wales
Saves
England

Europe is the museum America is the attic

PART II

Rain Clouds

Cumulonimbus

Remember Big Harpe and Little Harpe, "their tawny appearance and dark curly hair betrayed a tinge of African blood." The Harpe brothers crossed out kindness, happiness and all forms of civilized behaviour from their minds except revenge. And with only that in mind they inflicted vengeance and bodily harm on anyone who crossed their path.

Pause

Paul Robeson (1898-1976) played football, graduated top of his class from Rutgers University, had the highest grade-point average, 15 letters, and membership in the Cap and Skull Honour Society of Rutgers University. He started New York University Law School, transferred to Columbia Law School and graduated in 1921.

All the time Robeson was going to school he supported his family by singing on Broadway, and at the Cotton Club. In 1928 he began his acting career in *Show Boat* on the London stage. By 1930, Robeson was a celebrity. In Europe nothing could stop this brilliant man. It seemed as if he could do anything he wanted. There were no boundaries, no borders. Robeson was a citizen with an international passport.

In 1933 Robeson returned to America and made the movie *Emperor Jones*.

In 1934 he went to the Soviet Union to see Sergei Eisenstein. There was talk of a movie between them.

Big Harpe and Little Harpe, "their tawny appearance and dark curly hair betrayed a tinge of African blood." The Harpe brothers crossed out kindness, happiness and all forms of civilized behaviour from their minds except revenge. And with only that in mind they inflicted vengeance and bodily harm on anyone who crossed their path.

The census taken in New Orleans in 1880 listed the cartoonist George Herrimans's family as Mulattoes. John J. Audubon's mother was a black woman, as was one of Paul Robeson's wife Eslanda's parents.

Pause

A beautiful black man who happens to be Paul Robeson stands in front of a beautiful white woman who happens to be H.D. H.D. crosses her legs, her long thigh is the Atlantic Ocean. Paul Robeson crosses his legs; his long thigh is the Pacific Ocean.

Another woman crosses her legs; her long thigh is the Atlantic Ocean. Another man crosses his legs; his long thigh is the Pacific Ocean. From the hip to the knee the landscape crosses the meridian. The subjective phrase "Mid Atlantic" Latitude 45 West, Longitude 30 North, is never mentioned.

    Bird
    Gossip
    Rain
    Modern
    Mix

        Daily finger-
        Tips cover our
        Foot-prints

The pencil has not left the paper and curves around a woman's face. The lips will never be finished. She has turned her head. We know she is smiling but at who. We will never know. The line continues to draw clouds.

    Get rich. Be rich. Get rich. Be rich.

John Constable is an overbearing mother he hovers over nature. The leaves are unable to breathe. They wish they could hide, but where. If they fall they will become mulch. So they refuse to give him the attention he craves.

On a large movie screen we see John Constable hunt "the chief organ of sentiment" clouds. Constable swiftly executes one oil painting after another. They are almost all annotated with the date, weather conditions, time of day (one is timed at precisely five minutes past five in the afternoon) using the 1820 treatise *The Climate of London*, in which the Latin-name cloud classifications in use today were first published.

Pause

During the Second World War in London Bryher and H.D. frequented a restaurant around the corner from where they lived. The restaurant wasn't doing well. Because of food shortages they were losing their clientele. Bryher gave the couple who ran the restaurant money to tide them over until things got better. Things didn't and eventually the restaurant closed.

Get rich. Be rich. Get rich. Be rich.

It was Kenneth McPherson who persuaded Bryher to get a divorce from McAlmon. Kenneth McPherson and Bryher were married at the Chelsea Registry Office in September 1927. Then McPherson, Bryher, and H.D. shared a honeymoon in Venice. Bryher became McPherson's benefactress, his older friend. She ensured his future and gave him all the time he wanted to continue his love affair with H.D. McAlmon said of H.D. that she managed to be cold and withdrawn and passionately beautiful – but – "Alas," says McAlmon, "passion withheld."

H.D. lives in England and on the Continent but retains her American citizenship. Bryher's father is Jewish, her mother a Christian. Bryher legally adopts H.D.'s daughter, saying it is for financial reasons.

H.D. was forty when she took the twenty-four-year-old Kenneth McPherson as a lover. He dazzled and manipulated both her and Bryher. Both of them wanted to please him.

McPherson's parents were fallen Scottish gentry. His father painted flowers, his mother was known for her love affairs with younger men, sometimes her son's friends. McPherson would have to make his way in the world on his good looks and charm.

Bryher gave McPherson a movie camera as a present. In 1927 he filmed young John Ellerman, Bryher's brother, wildly dancing in a film called *Wingbeat*. After that he filmed *Foothills*. At the time he was making these movies Brhyer came up with the idea of a film magazine. McPherson edited the magazine *Close-Up*, and for over six years Bryher and McPherson called on everyone they knew to express their views and write criticism about film.

Close-Up was an instant success. H.D., Gertrude Stein, Dorothy Richardson all wrote about the importance of this new craft. Or was it to be a new art. *Close-Up* was an open letter and some of the best artists of the day confronted the social and commercial implications of film.

McPherson never took his pencil off the page while making the movie *Borderline*. In a series of over nine hundred pictures he drew and wrote his scenario for the film. In the movie *Borderline* Astrid, played by H.D., and Thorne (Gavin Arthur) quarrel. Thorne accidentally kills her. Thorne has been having an affair with Adah (Eslanda Robeson). Adah is black. She is blamed for the murder. The judge and the town's people are bigoted and Thorne is acquitted. Adah does not know that her husband Peter (Paul Robeson) is in the same town working in a hotel-cafe that is run by a cigar-smoking manageress (Bryher).

Eslanda and Paul Robeson are man and wife. Adah and Peter and the white actors are acting out a drama that could be taking place in Woodstock, New York, Key West, or Cornwall. Class, colour, and gender cross. And everyone knows that privilege expects to cross every border without penalty. McPherson's *Borderline* never makes conclusions. Only McPherson's cast of characters corroborate that the movie *Borderline* is not about evil. It is about men and women who do not have homes, children, occupations. They are consumed with self. Narcissus dissolves into the colossal ambiguity that McPherson calls BORDERLINE.

Kenneth McPherson was a very practical man. When he got up in the morning his first thought was what can I do for myself today. He wanted to have the best of what being an artist can give you. And he was willing to work very hard for its accesses and privileges. John McPherson, Kenneth's father, stopped painting flowers and helped his son with the lighting for the movie *Borderline*. The family was energized. After making four movies, editing *Close-Up* for six years and using the money that Bryher gave him, he earned a reputation as a modern master and was able to re-establish his family and himself. As a gentleman McPherson bought paintings, villas, and travelled.

The pencil has not left the paper and curves around a woman's face. The lips will never be finished. She has turned her head. We know she is smiling but at who. We will never know. The line continues to draw clouds.

Pause

And what about Robert McAlmon. Did he want access to something he could never talk about. He wanted Bryher, and that he could never have. He wasn't lazy. Did he want people to be better than they are. He wanted equality, in a better world. With Bryher's father's money he published *Contact*. No one paid him to type the first draft of *Ulysses*. Did he know that he was saying: "I want nothing for myself." Maybe he never knew that the people he cared about were jealous of him.

After McPherson married Bryher, McAlmon, being the cowboy that he was, could do nothing else but get drunk and ride away.

THE REAL THING HAS FOUR PARTS

PART I

James Cagney started his career in show business just after World War I. A fellow employee at Wanamaker's told him a troupe of vaudevillians were auditioning singers and dancers, and paying $35 a week. Cagney auditioned, and although he could neither sing or dance, he got the job.

James Cagney was born in the Yorkville section of Manhattan, New York. His father was a bartender and amateur boxer. As a youth, Cagney had a fine reputation as a fighter.

James Cagney was an intuitive actor, a master of improvisation, he could change his personae from gangster to clown. However superficial, violent, brutal or downright nasty his characters are, he gives them an understanding that cannot be faked.

Pause

Private Lattie Tipton, a lanky 33-year-old Tennessean who had become Audie Murphy's closest friend and a father figure of sorts, followed Murphy forward to take on the Germans. Murphy urged him to head back and get a wounded ear treated, but Tipton refused. "Come on Murphy," he said, "let's move up. They can kill us, but they can't eat us. It's against the law." Minutes later Tipton was dead. The Germans had waved a white flag, and Tipton, though an experienced infantryman, made the mistake of standing up. German machine guns treacherously shot him right back down.

Tipton's death swept Murphy into a blur of fury. "I remember the experience as I do a nightmare," he wrote. "A demon seems to have entered my body. My brain is coldly alert and logical. I do not think of the danger to myself. My whole being is concentrated on killing. Later the men pinned down in the vineyard tell me that I shout pleas and curses at them, because they do not come up and join me." Using a captured German machine gun, Murphy methodically mowed down the Germans who had killed his friend. "As the lacerated bodies flop and squirm, I rake them again," Murphy wrote; "and I do not stop firing while there is a quiver of life left in them." Murphy won the Distinguished Service Cross for his actions that day. He gave the medal to Tipton's daughter.

Pause

George Herriman a small, slight, handsome man with twinkling grey eyes and curly close-cropped black hair the hair was hidden under a Stetson hat which he wore *all the time.* A vest, suspenders, a piece of Navajo jewellery and a shirt with the sleeves rolled up were the distinctive features of his daily dress. Herriman was enamoured of the desert, of Monument Valley, and he loved the Navajo people. In his shirt pocket a pouch of Bull Durham tobacco with the pull cord hanging out was always on display. Herriman always rolled his cigarette with one hand.

Pause

With gloved hands Raymond Chandler writes his stories. English Raymond, drunken Raymond marries an older woman. He mothers her and documents the wealthy and the corrupt of L.A.

Pause

I'm in L.A. in a car with Jack Rice. The police have pulled us over and tell me to get out. They check my I.D., handcuff me and drive me to a police station. I'm finger printed and put into the bullpen. A half an hour later a sergeant walks me downstairs and tells me I'm free to go. I ask why was I arrested. I fit the description of a kid that escaped from a correctional facility upstate. My fingerprints had saved me they didn't match my look-a-like's prints.

Pause

I told the butcher I was a boy in England during World War Two. There was a shortage of food and to this day I think of rabbit as a delicacy. I told him at our end of the road Mrs. Haynes had the rabbits, Aunt Jenny and Uncle Lew had the chickens and sometimes there were eggs. My father grew potatoes, tomatoes, cauliflowers and Brussels sprouts in the backyard. Up and down our road nothing was wasted nothing was thrown out.

The butcher answered. I was born in Italy and we were so poor that my father killed our dog's puppies because we didn't have enough food to feed them. We never ate chicken my grandfather sold them. He looked at me. The waste in this country, the waste, restaurants, supermarkets they all throw good food into the garbage. We had a store in Manhattan and with bread you never know some days all of it goes and other days I took the leftover bread to a church and would leave it by the church door. I told the nuns to give the bread to the needy. I was in the pizza parlour across the street from the church eating a slice and I see this guy come out of the church pick up the bread and throw it into the garbage. I don't know I almost gave up religion those lying nuns.

The line comes from outside

Plagued by nightmares and sounds he thought he heard, Audie Murphy began sleeping in a bedroom made up in his converted garage, with the lights on and with a pistol under his pillow. He tried using tranquilizers but got addicted to them, finally throwing away the pills and locking himself in a hotel room until the withdrawal symptoms ceased. He acted in more and more forgettable movies, invested in real estate, bred horses, and gambled. "I didn't care if I won or lost," he said, "it was as if I wanted to destroy everything I had built up." In 1968 he went bankrupt. Two years later, he was in the headlines again, when he and a friend were charged with beating up a dog trainer. In every news story, he was invariably identified as "America's most decorated soldier". Today, his symptoms would be diagnosed as post traumatic stress disorder, but that term didn't exist during his lifetime. He had seen men die – ripped apart by machine guns, run over by tanks, obliterated by mortar fire. He had killed many men himself, supposedly accounting for 240 Germans single-handedly. "To become an executioner, somebody cold and analytical, to be trained to kill, and then to come back into civilian life and be alone in the crowd – it takes an awful long time to get over it," he told journalist Thomas Morgan in 1967. "Fear and depression come over you."

At war's end the most decorated soldier needed another war. Being that there wasn't one there was no place for him to go. That he gambled and was not concerned if he won or lost, made movies wrote songs wrote poetry got married, got divorced, had children that he did it all with the same indiscriminate intent – he was afraid. He had always been afraid and when there was no outlet for his rage that he was afraid Murphy became one of the living dead.

James Cagney retires from movie making in 1961. With his wife, Frances (Bill) Willard Cagney, he moves to his 800-acre ranch in Dutchess County, New York. On his ranch he swims, paints, plays tennis and writes poetry.

Pause

It was crowded in McSorley's all the bartenders knew Leroi Jones, Gil Sorrentino and Basil King. From one of the tables racial slurs were being directed at Leroi. There was no mistaking what the cops from New Jersey were saying. The cops were without their wives and girlfriends. They felt entitled to say anything they wanted and there was no one who could stop them. They didn't have any jurisdiction but that wasn't stopping them and if they didn't know it they were inciting not only the three of us they were pissing off most of the clientele. They were told to stop by one of the bartenders. They didn't.

Was it Gil was it Leroi was it someone else. Movies always tell and show who started it. Gil was a large man I'm a few inches taller than Roi (Amiri Baraka) what I remember is a free-for-all arms chairs and fists and in the midst of it I heard Brian the bartender croaking "Gil it's me, Brian." Gil had his hands around Brian's throat and he was choking him. Did the police come I don't remember but the New Jersey cops who had demonstrated what they were made of went back to New Jersey. Gil was licking his knuckles and he went home.

Martha wasn't home she was visiting her parents in North Carolina I went with Roi back to his house and we climbed the stairs and told our story to Hettie. Big Hettie is what my kids called Hettie Jones at that time she was taller than her namesake our daughter Hetty. Big Hettie got the iodine, band-aids cleaned the two of us up and I stayed and slept on their couch.

> Pause

The Cagneys adopted two children, Cathleen (Casey) and James Junior. They had married in 1921, and remained together until his death.

> Pause

George Herriman's Ignatz and Krazy Kat tell us if you've never spent time in the desert, you will never understand what makes America different from Europe.

> Pause

> Alice Neel
> Looks out the window
> Snow
> White's
> Climbing up the Fire
> Escape
> Alice says
> You are accustomed

To being the most informed
Speaker
On the street
Last night
You drew a rainbow
Leaning
Against
An urban landscape
Of a nude
In high heels
That asks

Do you trust your neighbours
Mine are troubled
By
The exaggerated menace
Of a secret
And of a time
That can never be
Forgotten

Miss White closes her mouth
And no amount of paint
Restores
Eve
And what of
Adam
He keeps
Watching
He wants
To be assured
The baby will be
What he wants
It to be

Eve's Poem

   I have committed no crime
   I am pregnant
   I feel
   Foreign movements
   Sensations
   My belly
   Contains

A future
Full of grist
Portraits
A retainer
When next
I climb
The Fire Escape
I will calculate
You will not
Come
Alone

Adam's Poem

I will surround
You
With a blue
Sharpened pencil
A little song
Made for
A mother
Who as yet
Has no song
Oh box wood
Bedlam
If I hired
An architect
To build you
A house
Would you ask me
To come and live with you
Bring our child
The floors are clean
And the door is open

Pause

Alice's children remember
Psycho was born
On their mother's canvas
The baby knows it is being watched
It knows because Alice has just
Finished painting its eyes
Before she paints its lips

She parks a nose on its face
The baby smells paint
And wonders will Alice
Paint my ears
Ouch!
That hurt
Am I a girl
Will I have tits
The boy's balls
Are scarlet
And because Alice has not
Painted
His arms
He cannot scratch
The surface
Of an artefact
That demands the attention
Of an idealist

                Pause

One of Alice's ancestors signed
The Declaration of Independence
She opens her legs
He has a hard on
The narrative and the monologue
The model and the libido
Fear
And
Pleasure

Did Alice ever
Tell
Any one
How she
Retraced
Her footsteps
The reprint of her life
Comes engraved
In the arch
Of her feet
Belts like socks
Wear shoes

Did Alice
Catch a chill
When she painted
Herself
In the nude
Alice wore glasses

Oh Grand Ma
You have no shame
You flaunt your disobedience
And want nature to turn its head
And see an old body
Contemplating a picture
of a man
You do not know
But you would like to
Send a Post-Card to
Johnny Carson
And the chicken
That laid
The eggs
We had
For
Breakfast

PART II

Lo, the line comes from outside.

In a town that shall be nameless Raphael invents the Western, ham, cheese, tomatoes, peppers and eggs. Eden is replaced with Daumier's biting condemnations, Monet's pale Camille, Lord Leighton's habitual pornography. Put them on a boat. Transfer them to a train, comb your hair, brush your teeth, ride the rods. In a deck of cards the Jack (the Prince) is drawn in profile.

Pause

John Wieners asked, and I said yes! And we went to Ma Peeks. After all these years I'm still not sure what possessed John to ask, and for me to accept. We didn't question it. We never never talked about it. The two of us went to a red-neck bar, in backwoods North Carolina with John in his blue flowered dress and high heels. Was it a challenge. Fuck you! We both knew they hated Jews and Homos. And knowing that, maybe, maybe that was what had us go where other angels would fear to tread. Maybe, but I'm not sure that either one us was that heroic.

At the time we were students at Black Mountain College, now famous for its educational experiment, for the poets, painters, dancers, potters and musicians who worked and taught there.

John attempted to sit on a farmer's lap. The farmer pushed him away and John went to the next table and grabbed a man's wrist just as he was about to put a piece of steak into his mouth. John said something like "Feed me big boy." The man was frightened and became abusive. John went to another table and then another table as the bar began to erupt. Barbara who managed the bar came over to me. "Ma Peeks phoned the sheriff." One of the men grabbed John. He managed to get away and I got hold of John's arm. He recognized me. We got outside and were about to run. If we had we probably would have been caught and beaten.

We stopped. There in the parking lot was the sheriff of Buncombe County, the sheriff, Ma Peeks' cousin, could take you off to jail and forget about you. Barbara was talking to him; he kept looking at us. It wasn't good. He had his head down and when he picked his head up he'd look straight past us.

I walked over to him. "Excuse me, sheriff … can I talk to you." He didn't say anything but because he moved away from Barbara and his deputy, I knew I could. "Sheriff, I, I don't mean to be rude, but I, I have to ask you," I hesitated, "have you lost your mother. John has just lost his. John doesn't know what he is doing. He doesn't always act this way. He doesn't. He works hard. I know of no one else who works harder."

The sheriff's body convulsed and at that moment he would not have denied anyone, no matter who they were anything that was in his power to give. He looked at me and said his mother was alive. That's all he said. He had no choice but to take us in his car and drive us back to school.

> The Keel Bone is the bone that goes down the front of the bird. All the flight and breast muscles are attached to the Keel Bone. This supports these muscles, so if a bird has a small keel bone it has short or small muscles, and if a bird has a long Keel Bone, it will usually have longer muscles, which are required for distance flying.

It was the early seventies. John bought a little red apron at the Waldorf Astoria. He wore it as he did the dishes. He told our daughters who at the time were seven and five years old that he was Joan Crawford. He told them all about his and Joan's life. He told them how pleased he was that their father was interviewing him for his magazine *Mulch*. John had said that he was willing to be interviewed if we would interview each other and for two days we did.

We were very pleased with ourselves until we listened to the tape. All we heard were gurgles, squeaks, laughter, Oh, yes, Black ink, the moon.

Pause

1945. James Cagney sees Audie Murphy, the most decorated soldier of World War II, on the cover of *Life* and invites him to Hollywood. Why did Cagney invite Murphy to Hollywood. What did Cagney see in Audie Murphy's photograph: "A touch of the gutter, ambition." Cagney knew that Murphy was a hero. Did Cagney know that Cagney was a hero and by what rule does an actor become a hero and by what measure does the hero paint a Self Portrait and say, I have become who I want to be.

Pause

Records show that there have been many artists who have been involved in brawls. After a printmaker messed up one of his prints Andrea Mantegna beat him up.

Gian Lorenzo Bernini was involved in a number of brawls.

Michelangelo Merisi da Caravaggio killed a young man in Rome after they quarrelled over a tennis match. Records show he was involved in three more brawls before his death.

As a young man Vermeer was fined for brawling.

I was ten years old and I had a fight with two boys who called me "an uppity kike." One of the boys knifed me on the wrist of my right hand.

America is the Attic
Europe is the Museum

Hans Holbein the Elder was the most respected painter in Germany. Hans Holbein the Elder's brother Sigmund worked with him.

Hans Holbein the Younger had a brother Ambrosius. He too was a painter. Like the Bosch and the van Eyck families all the Holbeins painted. The brothers were volatile and records show they were fined in Basle for being in a brawl. A year later Hans Holbein the Younger is fined in Lucerne in connection with a knife-fight.

> After 1517 Ambrosius is never heard of again
> Did he quarrel with someone in the family
> Did he swallow too much water
> Did he do something unspeakable
> Did he simply walk away

Pause

Hans Holbein the Younger arrived at the dining hall at Black Mountain College with a suitcase and a small hamper full of brushes and paint. Erasmus the philosopher sent him to de Kooning and Bill de Kooning told him Black Mountain College is a community where everyone learns. Classes are small intense the atmosphere can be volatile. The faculty their discipline will humble you. Black Mountain welcomed those who were willing to leave home, meet strangers and learn to draw.

There were those who came who stayed two to three days and were gone saying goodbye to no one. Did they find the place dangerous, disorganized. I never knew. Black Mountain was a democracy no tests, card markings, lights out. Faculty and students alternated on garbage details shovelled coal when there was coal and of course there was the dish detail.

Lo, the line comes from outside.

1955. Mike Rumaker and I were on dish detail. I think he was washing and I was drying. I can't remember what was being played on the radio when a voice we'd never heard the likes of threw caution to the wind and the air became flamed. Little Richard's "Tutti Frutti, all rooty, tutti frutti, all rooty! Tutti Frutti, aw Rudi, Tutti Frutti, aw Rudi…"

I don't think we said a word we just stared at each other. Fifty-five years ago the South was separated by colour. White people lived by entitlement. Black people lived in servitude. Everything was restricted to colour the water fountains, hotels, black people could only sit in the back of the bus. A white woman could have a black man lynched if she said he had looked at her the wrong way. Little Richard a black man and a homosexual had the audacity to flaunt his colour and his sexual preference. The result was phenomenal and almost unthinkable. Not just me and Mike but the North and the South loved it.

Pause

1932 Roosevelt is elected president
1933 Hitler is appointed chancellor
Black Mountain 1933-1956

At Black Mountain
If it fails begin again
For more than twenty years
There were no knife fights
No one stole food
At Black Mountain
At Black Mountain
In the pot shop
In the Studies Building
If it fails begin again
In New York and San Francisco
Voices never heard before
Gave themselves
Permission to speak
And speak they did

The road between Black Mountain, New York, and San Francisco was unpaved but well trodden information was transported via mail, books, performances and visitors.

Oh, Black Mountain, wonderful place, desperate place. I was blown to where light abstracts the smallest thing, into the core of a vernacular, into the heart of the abstract. No wind but the stillness blows me, no reason; no existence blows the shapes that have lost their edges. Oh, Black Mountain, wonderful place, desperate place. Blow your feathers and your worms. Your mulch protrudes the surface. Your bravery blows forgiveness. Your anger blows freedom. Oh, Black Mountain, wonderful place, desperate place. I was blown to where light abstracts the smallest thing, into the core of a vernacular, into the heart of the abstract. No wind but the stillness blows me, no reason; no existence blows the shapes that have lost their edges.

PART III

Drive at night and you drive America's profile
The King of Diamonds draw it and you draw
Highways
Lines

Profiles
My nose
The setting of my eyes
My chin directs you to
A white line
Passing cars and trucks
Finds more of the past
Things that took place
And were never recorded
The driver's wheel
The gas pedal
The motion of the car
Cupped hands
The view reads

My name is Basil King and I am the son of Basil and Martha King. Before I began to write I drew and painted. Now I paint draw and write. I paint my drawings with a mix of authorities. Colour is crucial. Colour enhances and compliments the source of the abstract. The mature shapes of the sentence dissect and divide lines all lines dissect and divide the mature shapes of the sentence. Say what you mean and before you sit down leave home, meet strangers and learn to draw.

Pause

In Galway Ireland we stayed at De Soto, a bed and breakfast. Margaret Walsh the proprietor a woman in her sixties told us she was selling the place. Her husband had died her mother was in the hospital and was not expected to live her two older children were married and her youngest boy was still in college. The house was in walking distance of the city centre one way, and Salthill the other.

The De Soto is on the corner of Newcastle Road and Presentation Road. Walk up Presentation Road cross over the River Corrib on the Salmon Weir Bridge and you get to Shop Street the main shopping centre. Walk up University Road cross over the River Corrib on the Salmon Weir Bridge and you get to Headford Road. Keep walking Headford to a Pub one of many Pubs whose names I can't remember. But there was one in particular that we liked. Our first night in Galway we heard an ecstatic young women singing in Gaelic accompanied by four young men. Walking home we crossed the River Corrib and got lost. We saw a cab parked on a corner and we gave him the address and he turned a corner and we were home. I can't remember what I paid him. He said he would be on the same corner tomorrow night and if we needed him he would take us home.

Lo, the line comes from outside
Flaubert's Madame Bovary
Sits in a parked car
As she waits
She whispers to herself
I want to see his face
I refuse to stop
Hoping

      Pause

The bartender said that there was going to be music. The Pub was crowded. The crowd was expectant and four young men were readying themselves a guitar two violins and a flute. A trim young woman not beautiful with pale skin dark red hair came in and sat between the men. As soon as she sat down and before she began to sing the men moved closer to accompany and protect her. She sang in Gaelic.

Her singing
Became
Animated
Then ecstatic
I couldn't take
My eyes
Off of her
She was a spirit
And she was
Making all spirits
Available
She melted my bones
And I became
Thrown out
Of
And into
An emotional identity
It was exhausting to be present
At something I didn't understand
But I did and that made it even more

      Pause

For almost thirty years the Czech Miroslav Tichý walked around his hometown of Kyjov photographing the women of the town posing them as he saw them. Everyone in town knew Tichý but no one knew why he photographed women. Without touching or feeling any woman with his hands he says she is everything it doesn't concern him if she likes him he likes her.

Get rich. Be rich. Get rich. Be rich.

Miroslav Tichý has been compared to Gerhart Richter. Gerhart Richter is brilliant but I think it is superficial to compare the two. If we lived in a better world Gerhart Richter might be considered the greatest forger who has ever lived whereas Miroslav Tichý is "The real thing."

The Communists tried to break Tichý they failed. He grew his hair lived alone and rarely changed his clothes. He became almost self-sufficient answering to no one he made his own cameras, enlargers, ground corn for his bread and printed his work. Tichý's resource never tired.

> Breast
> Torso
> With
> Or
> Without
> Clothes
> Her
> Thighs
> Activate
> The
> Pleasure
> Of
> His
> Purpose

> Pause

Miroslav Tichý is not ignorant of art history and the European classics on the contrary before he began to take photographs he painted. None of this is forgotten when he looks through the lens and deliberates he clicks his shutter he knows Cranach, Titian, the Velázquez Venus and all the distortions pornographic clichés pose to titillate. Miroslav Tichý focuses all of this on the female body and says to them you are endowed with something I need. You are everything there is nothing else.

Maybe this is madness. Was Henri Rousseau. Was Albert P. Ryder. They were queer not gay, queer, different. Were they born that way is a question I cannot answer. What I do know is "decide" and collapse the void.

I ask myself is Miroslav Tichý going to attack he calculates he threatens. And if he isn't going to attack why is he a threat. He is not afraid to be called "mad" or "queer." And maybe it takes madness to step out and say you protect your mothers, wives and daughters, I don't.

Pause

The class assignment was to write a book report on a famous person. Less than one year after my family came to this country 1948 the state of Israel was founded.

Who else but Theodor Herzl the father of modern political Zionism! I read and talked Theodor Herzl. Never before had I been so involved I wrote and rewrote what became an essay. The paper was returned it had not been given a grade instead at the top of the first page the teacher wrote in capitals and with quotation marks, "QUEER."

Pause

In the 1980s I painted the four aces the joker and two through seven of the playing cards. Ninety-nine paintings and I stopped. And now it's 2010 and I haven't played cards since 1968 but cards have always remained a powerful presence.

The architect builds a long poem
His autobiography endures brutality
The wrath of infinite numbers
Visualize a prescribed iconography
A method that never fails
Inherit a poem and you inherit a city
A deck of cards with a joker
The Queen blames no one
Her son Jack wants to be an architect
She tells him leave home meet strangers
And learn to draw
She says I can tell you about
The poet H.D.
And the photographer Evelyn Flowers
They left home and they became architects
They drew in what was not given to them
And in so doing they found
Fountainheads for strangers
Men and women who are
About to leave home

Pause

In England Cyril Flowers, Evelyn Flowers's half-brother, was considered the handsomest man of his day. He married Constance de Rothschild, became a Member of Parliament, and was later raised to noble rank with the title of Lord Battersea. Amongst his many accomplishments Cyril Flowers took photographs, won prizes for his photographs, and had them framed for the walls of his many elegant houses. He was a Victorian, an uncrowned prince. It never occurred to him that he had to protect himself from anything.

Evelyn Flowers's father, Philip Flowers, a successful East India merchant, headed a very large and comfortable household that was connected in high places. Growing up in her father's prosperous house Evelyn learnt to ride side-saddle, and to read and write French and Italian.

When Evelyn needed privacy, she wrote in French. She wrote in her journal, "I am not beautiful. I am strong, and I love to work. I didn't want to live in polite society as a spinster or marry down." According to the census for 1871 Philip Flowers's house contained fifteen servants, and six small children. Five of the nine offspring born to Philip Flowers were from his first wife Mary; she had died in the late 1850s.

Two Italian railroad workers in Montana are shocked when Evelyn began to talk to them in Italian. She photographed them two, three times and later when they settled in California and had families she corresponded with them. But mostly she kept her distance. She never went to a picnic or a dance unless she was photographing the event. Evelyn Cameron got paid in hard cash for her photographs.

Evelyn Jephson Flowers Cameron migrated to Montana with her husband to breed polo ponies and make money. Ewen Cameron was a penniless wildlife scholar from Scotland. Fifteen years her senior, Evelyn Flowers married Ewen Cameron. His family had fallen on hard times and his mother had retired in genteel poverty to Tunbridge Wells. Polo breeding failed and Ewen wanted to return to England. Evelyn convinced him that they should stay. She knew there was nothing for them in England. In Montana they were free to live a life that would not restrain their energies.

> Shakespeare let her go. Your tongue is in her
> ear. You bite her lips. Her ears conjugate your
> language. Tea is served. Play Bach before
> Brahms. She needs the piano. She has married

a man who spends his time looking at
large worms that wiggle and make hideous faces.

Evelyn Cameron photographs Montana's big sky,
Raw Badlands, and birds. Birds replace flowers.
Birds replace the children she and Ewen never
had. Birds, flowers, medieval thorns, calluses.
She picks up her leg; click goes the shutter.
Birds, self-deceit, woman and children
Mountains, a horse between her legs.
Evelyn Cameron speaks English.

America hold her. Her tongue is in your ear.
She bites your lips. German, Russian,
a taste of French. Montana's breath
powers the silence. Tea is served.
Play Bach before Brahms. Evelyn needs the piano.
Large worms that wiggle and make hideous
faces come into her house and sit at her table.

Evelyn is the woman with the beautiful brother.
He's a Prince, a Jack of the realm. Evelyn's nose
is too long. Her eyes are too close together.
Smile. She remembers wearing corsets, elocution,
nibbling sweets.

In Montana Evelyn and Ewen lived without running water. Evelyn had to learn to farm, cook, and sew. She did all of these things by herself. Ewen never helped her with the farm or any of the household chores. In her father's house she was expected to be a lady. In Montana she never would accept electricity.

Evelyn Cameron's photographs tell us how frightening it was to be a pioneer. How cleanliness survives in the hardest of situations. And modesty becomes those who are kind to themselves.

Pause

But for a few short return visits to America, H.D. (Hilda Doolittle), the poet, spent her maturity in Europe. When she came home, she came home to die. Evelyn Cameron, the photographer, except for a few visits to England, spent her maturity in Montana and there she died.

Pause

Two young women ride the same subway train. One is Asian. The second is an Arab. The young Asian woman is reading a book. She is beautiful; the calligraphy she reads is beautiful. The young Arab woman is reading a book. She is beautiful; the calligraphy she reads is beautiful. Lo, calligraphy is for lovers.

    blue   brown
    green   yellow

    Maybe the migrant understands
    when it is favourable
    and when it is unfavourable
    to rise like bread
    like sand in the desert
    calligraphy is for lovers

    Get rich. Be rich. Get rich. Be rich.

Dan Rice and I were uptown near the Dakota. We stopped in a bar. Jason Robards was sitting at the bar drinking a beer watching The World Series. We left the bar walking east and heading downtown we stopped in another bar The World Series was playing. In walks Jason Robards. This time he left before we did. We resumed walking downtown and went into another bar the game was still going on and Jason Robards was sitting there with a beer. This piece of theatre this happening if you can call it that repeated itself a few more times but at no time did we leave or did he leave or go into a bar at the same time. Hours later we walked into McSorley's the game was still going on and there sat Jason Robards he saw us and before we could order Danny Lynch the bartender put four ales in front of us and says compliments of Mr. Robards. We all smiled raised our glasses and nodded in mutual approval.

Playwrights, politicians, firemen, drunks, cops and actors stood at McSorley's bar and hoisted a few. There was the time Arthur Kennedy and Ralph Bellamy came in looking as if they had slept on a pavement. Finlay Currie came in with three other character actors whose faces I remember but not their names. What I do remember is every one of the men wore beautifully cut expensive suits. Van Heflin, Hal Holbrook and James Mason I wanted to tell him that I took my parents to the West End of London just before we left England to see *Odd Man Out* and how much we enjoyed his performance. But I didn't.

McSorley's Old Ale House was all male no female was allowed inside until 1970. But in 1937 Berenice Abbott took photographs of the bar at McSorley's. Men drink at the bar and others sit at tables eating and drinking. If it weren't for the 1930s clothes the men are wearing it could be 1867 or it could be 1967.

Pause

The flowered wallpaper is beautifully drawn. Medieval lions are woven into the hallway's carpet. A figure with its back to us knocks on an interior door. The door does not open. The figure knocks again.

H.D. asks the surreal, why do you knock on my door. The surreal answers: I knock because you are afraid of fire and war, because you do not have a job and you are dependent on your father. He sends you two hundred dollars every year. I knock because you are disappointed that you never finished college, you educated yourself. You taught yourself. When it fails, begin again. You go to parties but you never give them.

Your mother was expected to keep house and do all the shopping. Serve seven to eleven people at breakfast every morning. Lunch was easier, maybe. At dinner seven, eleven, fifteen and sometimes more visitors, relatives, faculty, and students sat down to a four-course dinner. It was constant and it wore your mother out. She was never able to give you the attention you needed. To add to your misery you were always tall, and as a girl you were never able to wear the clothes that other girls wore. Now you have all your clothes made by a seamstress.

> Every minute fold in her
> Dress finds a brush stroke
> Raise the skirt
> Lower the bodice
> The seamstress
> Never wears what she sews

Pause

Foreshortened sometime by shadows and self portraits James Ensor draws and paints his own skull and then with magnificent insight he struts across the canvas wearing the temperament of a short story. James Ensor wasn't the first person to be aware of his demons but I think he was the first artist to acknowledge that their presence was personal. Like *Adam and Eve Expelled from Paradise* Ensor was expelled. I don't know what caused this traumatic event but I do know that a year after his father's death he started his great work. Like Hamlet he had to revaluate his existence. The imagination and something unexplainable transcends our knowledge and what we think of as miraculous is, in James Ensor's paintings, given new meaning.

There was the fiction that the world
And everything
In the world was flat
And every third day
A father figure
Would put on a mask
Walk into the market square
Eat herring and provoke death
Because death had never
Had sex
Death did not know
How to dance
And because death did not know how
Children laughed
And the father was made grotesque
Death was born
So that we can be born
And people wanted to pray
But whom should they pray to
And what should they pray for
There was the fiction that the world
And everything
In the world was flat
Nevertheless Ensor's mother
Sold baubles
To customers who thought her husband
Drank too much

James Ensor's father was an Englishman educated as an engineer. When James was one year old his father went to America to look for work. He was unable to find any and returned to help his wife's family maintain a curio business in Ostend selling carnival masks, china, and stuffed animals.

James's father was not a good businessman and when James is fifteen the family declares bankruptcy and his mother's brother takes over the responsibilities of running the shop.

At sixteen James Ensor leaves college
And enrols in art school
The family's attic is his studio
Studios are curiosities in themselves

Depending on the height of the ceiling
The width and length of the floor space
Are there stairs
And where does the light come from
The artists who created
The illustrated medieval manuscripts
Drew angels, bells
Dante's intricate motifs
Rimbaud's Celtic fury
Combine solace and terror
Devotion
Wants to know what is love
There was the fiction that the world
And everything
In the world was flat
To ward off despair
Christ
Visits James Ensor's
Attic
Christ is bewildered
James Ensor and Albert Einstein
Enter Brussels and illuminate
James Ensor's love for his father
Death was born
So that we can be born
There was the fiction that the world
And everything
In the world was flat
And because no one has been able
To deny it
Christ remains

PART IV

At Black Mountain College Fielding Dawson said, "There are always things under the surface of your paintings. Do you know what they are." Fielding, they are unknown to me. And years later in another studio Fielding said, "You paint your Toons, your Gremlins."

The Toons had to be brought to the surface so that they could be seen. Even the ones that I still haven't come to terms with I call mine.

THE REAL THING HAS FOUR PARTS

To paraphrase something that I have already written:

I build houses for their grief and feed their grief three times a day. I make love to everything that has been given to me and to everything that has been taken from me. I understand that if their grief starves I too will starve.

>   Pause

>   For George Stanley
>   From the GREEN MAN
>
>   There is hunger
>   There is always hunger
>   A mouth a page a canvas
>   A coloured eye
>   A thirsty tongue
>   Bring him in bring him in
>   Bring in the forgotten
>   The twin the initiator
>   The sky Blue
>   Green initiator
>   Bring him in bring him in
>   The car the automobile
>   Side walls the house
>   Between continents
>   A perplexed roof
>   Bring him in bring him in
>   There is hunger
>   There is always hunger
>   A mouth a page a canvas
>   A coloured eye
>   A thirsty tongue
>   The country is in trouble
>   No one will come forward
>   No one will initiate
>   The New Year
>   Bring him in bring him in
>   Bring in the forgotten
>   The twin the initiator
>   The sky Blue
>   Green initiator

>   Pause

Can you find a brush stroke a hair out of place. The master never had any trouble painting texture. Jean-Auguste Ingres painted Madame Moitessier and what he thought was her profile reflected in the mirror. But the woman in the mirror is not Madame Moitessier. Ingres did not paint the same woman when he painted the woman in the mirror. The woman in the mirror, the one whose back we see, the woman no one mentions, is nameless. She looks nothing like Madame Moitessier. She's the woman the Cubists painted. She is a modern woman. When she turns her back on us, she will have her own reasons for doing so. We know her. She went to the movies with us last night. She sat watching the movie with her right hand propped up against her chin, and afterwards she said she wanted to go home, alone.

Madame Moitessier's right hand is propped up against her face. She sits facing us. A beautifully glazed surface picks up every tassel, every minute fold in her dress. Her eyes are like a highly fired vase. She stares at us. We cannot get close enough to her. Her soft body cannot be harmed. She is Empire.

Ingres painted two paintings on one canvas. Madame Moitessier is an autocrat. The woman in the mirror is a romantic. Is she listening to a manifesto. Is she a Socialist. She is listening to nothing. She strokes Ingres's unconscious and says to her children: Boots are as important as trees. People are important. Bread is important. The woman, the one Ingres painted in the mirror, is a modern woman. When she turns her back on us, she will have her own reasons for doing so. We know her.

In defiance of myth science reveals some mysteries. What Titian so capably did in old age by blurring his edges, impressionism turned upside down with vibrant colours that could be manufactured in a factory, Impressionism, socialism, and communism, boots as important as trees juxtaposed a social and aesthetic walk through the park. A tube of paint and the steam engine competed for importance. With this new vocabulary Ibsen, Henry James, and D.H. Lawrence used language, not paint, to assault beauty.

He wore her hat and she wore his. He rarely wore a skirt. But she wore pants. A man paints his nails. A woman changes her shoes. Who is going to take the garbage out.

Picasso and Braque reconstructed the excesses of the industrial revolution melding classical propositions and modern times into the collage. And last night she sat watching the movie with her right hand propped up against her chin, and afterwards she said she wanted to go home, alone.

The line comes from the outside

I had taken an earlier train than the one I had said I would. I knew some one was going to meet me Dan had said he was unable to so I sat down on a bench and read my book. A young woman who had been sitting in the back of the station came forward to meet the incoming train. She had a big sign with my name on it. BASIL KING. I introduced myself and told her I got to Penn Station earlier than I expected and a train was about to leave and I took it.

Driving to Dan Rice's house she told me she had known Dan for more than a year that she was one of Dan's students in his painting class. And in all that time she had never heard my name mentioned by Dan or Virginia until two days ago when Basil is coming. Basil likes bourbon. Basil likes chicken. Basil likes Basil doesn't like… She said she was puzzled why hadn't she ever heard my name mentioned and now they were making so much of my coming.

I told her I had known Dan since the early nineteen fifties. We were students at Black Mountain College. And through the years we had kept in touch. And I asked her if she knew the poet Andrew Crozier. She said she didn't. I told her he had called me

"The man who
Was never there"

Dan lived on a beautiful marsh and he painted the marsh. It was in those paintings that Dan painted his Self Portrait of a lonely man. Dan looked sick. We went inside and the young woman followed us in and sat down. It was obvious she was observing us. Dan had asked me to come and spend time with him while he still had some energy. Dan Rice knew he was dying. After a few minutes the young woman got up and excused herself.

What's that young woman's name. Dan gave me one of his John Wayne smiles. Did he say she was Alfred Stieglitz's great granddaughter or was it great grandniece.

Pause

In 1942 at the age of seven I went to a private Jewish boarding school modelled after Summerhill. Geography, history, French lessons. I wrote in a very large script and I drew trees and a young German teacher who later became a rabbi read me Holbein the Younger's letters to his father and his wife in German.

In Basle Switzerland I walked up a very narrow alley and there was the university and further on the path the Cathedral and Saint George and the Dragon. I've lived here in that house and I know that window that courtyard. It was months before I remembered the young German teacher and his reading me Holbein's letters.

There is no work. The Protestant Reformation forbids religious painting and Hans Holbein the Younger has to leave Basle. Having studied with Erasmus he goes to him for advice and is given letters of recommendation to William Warham Archbishop of Canterbury and Sir Thomas More.

At the breakfast table
Hans Holbein the Younger
Tells his wife
And children
He is leaving
He is going to England
Witness the bereaved
Their bravery
Is almost unnoticed
If I am not to paint Christ
Who shall I paint
Thomas More
Knows
The King of England
His bed is never empty
His belly never satisfied
Henry VIII lost his son
As did the painter
Gilbert Stuart
Hans Holbein painted faces
Gilbert Stuart painted faces
Chuck Close paints faces
Within each composition
Polka dots
Water Falls
Chalk
The curve
Returns the prodigal

Be Rich. Get Rich. Be Rich. Get Rich.

In London, the same year that I had the knife fight I had Mr. Cook as a teacher. Twice a week Mr. Cook crossed his legs adjusted his scarf and read

Shakespeare. At the end of the hour he closed the book. There were no discussions there were no tests. There were teas at Mr. Cook's house. Five or six of us would be invited at a time. Mrs. Cook served tea and biscuits. We talked. Mr. Cook listened. And then we were graded.

Pause

Olson at the blackboard with a cigarette in one hand and a piece of chalk in the other I was never sure did he follow culture or did culture follow him. He was the diesel the energy that propelled my Black Mountain.

When Charles watched Merce Cunningham dance his face would be so sublime if he could have he would have fathered all of us for his army Gloucester was the tabletop the field that suckled the wheat that fed him.

Pause

Before he painted Erasmus Hans Holbein the Younger
Studied with Erasmus
Before he painted *Body of the Dead Christ in the Tomb*
He internalized Grunewald
Hans Holbein the Younger went to France and learned how to use chalk
Holbein made paper and would have made books
At Black Mountain
It was nailed to the walls
By those who were present
Creeley's "The darkness surrounds us"
Duncan's the edge is the wonder of instability
It was nailed to the walls
By those who were present
Calligraphy is for lovers

Delacroix never finished the double portrait of his friends George Sand and Frederick Chopin. After Delacroix's death the picture was cut into two separate portraits. The only evidence of what the original painting looked like is a pencil sketch showing Chopin playing the piano with Madame Sand sitting beside him. She wears a black dress. Her black hair falls onto her bare shoulders.

Madame Sand bares no resemblance to the notorious George Sand. George dresses in men's clothing, puffs on cigars and blows smoke rings into the air. This very brave woman threw a gauntlet down in front of gentility and was willing to take the consequences of being a mother, a lover, a writer, and a breadwinner; so was George Sand.

Pause

Alice Neel painted men, women, young people and babies.
Sometimes we see her confront a personal locality. Sometimes elongated features waver between space and apartment walls. When Alice takes us outside to the city's back yards walls and windows the roofs fire escapes covered in pristine snow introduce a silence where if you have the patience you will hear voices and the chimes of sex. Creased foreheads with unexpected nerve endings are required to jab the paint. Alice Neel can be sympathetic but never is she sentimental. She learned a long time ago the idealist is capable of turning and becoming untrustworthy sometimes brutal.

Pause

At 5' 4" and with boyish good looks Audie Murphy looked like a pushover. But don't cross him he'd more than likely go into warp spasm and want to kill you. Murphy's parents were sharecroppers who barely eked out a living. One of nine surviving children his father walked out of the house one day when Audie was 16 and was never heard of again. His mother died the next year and the three youngest sibs were put in an orphanage.

He was a crack shot, his battlefield instincts were razor-sharp, and to others he seemed to be fearless. "If I discovered one valuable thing during my early combat days, it was audacity, which is often mistaken for courage or foolishness," he said. "It is neither. Audacity is a tactical weapon. Nine times out of ten it will throw the enemy off balance and confuse him."

Audacity or not, his fear never completely disappeared. "In the heat of battle it may go away," Murphy wrote. "Sometimes it vanishes in a blind, red rage that comes when you see a friend fall. Then again you get so tired that you become indifferent. But when you are moving into combat, why try fooling yourself. Fear is right there beside you."

America is the Attic
Europe is the Museum

Some time in the late 1970s Robert Kelly asked me if I would do a drawing of Lenin and a drawing of Robert for his long poem "Lenin's Necktie".

I went to a few bookstores and didn't find a photo of Lenin that I could work from so I phoned the Russian Embassy and told the woman on the phone I had been asked to do a drawing of Lenin for a poem that was to be published in a small magazine and I needed some photographs of Lenin.

Come at your convenience. The day I went to the Embassy it was being picketed by a Jewish group protesting Russia's inhumanity. Being a Jew I paused and asked myself should I cross the picket line.

After the seventh or eighth sizing the canvas comes alive and my brush skates as if I were on ice and I know maybe after one or two more sizings I can begin to paint.

A young officer let me in. "Can I help you." I repeated what I had said when I called the Embassy. "I've been asked to do a drawing of Lenin and I need some photographs and I was told that you will be able to help me." "Please follow me." The room was lined with chairs, bookshelves and cameras. The door closed and I went to the bookshelves thinking I would find a photograph of Lenin. All the books were in Russian and there were no photographs of Lenin. Fifteen minutes passed then another ten and I became alarmed. I tried the door it was locked. I banged on the door. I banged again. I'm in trouble I'm being watched. They think I'm a spy. I waited a few more minutes and banged again and the door opened. A very attractive young female officer stood in the door. She was smiling. I felt a rush I was afraid. "Can I help you." Again I repeated my request. "Please, follow me." and we went up a flight of stairs. We went into a room where there was a young officer. "Will these be of any help." There were a half a dozen books on the table all of them contained Lenin's photograph. "You can take all of them if you wish." I took all of the books and followed the young woman downstairs. She opened the door I was free.

BRING IT HOME

Squares and Circles
Oblongs the size
Of a Torso
Surround
The
Mouth

The mouth sometimes abrupt
Sometimes slow
Sometimes not altogether quiet
Moves
The challenge last seen
Reflects the disorder
The discomfort the newness

Pause

A
Serial
Tune
Sprouts
Roots
And
Repeats
Kiss
Me
I
Repeat
Sprout
Your
Lips
And
Kiss
Me
The
Milky-Way
Is
A

Continuous
Creation

Yesterday

I thanked Bob Rauschenberg for putting two primed canvases together and not painting on them.

Pause

William Herschel and his sister Caroline
Spent last night and the night before that
And the month before that
And the year before that
Looking into the heavens
For a place to live
They were displaced
By birth and country

William was 18 when to avoid the army
He and his older brother went to England
After a few years
His brother Jacob went back to Germany
But William stayed and didn't return
For twelve years

Born in Germany William Herschel (1738-1822) was twelve years older than his sister Caroline. Their mother was Prussian. She was a stern disciplinarian and remained illiterate all her life. Their father like his father before him began as a gardener. Herschel's grandfather was a Jew a gardener who made instruments and played the Oboe. Herschel's father Isaac taught himself to play the flute and became a military bandsman with the Hanover Foot Guards. He read philosophy, poetry and had an interest in astronomy.

The Milky Way promotes serial music
A universe of dark telling tells us
The stars conceal the innocence
Of the brash nebula
Spores
Seedlings
Feathers
The planet
Uranus
Incites

Change
Spores
Seedlings
Feathers
The planet
Uranus
Incites
Change
By the third cup of coffee
Something in the eighteenth century
Intersects
William Herschel believed
People live on the moon
Leave home meet strangers
And learn to draw

William and Caroline's mother had twelve children of which six lived. William was the second son and Caroline was the youngest. Their mother doted on the first son Jacob and Sophie the beauty of the family. Caroline was a sickly child at the age of 5 she caught smallpox and when she was 11 she caught typhus. As an adult she was pockmarked and not five feet tall. She could read and write and when her father was away with the regiment she wrote the letters to her father for her mother. She also wrote letters for other women in the regiment. Even so her mother and her brother Jacob treated her badly they whipped her and had her scrub the floors and do all the menial housework. She was a servant doomed to a life of drudgery.

William Herschel loved his sister and when he could afford to he went back to Germany and literally pulled her away from their mother and their older brother. He taught Caroline to sing and to play the piano. He taught her how to measure the sky and she distinguished herself she discovered many comets and she never scrubbed another floor.

Pause

At the start of *Art Is* George Quasha asks: "What is your name." It's a wonderful question to begin an interview. It's as simple as *Art Is* and it's as complicated as getting to the root. It creates a continuous dialogue.

My name is Basil Herschel King. My original name was Basil Herschel Cohen. The name was changed when we came to this country in 1947.

I was in my teens when my father told me that I was not named after his father or my mother's grandfather whose names were Hershel. My namesake is William Herschel (spelt with a c) the great astronomer; his first discipline was music he played many instruments conducted and composed. It is only recently that I read that William Herschel taught himself mathematics, Italian, and made his own telescopes to observe the stars.

William was reading while riding a horse. It was at night and the horse must have stumbled. He did a summersault over the horse's mane and landed on his back.

Looking up at the stars
Did William Herschel see a face
A beautiful Beatrice
Or did he see a lovely young woman
In a white dress on the Staten Island Ferry
Whatever he did see what ever it was
William Herschel was in love

LOVE

I have promised myself
I will not look
At anyone else
But you
You
With you
With you
I vanish
With you
The moons
Quartered
Limbs
Flower
Tenacious
Music
With you
A unicorn's
Horn
Pierces
Deceit

                        Pause

Every morning she goes into the kitchen
Before she makes herself coffee

She washes last night's dishes
She is a large young woman
She always wears a black slip
Her back does not speak to her torso
Her eyes are blue her lips
Repeat the sounds said last night
On a programme she watched on TV
She leaves the apartment
Closes the door and goes to a job
That reminds her she is lonely

For several mornings the lights
Do not go on in her apartment
Nor do they go on in the evening
Then one morning a large young man
Is at the sink he washes the dishes
She appears wearing the same black slip
They say something and leave the kitchen
It's evening he's cutting vegetables
She gets the frying pan
Is about to light the stove
When he pours two glasses of wine
She smiles he smiles
They left their parents
On the 8th floor
And in an elevator on the 23rd floor
She touched him
Silence interrupts the lovers
Silence interrupts the swimmers
When they reach dry land
The apartment is painted in subdued colours
Roses defend their status
Two moons of Jupiter
A thousand double stars
Two halves of an Avocado
They have been joined
By the unexpected

                    Pause

A man in his early forties he's one of the owners of the hardware store that is next door to the butcher shop he is telling the butcher that last night when he and his wife came home from being away for the weekend their daughter was with a young man who had been with her all weekend. "Our father would have killed me and my brother if he and my mother had come home and found us with a girl."

The butcher who is also a man in his early forties supplies his clientele with expensive cured bacons and smoked meats. Some mornings on his way to the store the butcher goes to Green Wood Cemetery to visit his father's grave. He has described to me the season's changes as he drives in from Long Island unconscious of the poetry he talks when he speaks of grasses clouds and the wild flowers. He is a man who is always making deals. He owns two boats and has offered me his Bose earphones next time I fly. Both men inherited their stores after their fathers died. Both fathers died of cancer.

The two men have known each other all their lives. They know me as a customer and are not distracted by my presence. The butcher tells his friend that times have changed. He wouldn't want his daughter to go to a hotel with the young man. I know your daughter and she'd never be with a bimbo. Isn't it better that she's not afraid to bring her young man home. The girl's father blushes and says "Hello MR. King."

We've lived in the same neighbourhood in Brooklyn since November of 1969. And some of the storekeepers call me Basil and some call me Mr. King. The butcher calls me Baa-zil and when I'm in the hardware store its always Mr. King. In the liquor store I am Mr. King in the pharmacy I am Basell either way it's impersonal. Their individualized pronouncing of my name can be Basil the herb or Basil the Greek and Welsh King.

PART II

A stage set that isn't painted by either Francis Bacon or David Hockney. The planet Uranus is discovered by William Herschel in 1781. William Herschel was a practical man. He internalized his passions and never abandoned the humanity that gave him courage. Courage that frail kernel of a thousand shapes if not worked disappears.

Bacon and Hockney thrive on courage they have installed it into their vocabularies into their language. England that miserable island has been expanded by what they have accomplished. England has green hills lovely valleys wonderful beer and Stonehenge. But England prides itself on insinuating into one of its best assets an acknowledgement that life is cruel it's in the island's prose and poetry but never has it been exploited in visual art with the possible exception of Graham Sutherland in his paintings. Bacon and Hockney's paintings abound with cruel mannerisms articulated references staged to show a tale that has been told before. (Chaucer, Shakespeare, John Donne, Hardy, D.H. Lawrence.) The surreal orbits the premise that everyone has a secret and is capable of harming another person.

Bring it home
Bring it home
As you would
A lover
As you would size
A canvas
As you would
Bring it home
Bring it home
Name a cave
That isn't minimal
A Vatican that isn't
Conceptual
Bring it home
Bring it home
The knowledge
The dispersed
Wisdom

I was 4 years old and my mother was entertaining some of her friends. I was on the floor playing with my castle and knights and I heard her say. "He made me, he begged me, I never wanted a child."

Pause

During the Second World War I don't think any man, woman or child ever forgot we could be invaded. I was 17-18 years old when my mother told me she had gone to bed every night with her knickers on. She was afraid that if we were blown up she would be exposed.

Honeysuckle and fog
Raspberries and thorns
Moss gardens Horse chestnuts and Marbles
Cricket and climbing trees
The 63 Bus
Johnny Haynes and Tony Bonny
Honeysuckle and fog

Raspberries and thorns
Moss gardens and anti-Semitism
Horse chestnuts and churches
V1s and V2s
Hymns
Mr. Cook and Shakespeare
Hide and Seek
Secrecy and mistrust
The urgency of not wanting
To be seen

                        Pause

Ted Wilentz phoned to tell me Fred MacDarrah had been at his house with hundreds of photographs and I wasn't in one of them. Ted said you were there at my store, my house, and at the parties.

When Ted read "mirage" he said, why didn't you tell us. I told him I couldn't I didn't know how. Not then. I told Ted every time Fred was about to take a photograph I ran into the next room or the bathroom. I didn't want to be seen. Not then.

                        Pause

Johnny Haynes was a carrot top. His father was in the Navy had been since he was 14. He'd had the cat of nine tails lain on his back for stealing a piece of bread and honey when he was 14. Mr. Haynes was tattooed from his neck down. Mr. Haynes was a chief petty officer and the Navy had wanted to make him an officer. He had refused. Mr. Haynes was out to sea during most of the war. He was rarely given leave. Every time there was an air raid Mrs. Haynes would call Johnny to come in and get under the table with her. When we played in the street Johnny would sit on the kerb and suck his thumb. No one made fun of him. He had hundreds of freckles and he could kick the hell out of a ball.

                        Pause

In 1942 at the age of 7 I went to a private Jewish boarding school modelled after Summerhill. My mother was ill, she was to have an operation and she would be a long time recovering. The school was very expensive. Because of my father's work as a fundraiser and organizer in the Jewish community he had access to wealthy families. The Montague sisters were identical twins and they were on the board of the school. They paid my tuition. The twins were tall, slender and dressed in Edwardian clothing. I remember they always wore hats and carried large pocketbooks. And there were always food stains on their clothing. Gas was expensive and it was rationed but a chauffeured car would bring them to the school and they would ask to see "the Cohen boy." They never sat down. They would ask me what was I reading, what were my interests. I would stand in front of them and answer their questions. They would always smile. It wasn't a condescending smile but because we never sat down they looked down on me. I wasn't afraid of them. There was something lonely and tender in their smiles.

The regular administration and faculty had been inducted into the army or some war-related work. The Matron had an adopted daughter. She took the bus to another school in the town of Brentwood. The Matron and her daughter were English so was the head nurse. The Matron and the head nurse were lovers. The cooks and all the help were Irish. The grounds were magnificent. We built imaginary towns and hospitals. There was a gardener straight out of D.H. Lawrence and every child had their own plot to grow whatever they wanted. The faculty except for one woman who taught English had been replaced with Europeans who were unable to find other academic positions. Education. Learn at your own speed pace your garden grow Sunflowers or tomatoes that feel like a girl's bum. Socialism, Communism, Fascism who projects the system. Do persons who wish to control invent systems.

We called the school "The Home" and in the Home there was cruelty inflicted on the children by the Matron the head nurse and some of the Irish help. Most of the children had compassion for each other. One of the boys used to sleep walk and we all made sure that he got back to his bed before he hurt himself. Breakfast, lunch, supper, Socialism, Communism, Fascism, we all learned to crochet.

All the children did their best to avoid being punished. Strapped down on your bed so that you couldn't move. Make a fist and have a large silver soupspoon whack your fist. Walk in the rain in a circle and then go to bed with wet clothes, you got chilblains. The faculty wanted to keep their jobs. They never interfered with the everyday running of the place. We learned that the Matron and her spies did things to have us mistrust each other. Someone's clothes would be missing from their drawer and would be found in another person's drawer. All the children wanted justice. I wrote in a very large script and I remember drawing trees. I remember geography, history, French lessons and a young German teacher who later became a rabbi who read me Holbein's letters in German.

We had to line up and watch as twelve-year-old Rosalind took off her dressing gown and her pyjamas and lay her nude body face down over the head nurse's thighs. The nurse would proceed to whack her bottom with a hairbrush. Beautiful Rosalind was growing tits; she had pale skin a crop of wavy strawberry blonde hair and the beginnings of a golden crotch. To this day I wake up and this sadistic spectacle that still haunts me always took place in the morning before breakfast.

Dear Clematis, it will take more than your purple bloom to forget the head nurse. Her thin face, her calculating smile as she cut off the ends of her toast. Which she would then dispense to her favourites. Socialism, Communism, Fascism we all learned to crochet.

Martha and I were in a farmers' market in Berkeley California. And I saw her. I said to Martha "There she is it's her." And I know my intensity scared Martha. It was those thin lips. Her arrogant cheekbones she was selling vegetables. I had to I buy something from her. She smiled it wasn't her but it was. She was there to say you won't forget me. She was a jailer, a guard not a guardian but a presence who was full of spite.

I wrote my mother every week telling her all the good things that I was doing, Geography, Gardening, History, Maths and reading books. Years later she said she was sorry that she hadn't saved all my letters. She read them aloud to all the women that were with her when she was convalescing.

Bring it home
Bring it home
As you would
A lover
As you would size
A canvas
As you would
Bring it home
Bring it home
Name a cave
That isn't minimal
A Vatican that isn't
Conceptual
Bring it home
Bring it home
The knowledge
The dispersed
Wisdom

      Pause

Stanley, what will it take to forget we had a plan. We were best friends and we went to the Matron and proposed that we would polish all the brass and all the silverware. She would pay us each a penny a night. We told her we would spend it when we went into Brentwood. She agreed. Stanley and I calculated how much it would cost us to take a train from Brentwood to London. At the end of every week we would cash in the pennies for a sixpence, a shilling, and then a half a crown. I can't remember how many weeks was it more than a month when some of us were taken into Brentwood to see a movie and we two slipped away. We went to the train station asked for two tickets to London. I don't remember. Did we talk about what we would do when we got there. The stationmaster told us there was a train in two hours. We went into the waiting room and it wasn't twenty minutes before two policemen came in and asked us our names and where we lived. They drove us back to the Home. We were sent to our beds and the Irish girls were told to strap us down.

What will it take to forget. My father promised me that he would phone the Matron to let me know how my mother was after her operation. I went to the Matron's office and the third time I knew I just knew that dad had phoned. She said he hadn't. I lost it. I tore books off the walls, kicked the furniture and screamed at the Matron. I was hauled off and shut in a closet. Dad was coming to see me so a little later the Matron told me that my dad had phoned and my mother was doing well.

I've already written about "Brian" and the engraved name on the banister in my long poem, "mirage." That was the second time I was put in the closet. It was horrendous. I peed and shit in my pants. First they sent Stanley. If I would say I carved the name, they would let me out. The next day they sent Jacqueline. Everyone knew we were friends. What the kids knew and the adults did not was that Jacqueline would climb into my bed and we'd sleep with our arms around each other. But I hadn't done it and I couldn't say that I had. I was in the closet from Wednesday till just before the Friday Sabbath when the door opened I was told to go and take a bath. With very red eyes I came down to supper.

Where shall I live
When will I know
It's safe for me
To be me
I want an arch
A cave a ceiling
Of my own
Michelangelo
Lying on his back

Sees figures
Eyes that rut
Alms Alms
Mr. Thomas banged my head
On the blackboard
Cohen
Either you are going to become
The prime minister of England
Or the world's biggest jewel thief

>Pause

PART III

I'm told that there are people who say, "We never know what he is going to do next."

I'm told I'm a living legend
I'm told I'm important
I'm told I sit on my ass
I'm told I'm the real thing
I'm told there is no one like me
I'm told I'm strong
I'm told I paint like a young man
I'm told I'm anti-clerical
I'm told I can have anything I want

Painters paint because they want to be famous

With the exception of my parents, my stay at the Home was the greatest influence on my future behaviour. The education was wonderful I learned to teach myself. Altruism, Anarchy, Yellow, White, and Red believe Grey comes out and is sent to the cleaners for winter storage so the moths won't eat him. Grey surprises everyone when Grey comes home all the other colours take note. Grey is the emotional divider, the sectarian that travels, and the altruist that asks that you give. Grey is a space, a volume I depend on as I depend on light.

>Pause

There are two large paintings downstairs
Both are titled "Looking for The Green Man"
Both of them are mixed media on canvas

Brushes rags and Bounty paper towels
Charcoal paste Higgins ink
Oil paint oil sticks Library chalk
Endless corners concrete illusions
The destination is clear
The edge is the wonder of instability
Square it rotate it
Digest it devour it
Divide it the edge
Is the wonder of instability
On the walls of the caves
Unfinished business
The male ruts
The female is swollen
Memory is a continuous fluid
From the abstract to the figure
From the figure to the abstract
If it fails begin again

Our garden isn't a garden
It's a Green backyard
Bricks and walls
Windows
Locust trees
Taller than the house
Watch the birds
Watching
JFK LaGuardia
Bring it home
Bring it home
Those who have
And those who will
Leave home
Meet strangers
And learn to draw

                        Pause

I was so determined to have nothing stop me that I didn't see what was staring me in the face. I paint because I want to. I paint because calligraphy is for lovers. The Cantata tells the story. I wanted everything and I wanted nothing. And I feared it would be taken away from me. Because of the ambiguities that I work into my paintings I would have had trouble having my painting accepted. It hasn't helped that I gave myself and I think everyone else mixed messages. Consequently a gallery has never represented my work. I do have to say that except for a few people who I will not name the rejection of my work has been impersonal.

Take stock
And drink
To the future
Horns
Drums
Strings
Sidewalks
A bass
Pastoral
Niagara Falls
The Maid of the Mist

                Pause

Last night I saw the moon was hand held
I saw faces relatives I never knew
Towns and cities I have never visited
I walked up a very narrow steep alley
There was a square and a church
St. George and the Dragon
The old university with very large wooden doors
And a house with a third floor window
I was certain that I had lived in that house
I was sure I had studied there
I was positive that I had
Grown old and been respected
I was disappointed with the sandwich
With the Swiss Deutsch that I didn't understand
Ah, but the Rhine and the naked
Men and women swimming
Cook fish to perfection

It was weeks before I realized I had come upon the square in Basle Switzerland that Hans Holbein described in one of the letters that he wrote to either his wife or his father. And then maybe it wasn't in any of the letters that the young teacher read to me. It's possible that the teacher described the square and the architecture it contained to give me a picture of where Holbein came from.

                Pause

Diaries, memoirs, denials, inhibitions the truth! True Caroline was always courageous. Intuition told her she had a future. We know that Caroline destroyed her childhood memoirs. She and William were disciplined romantics. But unlike Anne Frank Caroline did not want anyone to know her family's business.

My cousin John Hershel Shepherd phoned. "We've done it you said you wanted to be an artist and I wanted to be a judge. I've been made an appellate judge. I open the books as our great grandfather did. (He was a judge in the London Beth Din, the Court of the Chief Rabbi and the oldest Jewish court in London.) Johnny said, "Most of my cases are routine but then there is the one that sets precedent."

Pause

King George III and William Herschel never spoke German to each other they only spoke English. The King and the Astronomer had accents. They were foreigners and they had something to prove.

King George was good to the Herschels he gave William a stipend and sponsored many of William's investigations. In time with diplomatic prodding from William and with the help from Joseph Banks Queen Charlotte bestowed a yearly stipend on Caroline. She became an independent woman and when William married a wealthy widow she was vexed because she had to leave her brother's house. But given their common interests Caroline and her sister-in-law became very close.

Caroline doted on her nephew John Herschel he got married had twelve children and a flamboyant career. As an old lady Caroline returned to Hanover Germany. Caroline the sister of William Herschel the aunt of John Herschel. She was *the lady comet hunter*. She built her own telescopes was admired by men and women. I don't know if Caroline fully recovered from the abuse she took as a child and young adult but Caroline combated the cruelty she received in her early years and fixed her telescope on a monster star of comparable courage.

> Bewitched by artefact
> Contradictions mount
> And memories exercise
> Our heart and chest
> Our heart and chest
> Breathe solitude
> A lone Oboe explores
> The unknown clause

The unknown clause
Calculates
Diction chimes
Bring it home
Bring it home
The desert
The Sphinx
The life we
Live
Springs
Green footing
PASS – OVER
PASS – OVER
Space is
The armature
A provider
The arbiter
Of things
To come
The past is
The past is
But one corner
Of a square
That contains
Two triangles
A pyramid
And an all
Seeing eye
And an all
Seeing eye
Mirrors
The Deep
Deep
Continuous
Creation

WILD CARDS

Prologue

Each time I fill a full house
I am called to an album of family photos
Wild Cards
The towering Ace
Black Jack
Don't call the accountants
Its too early people are moving
New structures are being built
Give me the egg
You keep the chicken
Each time the hand
Finds three of kind
Space equals the information
Not everything can go into
One painting one poem
Not everything can go into
One painting one poem
Scare Crows Blackbirds
Pumpkins and biting fish
Naples Trafalgar
In Venice there are canals
Ancient whorehouses
Torture chambers
Lady Hamilton
Giorgione Titian and Jews
Ladino codfish
Not everything can go into
One painting one poem
Not everything can go into
One painting one poem
The painter puts his hand
Through the canvas and finds
Wild Cards
Music Grass
A Dandelion gone to seed
Protracts the winds
Course landscape

And builds masks for everyone
Who has had their face shot off
Not everything can go into
One painting one poem
Not everything can go into
One painting one poem
She said I am an actress
I should have seen through him he was acting

Pause

King of Hearts
Eight of Hearts
Ten of Diamonds
Two of Diamonds
The Ace of Spades
        Black Jack

Part One: Wild Men

In 1875, Monet paints "Woman with a Parasol – Madame Monet and Her Son." The wind is behind her skirt. A green parasol and green vegetation articulate the sky. The boy, her son, looks at his father. His mother looks down at her husband. *Family Photos.*

"Camille Monet on her Deathbed" (1879)

In 1879, Camille is the vehicle that chronicles Monet's own death. White, blue, black and red she leaves her son, an unborn child, and her husband.

Photography can be the most judgmental of disciplines.

> Monet walks across the "Japanese Bridge"
> Stopping to look at "Green Reflection"
> Orange tells him take your time
> Don't rush there is a high tide
> And a low tide a vortex for water
> Don't rush dusty blue deep green
> "Water Lilies at Twilight"
> Will shake your hand and tell you
> How glad it is to see you
> Oh virtue Ochre mumbles
> And no one knows

It is saying
The brush like a good parent
Keeps the rain from falling
On the evening meal
   Not everything can go into
   One painting one poem
   Not everything can go into
   One painting one poem
   Cleopatra sails the Nile
Dressed in white and pale yellows
"Water Lilies" sprout leaves
And hide behind
"The Two Willows"
The clouds return and
Peel away Camille's swollen body
That is unable to abort the child
That was never born

In 1901, Claude Monet paints "Haystacks." In 1901, Nadar takes Claude Monet's photograph. Monet is sixty-one. Nadar is eighty-one. Born Gaspard-Félix Tournachon, he legally changed his name to Nadar in 1856. He began to take photographs with his brother in 1854. By 1856, he has quarrelled with his brother and takes all the photographs by himself. He, like Monet and their counterpart in America, Frederick Law Olmstead (1822-1903), is an Impressionist.

Frederick Law Olmstead hung the keys to his house on a tree and put his boots on. America's greatest impressionist did in his parks what Claude Monet did in his "Haystacks" and "Water Lilies." There are no right or oblique angles. All this came before the migration. Before Picasso moved to Paris. Before Monet and Renoir shared a studio.

It was the sixteenth century and Giorgione and Titian painted the magnificent "Pastoral." They were Venetians, and the Venetians were literal in their politics, religion, and in art they were incapable of having an impression.

Art of the late Industrial Revolution created public spaces that didn't speak down to the public instead it flooded their moral codes, and educated generations of romantic professionals.

"The Bridge with Water Lilies" (1919)

Monet painted "The Bridge with Water Lilies" as a room
With no windows no doors where does the light come from
Imagine a place where no light
But shadows menace the unprotected
Where but in the dark do we watch movies
Where but in the dark
Does the unspeakable sit next to us
Not everything can go into
One painting one poem
Not everything can go into
One painting one poem
A mother carrying her unborn child
Her womb has possession of the child's ego
And the child who knows this reinvents itself

                Pause

The photograph
Reveals secrets
Invisible things
Hidden expressions
Caricatures
Kindness
Regrets
Resentments
Tall redheaded Nadar
Invented and reinvented himself
Nadar (1820-1910)
Lived to be 90
Was a friend of Daumier
Honouré Daumier (1808-1879) had sympathy
For those who suffered
His father had been a poet and playwright
Had started a school for boys which failed
Daumier was a great draftsman
Maybe one of the greatest
He loved the theatre knew how to use
Drama in his lithographs and paintings
Not everything can go into
One painting one poem
Not everything can go into
One painting one poem

Daumier the pedagogue would say
"One must belong to one's own time."
One must belong one must
To one's own time
One must
Take stock
And drink
To the future

                Pause

There are rooms with no windows
No doors
Where does the light come from
Imagine a place
Where no light
But shadows menace the unprotected
Where but the unconscious
Where but in the dark
Do we watch movies
Where but in the dark
Does the unspeakable
Sit next to us
Not everything can go into
One painting one poem
Not everything can go into
One painting one poem

                Pause

John Chamberlain may have derived his shapes from abstract paintings. But it's Chamberlain's imagination that transforms coloured scraps of old car parts into those wonderful sculptured miniatures of the 1960s. Random parts, scraps, metal leftovers, excesses of the car-buying public are made into artificial flowers that have no need of vases, crystals, or chandeliers to promote their elegance. Sometimes these small pieces become last night's stews. Chamberlain doesn't hesitate. Strike, sweet stew. Action is the aesthete's first weapon. Miniatures don't always sit still. They get hungry. They thirst for structure, for materials that will excavate the core. Apples and lumber and strands that twist the heart claim the workers lining the avenues praying for a new car. Popular icons blink and shudder. No one is reproached for not working. Not even the bountiful Chamberlain knows how long this will last.

Chamberlain moves his arms and we learn that he can smile. His totems entitle families to migrate to places that they would never have dreamt of. His grandfather was a bird and his bride was a snake. When they mated, they had his father. His father said he didn't want to fly and he didn't want to be on the ground. Their children are the ones that I speak of. I've heard them talk about their parents. What they have to say is, you can get lost. You can walk into a wall. The night is not the only darkness. Remember your Totem. Remember there are no windows or doors in Chamberlain's miniatures. Where does the light come from. Remember your Totem. Click … turn on the lights and go outside.

Be rich. Get rich. Be rich.

Pause

George de La Tour (1593-1652) painted "The Cheat with the Ace of Spades" in the 1620s. There are no windows or doors in the painting. Where does the light come from. De La Tour paints scoundrels earning their living by cheating and robbing the innocent. He uses candles in "The Flea Catcher" (1630s). "The Penitent Magdalene with the Night Light" is also illuminated by candlelight. De La Tour's paintings have no windows or doors. Where does the light come from. George de La Tour tells his stories in an artificially lit studio. "St. Jerome" reads, and in the next frame "The Flea Catcher" sits exposing her breasts. No one is spared. De La Tour's characters are an early *noir*. Sin, corruption, and penitents are controlled by outside forces. The inner voice waits. "Carpentry by Candlelight." The heat is in the tip of the flame. For love, another painter burned his hand, cut off his ear, and ate Black Birds.

Pause

> Paint – have you ever inhaled it
> Tasted it chewed it resented it
> The King of Clubs looks at itself
> In the hallway mirror
> He wears a Black suit
> A White shirt
> And a Black tie
> Black socks and Black shoes
> He is clean-shaven
> And his hair is combed
> He is the Man
> He distributes candles
> Mocking birds

And is a shill
For all the houses
That play games of chance

Part Two: Family Photos

Pop Art, the genre painting of the 1960s and 70s, might not have existed without John F. and his wife, Jackie. The Kennedys were stars. When they began to talk Aphrodite and Aristotle went to the park, held hands, and had their photograph taken. For love we pursue. For entertainment the movies give us an endless supply of androgynous characters.

> Pause

In Nadar's photographs of Daumier, and I've seen four of them, there may be more, Daumier thrusts his hands into his pockets. He turns his head and squints. Everything about him is dangerous. We don't see his feet. No one can mock their victims as thoroughly as Daumier without mocking themselves.

Photos, family photos. Only four and a half blocks from Olmstead and Vaux's Prospect Park our back yard is in summer a large dining and sitting room. And it's Martha's garden. There are always flowers.

> Get rich. Be rich. Get rich. Be rich

Édouard Manet (1832-1883) his fast brush, his Greys, his contradictions, his inability to accept the professions that were assigned to someone of his class.

Manet sat in his boat and picked up tubes of paint. It was an intimate moment. Even when it jeopardized his social standing he would fight for the paradox to continue. Boots became as important as trees. The camera the tube of paint, the train's smoke, the colour grey. Paris was changing; France along with the rest of the world was resisting that change.

Manet was entering the final phase of locomotor ataxia. His muscles were wasting away. He was in pain and tired easily. At the age of 52, Manet is dead.

No one, not the fields waiting for the clouds to deliver water or the promise of further rain can finish a short story. A short story never ends.

> Pause

Family photos. In defiance of myth science reveals some mysteries. A tube of paint and the steam engine competed for importance. It was different in this new place where the abstract made Manet's fast brush and Turner's reveal something of the unknown. In this new place Impressionism made it different. Overnight, both intimacy and nationalism where struck with a democratic force that blurred the edges. Borders were crossed. The androgynous figure that Giorgione and de La Tour had painted ceased to be. Ibsen, Henry James, and D.H. Lawrence used language, not paint, to assault beauty. And beauty changed. He wore her hat and she wore his. He rarely wore a skirt. But she wore pants.

With the invention of the tube painters could work outside. Before that, small paintings (studies) done outside had been considered merely part of the working process, and were to be seen only by the painters themselves, their friends, and perhaps their students. Now these expressions began to be looked at as legitimate works of art. The paradox continues.

Part Three: American Hands

Winslow Homer (1836-1910)
Thomas Eakins (1844-1916)

Homer and Eakins
Dismiss
London
And Paris
They want
America

                             Pause

James Abbott McNeill Whistler (1834-1903)
Needs the English Channel
It gave him time to change
From English to French
High tea and Hyde Park
To the Tuileries

John Abbott McNeill Whistler was born in America. His father, a civil engineer and a graduate of West Point, was employed in 1842 by the Czar to build a railroad from St. Petersburg to Moscow. In Russia, Whistler learns French and studies drawing.

In 1848, John's father, Major George Washington McNeill Whistler, dies of cholera, in Russia. Whistler's mother brings the family back to America. Whistler is 15. The next year Whistler enrols in West Point. He is dismissed and doesn't graduate. When he decides to be a painter, he goes to Paris, then to London. Whistler's mother, half-sister, and brother all move to London, and Whistler never returns to North America.

Whistler hung his hat and coat on wooden pegs. Possibly the same pegs his great-great-grandfather had used before he left England for the colonies.

Pause

"It's always the same work that's so hard and uncertain," Whistler wrote Fantin LaTour. "I am so slow," said the man who signed his paintings with a butterfly. I am so slow, lotus blossom. Amour. To know what to paint, and then to paint it.

Whistler loved Franz Hals
Loved his defiance
Alms give me "Nocturne
Symphonies" –
Give me "The White Girl"
Her tranquillity
Bewitched by Butterflies
Japanese prints Degas Mallarmé
Oscar Wilde and Thomas Carlyle
Whistler was not like his friends
Not everything can go into
One painting one poem
Not everything can go into
One painting one poem
Oh! St. Luke, patron saint of painters
Whistler's literal translations
Can be mistaken
For a mistake
Consider the originator
Whistler is an expatriate a migrant
A whistler challenging beauty
Calculates
Find the question
Before you find the answer
Not everything can go into
One painting one poem
Not everything can go into

One painting one poem
The ancient seamen believed
The ocean was flat
And if you went far enough
You would fall off the edge
So it is with a painting
Its edges are liken to a waterfall

    Get rich. Be rich. Get rich. Be rich.

Dr. Gross never falters. In the pyramid that Thomas Eakins builds in his painting, "The Gross Clinic," everyone is positioned. Only the patient is interchangeable. As in "Max Schmitt in a Single Scull," Eakins defers to Velázquez and Rembrandt.

Thomas Eakins stands bare-assed on a beach. Do not mock him. Eakins loved photography. It is in Eakins' photographs that he breaks with Velázquez, Rembrandt, and his conservative father. His young men and women with their clothes off are not Greek statues or monuments. They have nothing to sell and nothing to hide.

She is almost beautiful
He is almost handsome
Today we don't wear clothes
We don't want to get married
Today we read Whitman
Long lines praise Abraham Lincoln
Lincoln is tall he believes
Evil can be checked darkness can be righted
Tall men see over every one else's head
Not everything can go into
One painting one poem
Not everything can go into
One painting one poem
Sex is to be enjoyed
Boxing Fishing Sailing
Science and the rotation of enjoyment
Her dress doesn't fit
His hat is too big his shoes are too
Psychological
Not everything can go into
One painting one poem
Not everything can go into
One painting one poem

The phone rings an anonymous caller
Wants to know what are you wearing
And have you photographed yourself
Some painters use photographs
Easels and pre-primed canvas
Is every nude beautiful
Can morality be overdressed
Is every nude beautiful
Are all landscapes overexposed

Pause

The next time I see Tom Eakins I should ask him, "Doesn't the sun ever shine in your house." Eakins lived all his life in the house where he was born. All his portraits are dark, weighted and without humour. The sitters look as if they are straining to be something that they cannot be. Maybe he was right. The sun never shines in his house. Oh, but on the Schuylkill River, boats and oarsmen, dogs and horses, and bare assed boys benefit from the light that never enters Eakins' house. Trample the grass, pick a rose, hear the bells. It's Sunday and everyone has gone to the park.

After Eakins was fired from his teaching job by the governing board of the Pennsylvania Academy of Fine Arts for removing a loincloth from a male model in the women's class to demonstrate the origin of muscles, Eakins went to New Jersey to see Walt Whitman. He asked to paint his portrait. Whitman was to say, "The portrait ... sets me down in correct style without feathers ... It never weakens." It infuriated their contemporaries that both men were willing to continue without status and without approval or material gain.

Get rich. Be rich. Get rich. Be rich.

In 1900, Homer wrote a letter to his dealer at Knoedler & Company in New York City about the painting, "West Point, Prout's Neck": "The picture is painted 15 minutes after sunset. Not one minute before. As up to that minute, the clouds over the sun would have their edges lighted with a brilliant glow of colour, but now (in this picture) the sun has got beyond their immediate range and they are in shadow. You can see it took many days of careful observation to get this (the high sea and tide) just right."

Homer managed the family's business interests on Prouts Neck, Maine – selling lots and care-taking the houses that the family rented during the summer. Eakins lived on the money his father had made in real estate.

Homer went to Key West and the Bermudas. Eakins went out West once and once he travelled to New Jersey to visit Walt Whitman.

Whistler was a Peacock. He borrowed, cajoled, and played people against one another. Whistler couldn't keep still. London. Brighton. Paris. Brittany. Venice. Homer's visits to Key West and the Bermudas don't have the same urgency.

Pause

Winslow Homer loved to fish and hunt. Eakins painted men rowing boxing swimming and hunting. Eakins became transfixed with Velázquez and Rembrandt. When he visited Europe Homer painted the fishermen of Cullercoates, England their wives and children.

> The Civil War is over
> Beaches are crowded
> Fields are ploughed
> It is November and the Lobelia
> Continue to bloom
> Bungalows Palm trees Turtles
> Key West North West
> A pond full of Frogs
> The Deer return to New England
> And the epic begins
> Not everything can go into
> One painting one poem
> Not everything can go into
> One painting one poem
> Does your stomach hurt
> Does your tooth ache
> The Civil War is over
> Beaches are crowded
> Fields are ploughed
> It is November and the Lobelia
> Continue to bloom
> The waves starch and press
> Your tailor-made clothes
> A "West Wind" mounts a whale
> And a "Winter Coast"
> Is a mime among the rocks
> "A Northeaster Kisses the Moon"
> "Hark! The Lark"
> The Civil War is over

> Beaches are crowded
> Fields are ploughed
> It is November and the Lobelia
> Continue to bloom

Pause

Mount Auburn Cemetery, Cambridge Massachusetts. "America's First Garden Cemetery Consecrated 1831." The cemetery's map reads in bold letters, "GRAVES OR MEMORIALS OF SOME NOTED PERSONS, Key 30 Section D5 Homer, Winslow." Winslow Homer is buried with his parents, his two brothers and their wives. Homer loved one of his brother's wives. Now he is buried next to her.

Pause

> King of Hearts
> Eight of Hearts
> Ten of Diamonds
> Two of Diamonds
> The Ace of Spades
>   Black Jack

Part Four: Three of a kind

Viscount Horatio Nelson fought his way up from the ranks. Joseph Mallord Turner's father was a wig-maker and a barber. William Blake did not fulfil his family's expectations.

No man's land

William Blake (1757-1827) went to no man's land without troops or maps. He had gone, knowing he had no other place to go. Where else would he be able to go and find nothing. In no man's land he was free to invent. In no man's land Blake had a partner, Kitty (Catherine Boucher Blake, 1762-1831). Blake taught Kitty how to read and write. Taught her how to mix paint and meditate. Blake brought Kitty with him to no man's land. Who else would have gone with him. Who else. Only Kitty knew what had brought them together. She was the only one who knew why she stayed.

> Everyone knew they were childless
> Their table was set
> Two plates two forks two knives

Not everything can go into
One painting one poem
Not everything can go into
One painting one poem
Oh, sister Kitty
Children dream of oval skies
Psalms of ingratitude submerge the mind
Until incompetence has been removed
Create a meditation
Industry has transformed what once was
Is now without breasts
She is childless she smokes
She opens her legs she is humbled
The man she knew has lost his prick
The gates of hell
Have been opened
Don't close them
Let them remain open
Self-hate
And all its intimidations
Augment the colour wheel
Not everything can go into
One painting one poem
Not everything can go into
One painting one poem
Dante brought us the vernacular
Blake is dead
Kitty is dead
Their childless children
Say you are never distracted
I say I have to concentrate
Pay attention I have to I have to
Pay attention
When all the leaves are gone
And the trees are bare
Having drunk
Both water and turpentine
No metaphor is necessary
No photograph is needed

    Get rich. Be rich. Get rich. Be rich.

Turner included the sport of cricket in his painting, "The Lake, Petworth," "Sunset, Fighting Bucks" (1829-1830). In Giorgione's "Pastorale Concert"

(1510) the women are naked, the men wear clothes. In Manet's "Luncheon on the Grass" (1862) one woman is naked, another woman in the background wears a shift and she is bathing. The two men are clothed. The naked woman sits between the two men and she looks out of the painting at an audience – or is it a camera. It was during the Industrial Revolution that pastoral power diminished and in its place Turner's "Rain, Steam and Speed" forecast the power of the short story.

From 1831 until Lord Egremont's death in 1837 Turner often stayed for months at a time and became, in effect, an artist-in-residence at Lord Egremont's ancestral home, Petworth Castle. Unlike most 19th century manor houses, Lord Egremont's Petworth had no schedules, no rules. Lord Egremont was a famous eccentric. Everyone came and went as they pleased. It was always chaotic. And Lord Egremont's guests became Turner's models. Turner had his own studio. It had a tall arched window and it overlooked the lake. In this commodious atmosphere Turner drew, painted, and did hundreds of watercolours. Deer cohabitated ladies and gentlemen of the castle cohabitated with each other, and sometimes with the servants.

The last thing the great Turner asked for as he lay dying was a crayon. Oh, Massaccio, there was a medieval artist who drew Roses. And the Rose needed to leave home, learn to draw, and meet strangers.

Ruskin, afraid they would ruin Turner's reputation, tore up most of Turner's pornography. Victorian hypocrisy loved the steam engine. Up, down, up, down, in out, in out.

Pause

Lucia Berlin asked me, who is Mrs. Booth.

Dear Lucia,
In the early 1830s the painter Turner used to stop in Margate, a seaside town, on his way to Petworth Castle. Petworth Castle was the estate of the very wealthy and egalitarian Lord Egremont. At Petworth, Turner had all the privileges of an honoured guest. He hunted and he fished. He loved fishing. He had his own studio and he was free to stay as long as he wanted. Turner painted, did watercolours, and I don't know how many drawings at Petworth. This continued until Lord Egremont's death. Then his children cut Turner off.

Sophia Caroline Booth with her second husband ran the lodging house Turner used in Margate. In 1833 Sophia's second husband died. Turner convinced her to move closer to where he lived. She moved to a small house on the Thames, at No. 119 Cheyne Walk, Chelsea, a street that James McNeill Whistler was later to live on. Mrs. Booth was fortyish, and more than twenty years younger than Turner. It is said that she was a good-looking woman. She had dark hair and was said to be cheerful. I don't know how much education she had but she must have been intelligent. After Turner died she had a correspondence with Ruskin, and the old snob helped her sell the drawings and watercolours that Turner had given her with the express purpose of her selling them when she became old and needed the money.

The house on Cheyne Walk was considered shabby but it had a spectacular view of the river. Turner had a passageway cut from his top-floor bedroom to the roof. There he built a little porch where sometimes he would sketch. Other times he would sit for hours looking at the unobstructed view.

Mrs. Booth's Chelsea neighbours called Turner "Mr. Booth" or "the Admiral." He wanted it that way. The old seadog Turner had a ruddy complexion and rolled when he walked. Being Mr. Booth explained Mr. Booth's long absences. He was at sea. Where else does a sailor go.

As you know a short story never ends. Mrs. Booth brushed Turner's clothes. Sent him to the doctor and the dentist. They took boat rides and strolled together. She cooked, he took naps, read, painted. If the reports are correct, he and Mrs. Booth had a good thing going. She understood her man. And Turner understood that she too understood love.

    I sent Lucia this poem:

Sunrise With Sea Monster, 1845

I told
Mrs. Booth
All I
Want
Is to
Sit on
My porch
And watch
The sea

She told me
I don't sleep
Enough

She told me
The sea corrupts
Frogs and men with
Out hats

I told her
I was going fishing
She told me
To wear my old boots
And not to forget
The imagination
Spawns monsters

I
Fear
The monster's
Big eyes
Its many teeth
Cross
My heart
Mrs. Booth
I am going
To paint
The Monster
At Sunrise

                Pause

Having lost an eye and an arm in battle Viscount Nelson illuminates his decorations by strutting. Everyone could see his wins and his losses. The Viscount loved Lady Hamilton. She was a beautiful poor girl who was passed from man to man until the elderly Lord Hamilton became her protector. He educated her and gave her his name. Nelson was married to a widow whom he did not love. Wellington never understood Nelson. His dour countenance refuted Nelson's love for Lady Hamilton, and she suffered after Nelson's death.

It is not our war
We are children
We hold a parent's hand
Our eyes
Watch their backs
It is not our war
We cannot fight an enemy

We do not know
Not everything can go into
One painting one poem
Not everything can go into
One painting one poem
They are not tall
And they are not handsome
And they are not kind
And they are afraid of us
We are not afraid of them
No we are not afraid of them
Viscount Nelson
Says
Sickness attacks me
Every time I step
On board a ship
I want to make room
For Lady Hamilton
England doesn't
Know it but they
Need her
She loves
The North Sea
Vikings Danes and Normans
The arbitrary Celt
Not everything can go into
One painting one poem
Not everything can go into
One painting one poem
Goethe's *Theory of Colour*
J. M. Turner's colour wheel – inherited
From Titian a Venetian apple
For Cézanne
Not always functional
Not always related
Aristotle loved his boys
Alexander benefited from his wisdom
And used it to conquer the known world

                Pause

King of Hearts
Eight of Hearts
Ten of Diamonds

Two of Diamonds
The Ace of Spades
               Black Jack

Part Five: Full House

What Giorgione had begun by not outlining his figures and bringing the foreground up to the figure, what Titian so capably did in old age by blurring his edges, Impressionism turned upside down with vibrant colours that could be manufactured in a factory. Boots became as important as trees. This seemingly simple coming together of objects extended into the family and gave families permission to migrate, change their lives, and live in a manner they were unaccustomed to.

AMERICA KNOCKS

BOOK ONE

As the fortunes of the American Patriots improved, Gilbert Hicks, the Quaker minister and painter Edward Hick's grandfather, had to flee to New York, which was held by the British army. Edward's grandfather sympathized with the colonists but felt that resolution should be sought through mediation and negotiation, not war. When the war ended, Edward's father and grandfather's properties in Pennsylvania were seized and auctioned off, leaving them both impoverished. Gilbert Hicks fled again, this time to Nova Scotia. Edward grew up never knowing him.

After the Revolutionary War the new country continued to persecute those who had not agreed with the Patriots, and an opportunity was missed. Had the Patriots forgiven their neighbours for being Tory sympathizers and accepted them as fellow countrymen, the terrible witch hunts that to this day drive the authorities to dehumanize a neighbour, friend, or relative if they are suspected of being "un-American" might never have begun.

On again, from the military outpost along Boone's Trace it is grinding going. One of the parties wanders into the forest and is lost. They wait; they fire their guns and beat about in the thicket, yelling his name: he is gone, his fate is unknown. The wilderness has gulped him in. Next day they move on again: What initiated the move? The poem is almost endless.

They were brothers, Big Harpe, born 1768, and Little Harpe, 1770, in North Carolina. It was rumoured that they were part Negro: "Their tawny appearance and dark curly hair betrayed a tinge of African blood."

Their father had been a Tory; he had fought the Patriots during the early part of the war. Later he joined them. But it was too late and he was never forgiven and was forced to flee. This kind of persecution was not uncommon. Properties were seized. Brothers became enemies. Children were farmed out to friends.

A Tory sympathizer was never allowed to forget he had made a mistake. The two Harpe sons and their mother remained in North Carolina. Maybe they were treated badly. We will never know. But in 1795 the two young men left North Carolina with two women, two sisters, Susan and Betsy Roberts.

Roaming westward into central Tennessee they lived with a tribe of Cherokee Indians – a tribe wandering like themselves, outlawed for some breach or other from the general confederacy of the Indian nations. For two years they travelled with these Indians; it was a dangerous life.

Big Harpe and Little Harpe wanted to be remembered. They wanted their portraits painted. They wanted everything that they couldn't have. They wanted pale faces. For the love of killing they killed. They opened their victims' bellies and scooped out the intestines. Would they have liked a photograph of what they had done. Would they have enjoyed a photograph of the two of them standing over a victim?

Two images, one on the left side and one on the right side are being shown simultaneously on one movie screen. On the right side of the screen a solitary figure paints on a canvas. The audience cannot see who the painter is; they can only see an artist at work. The artist could be a man, and it could be a woman. Could be. The painter could be Benjamin West, 1738-1820, but it isn't. In 1797 West is in England painting large historical scenes for the King of England, George III.

On the left side of the screen five figures pass the painter. Two men and three women are walking in the wilderness. One of the men is very large. The other is smaller. There are no horses, no children. Both men wear Indian clothes, buckskins and moccasins. The women are as ragged and as unkempt as the men. For a long time they say nothing; the audience hears the birds. The party of five does not see the painter and the painter does not see them. 1797, The Wilderness Road. The surreal knocks. The two images merge.

Big Harpe and Little Harpe are on the movie screen. There is a rustle of leaves and a few birds cross the screen. The screen looks huge. The Harpe brothers don't move. The trees behind the Harpes are still. This could be a photograph. Grey, white and some black predominate. Again a few birds cross the screen. The brothers stare at the audience. One of the Harpes says, "I hate you, whoever you are. I can't see you, but I don't want to. I don't want to hear what you have to say. If you are afraid, if you come any closer I will kill you. You don't give a shit about me and my brother." Colour begins to show. Simultaneously, the brothers are shrinking; buckskins and moccasins become a blur. Big Harpe and Little Harpe's faces fade and no longer exist.

Get rich. Be rich. Get rich. Be rich.

Edward Hicks was always in poor health and complained about it constantly. John J. Audubon enjoyed good health and was able to do strenuous work. He never complained. Audubon was born a year after Hicks and died two years after Hicks did. The Lion's face becomes a human face documenting Hicks' age and emotional state. The same can be said of Audubon's birds. They too have human features. Did either of them know they were painting their self-portraits.

Remember the Harpe brothers and what they did when they lost their father. Edward Hicks (1780-1849), Quaker minister and painter, was ten years younger than Big Harpe. Eight years younger than Little Harpe.

Edward's mother died of grief and his father had to board his children out. Edward went to live with the Twinnings. The Twinnings were Quakers. They were not his people. They were pleasant to him but they never loved him. His father remarried, raised another family, and had little to do with Edward. Young Edward never became close to any of his siblings.

Two images, one on the left side and one on the right side are being shown simultaneously on one movie screen. The Harpes are on the left side of the screen. Edward Hicks is on the right side of the screen. The Harpes are watching Edward Hicks paint. They do not know what to make of it. Edward Hicks is all hunched over. He paints on a small board. He paints very slowly. He is talking to himself. The Harpes cannot hear what he is saying. The Harpes are waiting for a victim. They are in no rush. They know exactly what they want to do. They are killers. If they are not stopped they will kill again. The surreal knocks. A Quaker shouldn't paint. Edward Hicks paints.

There's a hint of Bosch in some of Edward Hicks' "Peaceable Kingdom" paintings. The trees, sometimes old, are cracked and hollow. Sometimes without warning, Saint Anthony sits next to the Lion. He brings with him the thought of monsters, of animals wanting to do harm. Save me from war says the elongated Leopard. Save me from crisis says the Lion. He knows George Washington has crossed the Delaware. Tell me more says the Lamb. Tell me contradiction abounds, but not on our land, not in our time. Not on the waters that separate us from the mountains. Not in the leaves, on the trees, or in the Ox that avoids the Bear.

In this land of coded behaviour where some animals stand and others sit on a hill, William Penn always negotiates with the Indians on the left side of the canvas. The sky and the water are always given the same position. Sometimes a ship is docked in the harbour. Two children are placed on the grass. Sometimes they sit next to a Tiger, sometimes an elongated Leopard stares at the congregation insisting that the line that separates William Penn and the Indians from the animals is an entitlement. Not all vowels move. But since Rimbaud, all of them have colour.

Pause

In Edward Hicks' painting, "Noah's Ark" (1846)
Pairs of animals enter the ark
The White Horses are dignified
The Leopards stare
The Lions implore the congregation to realize
The importance of the situation

Elephants
Birds
Snakes
William Penn
Continues to talk
To the Indians
No one knows
How long
We will have
To stay
The door of
The Ark
Is closed
Where does
The light
Come from

Inside the Ark
No one speaks
Language
Is forbidden
The door of
The Ark
Is closed
Where does
The light
Come from

Imagine a place where no light but shadows menace the unprotected where but the unconscious. Where but in the dark do we watch movies. Where but in the dark does the unspeakable sit next to us. And only then do we realize the night has stars, gods and goddesses, the Milky Way.

Pause

She said she didn't believe in god. She said she didn't believe in sin and she got pregnant. Her parents were southern Baptists. They took the baby and gave it to an orphanage and had their daughter committed.

She realized that she was never going to get out. And after a year she escaped. She had a coat covering her regulation uniform. No suitcase, no hat, she didn't know where she was going.

She was standing on the highway. A car pulled up and a young man asked her if she needed a ride. She didn't hesitate she got in and he drove. He asked her where was she going and she broke down and told him everything.

He took her to a Howard Johnson and after they had ordered he said he would be right back. She thought maybe she should bolt maybe he was going to turn her in but she didn't leave and he came back and said, "I'm taking you home."

She had her coat on. And he said, I phoned my mother and she says I should bring you home and she asked herself what does that mean.

I met this young woman when she was a student in my art history class and I was her adviser and she told me that after she told her story to the young man's mother and father, the mother said you are going to stay here with us and she took her to a room and said this is where you are going to sleep and the next day she brought her some clothes.

The family did not tell their friends about their new ward. They retained a lawyer. It took months before the young woman was cleared and was free to leave the house.

If she was scarred by the trauma she had lived it was mostly hidden. Except when her handsome face would look as if she was living something that was remote and far away.

It was on one of those days that she looked at me and said
I'm to be married and I want you to meet his parents.

The four of them came to our house for lunch. They said they voted Democratic in a district that was predominately Republican. They said they went to church and that their son had fallen in love with the girl he had picked up. They said that they had an older son and he was married and his wife was pregnant. The mother said she had always wanted a daughter and she smiled at the young woman who was going to marry her son. The mother said that there are only a few times in your life when you can do good and you have to recognize when that is and do it. The father didn't say much. Maybe he never did. But I knew he was checking Martha and me out. And the son he sat coolly occupied with the future.

It Is Said
Light Gives The Peace Maker Time

Time Is A Giver A Feeder A Swamp
A Dam Builder Is Thirst

The Thirst Giver Renames
A Peaceable Kingdom

A Peaceable Kingdom
Gives Light To Offend The Caustic

Pause

At thirteen, I was apprenticed for seven years to local coach makers where I developed my talent for ornamental painting. I painted signboards for Carpenters & Joiners, Hatters, Libraries and Miniature Chests. I decorated boxes and chairs. This trade that is as abstract as it is imaginative I have pursued all my life. Knowing this, I paint.

As a young man in Philadelphia I drank and slept with women. I had bad days, I worried. I had much to think about. When I was eighteen months old my mother died. My father and grandfather had been Tory sympathizers during the Revolutionary War. They were severely punished for it. They lost their wealth and position. Grandfather Gilbert Hicks fled to Nova Scotia. Never to be seen again.

Years pass. Edward attends Quaker meetings, gets married, has children and becomes a Quaker minister. And still the sleepless nights persist. Sometimes followed by periods of extreme sadness, anger or joy, any one of which are capable of bringing tears to his eyes.

Edward Hicks said, "Where early impressions are neglected the loss that children sustain is almost incalculable."

Get rich. Be rich. Get rich. Be rich.

Loretta's mother had been an alcoholic who, when not drunk and abusive, was sick. The court had intervened. Loretta and her two sisters were placed in foster homes. Loretta lived with her foster mother for eight years. From the time she was 10 to the time she left, her foster mother made sure that Loretta saw her two sisters on a regular basis. It was important to the foster mother that the sisters remain a family.

Loretta doesn't smile very much something prevents her. She cannot describe what frightens her. She feels that she is in danger, of what, she does not know. She isn't afraid of having an accident or being run over by a car. She flies and she shops, and isn't interested in details; she wants to escape the emptiness the dour consequences of her childhood. She is pursued. According to Aristotle and other ancient authorities, a baby awake does not smile until forty days after birth, when both mother and child are out of danger. It could be said, "The infant's first smile, then, becomes a formal taking possession of life." Loretta has never been able to take possession of her life and it has stunted her perceptions. Her education is limited. She is never able to finish. Few things get completed.

Loretta married young, had two children, a boy and a girl. She divorced the children's father, and married Bob. Like her first husband, Bob was in the army. Bob had a daughter from his first marriage. Loretta and Bob had one daughter. Her two older children lived with their father. Loretta doesn't see them very often.

When Loretta and Bob's daughter was 4 years old Loretta's mother died. Following her mother's death Loretta received some legal papers. She discovered that her mother had been married two other times. First to another man before marrying Loretta's father Loretta's story repeated itself. The mother had lost custody of the children and they had been placed in foster homes. By the time her mother married for the third time she had sobered up and had a daughter and raised her without any intervention from the courts. This daughter described their mother as kind and considerate.

After Bob's discharge from the army Bob became a successful businessman. This enabled Loretta to hire a private detective. She wanted to find all of her brothers and sisters. It took the detective ten years. He found 16 in all. She also discovered that her father too had been married before, and, I think she said, that he too had married again after leaving her mother.

The last half-brother she found was serving in the army. A friend of Bob's, a man who had been his commanding officer, was driving Loretta to meet

this brother when she said, "There he is."
The friend said, "How do you know?"
"I can tell by the way he's walking."

Loretta prefers not to see some of her sibs. "They aren't people I want to know," she says. Her father now lives in Florida. He has become a Bible-thumping fundamentalist whose idea of preparing to meet his maker is to straighten out everyone else, including Loretta. She doesn't visit her dad very often and when she does it's not pleasant. She has divorced Bob and their daughter doesn't always go with her to see the father.

BOOK TWO

They brought with them their border wars. They came from the north of England, Scotland, and Northern Ireland. Seven centuries of fighting between the kings of England and Scotland over the borderlands they inhabited had made the people inured to their towns being sacked and burned and their kinsmen tortured to death. Their hatred and contempt for one another marked everyone who came in contact with them.

Many had been forcibly resettled in Ireland. When they came to the American South, they brought with them a penchant for family feuds, a warrior ethic that demanded vengeance. Their prevailing principle, "lex talionas," the rule of retaliation, helps explain the bloodiness of the fighting in the backcountry from 1760-1785.

As far back as the middle ages blood feuds between families and clans claimed the ethic of "primal honour". Above all, honour meant reputation; honour also meant valour; a man had to be prepared to fight to defend his honour if challenged or insulted.

White tenant farmers photographed by Walker Evans in the 1930s are the heirs to this insulated cruelty. Their ancestors came to America with their anger and excesses and invented Dog-patch.

Pause

Sit on the bed with Granny, her son, his wife and their three children. Twenty-five families have bred with each other for two hundred years, or more. There are exceptions; there is the orphan girl. Her parents had taken her up north to Detroit. In Detroit her mother stocked shelves at Woolworth's. Her dad worked at Dodge on the assembly line. Things went well for a few years. The three of them lived in an apartment. She had her own room. They bought a car. She had started first grade. It was a Saturday. She was at a friend's house when the police came and told her that her parents had been killed in a car accident. Her uncle came up to Detroit and took her back down south. Her uncle's wife didn't want the girl to live with them. She had never liked the girl's mother. So her uncle took her to his friends who lived on the other side of the mountain. They took her in and she has lived with them ever since. She is fifteen and she doesn't want to become pregnant. She really wants to get married to a boy she's not sleeping with. Her adopted father always has a sore on one or two parts of his body. And he's tired all the time. His wife can't remember. Did she ever love him. She never has had much time for her children. Because of her husband's ailments she works the fields with the three children.

Walker Evans photographed these families, their pain, and their shame. On Sunday, Praise the Lord! Praise be the perfectly proportioned 18th century garden. Praise be the sculptor Jean-Antoine Houdon who produced a perfectly proportioned likeness of Thomas Jefferson. Walker Evans photographs one of their clapboard walls the one that has the print of Gilbert Stuart's painting of Thomas Jefferson.

Oh, wilderness, have the sun filter through the trees. Have the wind stir the birds. Have a bird sing. Have the Harpes and their women tear at the flesh of one of their victims. Have the Harpes repeat this. Have the photographer make a series repeating what the Harpes do. Have all these photographs numbered and catalogued. Have the Harpes describe verbally what they do. Have the poem continue to dismember chains and whips, fear and pain. Oh, wilderness, the Harpes knew they had no future. They never considered the consequences of what they did. They thought they were the only ones. The only ones that had ever been hurt.

Edward Hicks said, "Where early impressions are neglected the loss that children sustain is almost incalculable."

BOOK THREE

It could be said there were no social problems on Jefferson's farm. He approved or disapproved. This tall six-foot three-and-a-half inch, red-haired Thomas Jefferson loved being master of his "little mountain." Monticello was sited, an installation. No one questioned his conspicuous consumption, his belief in patronage, his promotion of democracy. No one questioned his contradictions. Maybe Monticello was America's first attempt to deadhead Europe. But there were too many words. It was words, inscribed in his own words, "and not a word more": "…Jefferson, the author of the Declaration of American Independence … and Father of the University of Virginia" sited and installed in Monticello, his conceit. The front hall was Jefferson's museum – his paintings, sculptures, bones, minerals, maps, and Native American artefacts were all words. Everything was for him. Words by him, for him, turned toil to pleasure. His house and his land were a pleasure ground where "the canvas at large must be Grove, of the largest trees trimmed very high, so as to give it the appearance of open ground."

If it is true we dream all the time and consciousness interrupts us, then Jefferson in the privacy of his bed freed his slaves. Add, divide, and subtract in addition to; no more worlds to conquer. Thomas Jefferson (1743-1826), statesman, third President of the United States, tore down the first house, built the new Monticello on the same elevated site, this time with bricks. To please his friend Mr. Madison, Jefferson sends black women, his slaves, to the north octagonal room.

She arrives in the dark and leaves before daylight. She works the fields or does she work in the laundry. At different times she thinks about Mr. Madison. Oh, wilderness dismantle her fears. Dismantle her grievances. On Monday she buried, was it her son. Tuesday she saw the back of, was it her husband they took away. Thursday there was a storm. She used the rainwater to wash her hair, and on Friday they told her Mr. Madison was coming on Saturday.

On Saturday Mr. Madison did what he always did. She blanked out. She lost her voice and she thought if she stopped eating she would get very thin, and maybe he wouldn't want her anymore. Oh, wilderness, she lost.

America is big. It's so big something is always left out. A person, families, a whole state disappears and is never heard from. Change your name. Change your religion. Grow a beard. Shave it off. The silent movies followed the gold rush. Oh, wilderness, this odd combination consolidates a dream.

Instant gratification became part of our heritage. Everyone who comes to America is given one more chance.

> Pause

> Gilbert Stuart painted
> Recognizable
> Politicians and Landowners
> Their wives and children
> Dictators and Poets
> Faces drawn without a ruler
> He wants to be forthright
> He wants to drive
> Futility out of
> His house
> Off of
> The canvas
> But he can't
> But what he can
> Do is concentrate
> On the sitter's nose
>
> She wants to be
> Loved
> He wishes he owned
> More
> The painter is discreet
> He tells them
> They will have
> What they want
>
> Witness
> His bad temper
> His kindness to
> Young painters
> Their bravery
> The bereaved
> The enlightened
> Posture
> Activate his secrets
> Gilbert Stuart spent
> Too much money
> He was always in debt

Pause

At the outbreak of the American Revolution Gilbert Stuart's family fled to Nova Scotia. Stuart's family were loyalists. Gilbert Stuart (1755-1826). Born North Kingston County, Rhode Island, Stuart doesn't go with his family to Nova Scotia. Instead in 1775 he goes to London.

There he studies with Benjamin West becoming his number one assistant. In 1784 West was to say. "He nails the *face* to the *canvas*."

Unlike his mentor Benjamin West, Stuart never drew or made any preliminary studies. Stewart's paintings – no matter what their subject matter – are comparable to Houdon's sculptures. Stuart and Houdon personified the Enlightenment.

Painted during Stuart's stay in Ireland "John, Lord FitzGibbons" (1789) shows "Black Jack" FitzGibbons, arrogantly displaying his office. During the later years of the Protestant Ascendancy, Black Jack was virtually dictator of Ireland.

Twenty five-years later (1814), Stuart paints "Josiah Quincy" – congressman, progressive mayor of Boston, president of Harvard.

In 1825 President John Quincy Adams persuaded Stuart to paint his father once more. Stuart was ill but finally consented. The two old men thoroughly enjoyed each other's company, and the painting was finished shortly before Adams died at the age of ninety.

Josiah Quincy said: *and this portrait of John Adams is a remarkable work, for a faithful representation of the extreme age of the subject would have been painful in inferior hands. But Stuart caught a glimpse of the living spirit shining through the feeble and decrepit body. He saw the old man at one of those happy moments when the intelligence lights up the wasted envelope, and what he saw he fixed upon the canvas.*

Stuart died at the age of seventy-three leaving debts. A memorial exhibition of more than 200 works, held "for the benefit of his family", raised $1,500 to purchase the portraits of President and Mrs. Washington. The bills were paid and Stuart's widow moved with the four remaining daughters back to Newport. There, Jane, the youngest, for more than half a century produced copies of her father's famous "Athenaeum Washington". Jane outlived her sisters, becoming a legend around Newport, and there in 1888 she died at the age of seventy-six.

Get rich. Be rich. Get rich. Be rich.

Every summer for more than twenty years Martha's parents, Lambert and Isabella Davis rented the Watkins cottage at Celo, in the Black Mountains of North Carolina. When all three of the Davis children came with the grandchildren, they also rented the Vernon, the other cottage in the compound. A hedge on two sides of the compound separates the cottages from the Westall property. The Westalls have been locals for generations and when Rhonda and Nollie Westall were alive they worked the farm.

Rhonda and Nollie Westall's daughter Imajean had a child by a man who deserted her before the boy was born. She and her son Barry lived with her parents. The grandparents raised their grandson, wild flowers, and buckwheat. They made butter, kept bees and always sold the young cow for veal. To supplement his income Rhonda arranged music for all the Baptist churches in the valley. He once spoke to me about the foreigner who now lived down the road. I asked him where the foreigner came from. And he gave me the name of the next county.

In 2003 after my reading with Julian Semilian at Reynaldo House Museum in Winston-Salem, Martha and I rented a car and drove up to Celo. It was a gorgeous day, blue and crisp. The valley didn't look as poor as it used to. There are fewer old wrecked cars on the front lawns and the houses are painted and look maintained. The Baptist church across the road from the Westall property has a large addition to its already substantial size. Rhonda and Nollie's small house is still there but the field that once grew their corn and vegetables now contains a large new house.

In front of the new house and to the side of it, right by the road, there is a small cabin-like structure. Something like "Robin's Hairstyles" is written in large letters above the window. Martha knocked and we went in. A local woman was getting her hair cut and streaked. Martha explained who we were and asked after Imajean. Imajean died about nine months ago. It was terrible. Heart attack, cancer, her kidneys, everything.

"I'm so sorry. How's Barry?"

"Barry's in a bad way," said the woman who introduced herself as Barry's wife, Robin. She stopped streaking the woman's hair and said: "You know, Barry never knew his father and Imajean would never speak of him. You know Imajean. It's been hard on Barry, Imajean's death. We are on a mission; we are looking for Barry's dad. Me, Barry and the children, we are looking for his dad."

"You have children."

"Yes, two teenagers."

I asked if we could walk around, go down to the river.

"Sure, take your time."

The compound is the same the hedges are there. And you still have to take a dirt road through the Westall property to get to the cottages. The porch on the Watkins cottage has been repaired and the Adirondack chairs that had been green are now red. The little table where all the grandchildren ate is falling apart. Otherwise it was like being in yesterday, more than thirty years ago. Barry was about four or five. His mother never got married. Imajean went to work at Glenn Raven Mills. The mill made socks and stockings and she became a foreman.

Our two daughters would carefully pick wild flowers that grew between Nollie's rows of vegetables. Our family would pick corn. Shuck the ears and get the corn into the boiling water right away. That way the corn kept its sweetness.

We took photographs of the cottages, the river, the Baptist church, the Black Mountains. We couldn't photograph the damage that had been done to the Westalls. That damage isn't visible.

Trust Me

I want to love
Your forehead
Your brow
I want to trust
Your mouth and the lips
That kiss my trust

I wanted to trust
You
I wanted you
You to be
What I cannot be
Trust me
I have come to
Hate you

Trust me
Trust me

My forehead has
Become creased
My thighs
Have become cold
Trust me
I have witnessed
My retaliation

Trust me
Trust me

You betrayed me. You left my bed knowing you would never come back. You didn't want our child or me.

Our son looks in the mirror and he sees someone he has never known. An older man who looks at him and says, I don't know you. I don't want to know you. You are your mother's son. I know my kind and you're not mine. Go away you silly boy. You Westall brat.

No one was in the hairdressers shop when we got back to it. We got in the car and quietly said goodbye.

TWIN TOWERS

Get rich. Be rich. Get rich. Be rich.

Before September 11, I'd see those Twin Towers every time I left my house on 4th Street and walked to the corner of 5th Avenue. I'd see the towers directly over the large tree that holds its own on the other corner of 5th Avenue. After September 11, I wondered what would it have been like if Frank Lloyd Wright's "The Mile High Illinois" had been built on the same location. A mile high.

Wright wanted his conception, his new city, to enter into the future with organic forms, calculations that would parallel the wind. Think of it. Open a window, walk out onto a cloud, find your Genii, the sky's the limit.

After September 11, My "Learning to Draw" takes on the scent of buttercups, Daisy chains, wetting my bed. I had not wanted to refer to my childhood or use any autobiography in "Learning To Draw." I had wanted it to be as secular a document as a drawing is. But childhood has a narrow brain. Hit it and your ego becomes a punching bag.

I remember leaving a Lyons Corner House with my parents in London during the Second World War. We went into the basement of a church. The minister had all of us sing. When the all-clear sounded and we returned to the street, Lyons Corner House had been hit. The firemen were looking amongst the rubble for bodies. A number of houses had come down. Only one staircase remained standing. Its banister and steps didn't have a scratch on them.

Why was that staircase still standing. Why amongst everything that had come down, why one staircase. My ego foraged for something that it could believe, something that I could comprehend. The ARP and St. Johns ambulances were there. Tea was being served by a young woman. No one was crying. Firemen were looking amongst the rubble for bodies. There were colours and smells, fire, silence and smoke.

Aeroplanes were coming back from a bombing mission. One of them, a Spitfire, tipped its wings and the silence was broken. My mother began to cry. My father took my hand. A young girl who had been standing close to me smiled. So did her mother. Her father asked: do you know where the nearest bus is. They began to follow us. And the six of us turned our backs on something that had become sculptured. A memory that stands after everything else has fallen.

Pause

I show you a conventional palette. A thin board with a hole at one end, and on this palette are laid out different whites. White: the opposite of black. White. I never want to shock. I want to squeeze the heart and remind us that there is still a shudder in us. Maybe the same shudder we saw in medieval paintings. White: there is the white that stays all the way in the background and there are the others: the ones that move all the time; the ones that take to the corners; the ones that show warmth; the ones that remind us that apples, lemons, and potatoes are food. I don't have to take to the pallet – the small bed, a bed of straw – to feel the surreal. As my tongue hits my palate, the roof that houses my tongue becomes wet. Olive. Peace be with you.

Pause

I'm sitting on my bag waiting for a car to come along. I look up. Clouds, changing metaphors, highway obstacles. "Here boy, read this" he said fifty years ago at Black Mountain College when I was sixteen Charles Olson gave me Arthur Rimbaud.

Pause

March 2001. Our house in Brooklyn is being renovated. Martha and I move into the top floor of our daughter and son-in-law's house in Jersey City, New Jersey. The space is too small to paint in. I put a table in the corner by the bedroom window and draw miniatures in mixed media for Arthur Rimbaud's *Drunken Boat, Illuminations,* and *A Season in Hell.*

Some children know they are homosexual when they are four years old. Some know they want god. I knew I wanted art. Sometimes, not all the time, knowing can be important. Olson and Rimbaud are sitting on the edge of the table swinging their legs. I will not be able to write. I will not be able to paint. I will lose what I have. Homage, I am about to begin a series of drawings for Rimbaud's letters.

Get rich. Be rich. Get rich. Be rich.

I'd take the Path train to The World Trade Centre. Walk through the concourse to the R train and take it to Brooklyn. Check the house out. Meet with Sean the contractor and Marshall the designer.

We moved back into our house July 30th. The house was still being worked on and it was another month before the stove was working. In fact, workers were still in our house in September when the stench of burning metal and gas drifted in from the World Trade Centre.

The Twin Towers had replaced the Statue of Liberty. They were capitalism's welcoming committee. Everyone, no matter where they came from, was welcome. Get rich, be rich, stay rich. Poverty's face is ugly. It is also sick and has learning problems. There are good guys and bad guys, good girls and bad girls. It's too hard to think anything else. It's too difficult to think what it would be like to be without possessions. No possessions, no self-worth. Not to have *money*. It's too difficult to think of. What would it be like if everyone had as much as you. If no one was considered less than you.

I insist light abstracts the smallest thing.

And because I believe this I believe the miniature is as powerful as a mural.

Pause

She was a little girl and she lost her father, and her mother never found her. Her mother went into the rubble with a man she didn't know and they fucked. Neither of them said a word. When they were finished they didn't say goodbye. They had tried to repeat something that was familiar, something that they had done yesterday. Everyone during the war repeated something they had done the day before. It was that way. But very few committed suicide. It wasn't that it wasn't done. There wasn't a thing that wasn't done. In between the rows of potatoes and carrots in the victory gardens flowers grew. H.D. was writing poems. Dame Myra Hess was giving open-air concerts on the piano. Vic Oliver was on the radio cracking jokes and playing his violin. Graham Greene was an air raid warden and spotter, and everyone carried a gas mask. The concrete pavements exuded faith. We were right and we would win.

September 11, 2001. Tod Thilleman and I were in his car. We were looking for a lumber yard that could cut some boards for shelving that I needed in my studio. We could see a huge plume of smoke over lower Manhattan. Fourth Avenue in Brooklyn was crowded with people who had walked over the Brooklyn Bridge and were going home. Some had remembered to take their brief cases and coats when they left downtown Manhattan. Every one of them had acquired a mime of their own, a partner to walk and hold hands with. Through the white dust that covered their faces, shock showed its contempt for their fears. Which one of them would have sex before or after tomorrow's breakfast. Who would jack off. They had survived but their survival had cost them. They looked at themselves in the mirror. Mirror, mirror on the wall, do I look as I did yesterday. And what will I look like tomorrow.

We deceive ourselves. We know what we look like. We know the size of our own souls. And we know that everyone else knows.

These young Moslem men committed suicide not because they had faith but because they had lost their faith in ever winning. By killing themselves they would never again have to contend with modernism, democracy, equal rights for women. They crashed into the Twin Towers believing they would be rewarded, and go to heaven. There they would be greeted by virgins and never have to face the hell they had left behind. They would never have to smell the stench they had created.

The Egyptian I buy my Lotto tickets from was frightened. He wasn't sure how the neighbourhood was going to treat him. After a few days he relaxed, no one was blaming him, and I don't think he received any threats. He goes back to Egypt every year with his family. He wants his children to know where they come from. His children are American kids. Noisy, well-fed and sassy.

Andrew Crozier phoned from England wanting to know if we were all right and had Martha's ride to work been jeopardized by the happening. Her sister Charlotte phoned from California. Her sister in-law called from Denver. There were emails, phone calls from Australia, Slovenia. My cousins in England, Malcolm, Renee and Penny, did not phone. Ted Enslin phoned. I had nothing to say. I was angry I had nothing to say. We were both angry. The Moslems want the twelfth century and the fundamentalists in this country want the eighteenth century. Pick your poison. None of them want what is contemporary.

> We paint from memory
> those things that are
> nearby even though
> the realism of your
> portrait dissolves
> I squeeze your heart
> and feel jealousy

Richard Serra's dog is barking at me. He says, "Richard is not mean. He doesn't beat me or kick me." I tell the dog, "I know he loves you. I know he is not a mean man, a cruel man. He is not a sadist. He is an artist and I love his sculpture."

But I don't agree with him, and that's my dilemma. How can I love his work. I am unable to agree with him. He insists on purity. And purity is the curse of the twentieth century. He wants nothing to do with disparate things, unruly things. And having said this I still admire his nerve, his reduction, his conservation.

After September 11, my "Learning to Draw" takes on the scent of buttercups, Daisy chains, wetting my bed. I remind myself, I had not wanted to refer to my childhood or use any autobiography in "Learning To Draw." I had wanted it to be as secular a document as a drawing is. But childhood has a narrow brain. Hit it and your ego becomes a punching bag.

Pause

Casper David Friedrich, the nineteenth-century German painter, is standing next to Rothko who is seated with his back to me. Both men face Rothko's painting. Jim Dine's bathrobe is floating like a cloud over the city. His heart is pounding. He is looking for his mother. She is missing. I see my mother. She too is looking at the Rothko painting. She has her back to me, she always did. She defined her borders years before I was born. She never relented. She never wanted me.

Rothko's edges are glowing, and from underneath the painting's surface magic crackles. Rothko's spaces have to fight Rothko's colours because his spaces are forever being pushed in a side down and then it's the colours that are being pushed to the rear. The shoulder of the three Blues retrace the edge. Green keeps trying to catch Orange. The intellectual yellow sun sets over the city.

Be careful not to go too far to the rear of a Rothko painting. There is no air there. Stay there too long and you will suffocate. You will choke as he choked when the three Blue shoulders retraced the edge. Green keeps trying to catch Orange. Red slowly dissolved and the intellectual yellow sun sets over the city. Forsaking trees for automobiles, Rothko ate a hot dog as he passed the vegetables for sale on the sidewalk.

> Oh muse that walks between our legs
> Have every word dismiss the unnecessary.
> Have every argument find a word.
> Have every word find an argument.
> Oh muse that walks between our legs
> Deplore the word deplore the argument.
> Oh muse that walks between our legs
> Have every word dismiss the unnecessary.

> Have every argument find a word.
> Have every word find an argument.
> Oh muse that walks between our legs
> Have every word dismiss the unnecessary

Manet and Franz Kline are crying. David Hockney is crying. The animators and the cartoonists and their comics are crying. Philip Guston is shaking his head. The towers have imploded, and there are heaps of rubble. More than Guston's junkyard can tolerate. There is so much to internalize and process. Why did America turn its back on all the events that had taken place in the Mid-East leading up to this huge happening. This happening that wasn't an Art Happening outdid all the Art Happenings of the past century. A cast of thousands couldn't have accomplished what those two planes did. Two planes crashing into the Twin Towers have shown the whole world that everyone is vulnerable. Not just Americans, but everyone in the world is at risk.

Rothko remains sitting. He never takes his eyes off his painting. Casper David Friedrich remains standing. Both men have their backs to us.

It was not easy being Casper David Friedrich. He preferred the twilight, the night. Daylight bothered him. He was a romantic smitten by an abstraction that lived in him but was not of him. The spiritual has a home of its own. It doesn't need his body. It can have a meal, drink a beer, and get into its own bed. But depression has no home of its own. It ate off of his plate and sucked off of his beer. Depression looked at him when he was painting. It looked straight at him and he had no assurance that it would go away.

In the late forties it's not reduction or simplification but Rothko processing the realization that the Psyche is figureless. And Psyche having been burdened with many sufferings is reunited with Cupid. When they make love, Flesh is Untitled, Blue maintains its solidarity, Black quivers and resists temptation. Grey has no equivalent. Plum and Purple, Green and Brown. Like Casper David Friedrich before him, Mark Rothko turned his back on something very basic. Neither artist saw a future where they could in good conscience fully participate. With brilliant foreboding each man establishes an independent evaluation of the past.

In 1983, I painted a baseball manager with his back to us. He's looking at an empty field. He'd grown up in a small town and knows nothing about farming. Baseball had brought him to the big city. As a pitcher he'd played for fifteen years on four different teams. He'd been a good pitcher, everyone respected him. Baseball was all he knew. He depended on it. When he stopped pitching he was hired as a pitching coach and three years later he became the team's manager. All he wants is two more years, then he'll retire. He isn't sure what he's going do after that. But he knows he won't be playing catch with his grandchildren. He'll have to turn his back on the game.

There's a horizon line with an ambiguous coloured sky coming as an afterthought as afterthoughts do. After the rainbow had finished telling him nothing is what he thought it was, the manager's hands go into his back pockets. He's lost a lot of games, and he doesn't want to lose any more. He wants his team to play without error. He hopes that his team will tower over the city that he loves.

> Get rich. Be rich. Get Rich. Be rich.

It was not easy being Casper David Friedrich. There is no summer, no heat in Friedrich's world. His men and women turn their backs and face the twilight, the night. Daylight bothered him. He was a romantic smitten by an abstraction that lived in him but was not of him. Friedrich may have been the first painter to recognize that this abstract other self could be painted. Wood, sunset, twilight, the gods who live in trees, birds and the backs of the ones you love.

Friedrich took this abstraction by its hand and manipulated it into his being, his soul, his internal doubts into the sublimations and shadows that must have haunted him. Nature that does not sing sang into Casper David Friedrich's ear and all the troubles he could never rid himself of overflowed like paint, insisting that independence come before night, winter, spring.

Turn left, turn right, childhood has a narrow brain. It is overfed by too much information. Friedrich lost his mother at the age of 7. The gods who live in trees, birds, and the backs of the ones you love sang into young Casper's ear and he became a craftsman, a maker of surfaces. At the age of 44 he became a husband, a father at 45, and four years later, at 49, his second daughter was born.

In his self portraits he could be as practical as bread. He doesn't show how smitten he was. Yellow, red, twilight penetrates the roof of Friedrich's house. In architectural clarity his lines hold the mean. He never drew the back of his own head. When he paints or draws men standing and looking out to sea he always has them wear an outlawed hat. The men wear medieval garb, a hat revived by radical German students in the wake of the Napoleonic Wars. Friedrich ignored the 1819 royal decree that forbade this dress. The staunchly patriotic Friedrich painted his figures in the Old German costume until the end of his life.

Pause

Writing about the towers, the Second World War, and death hasn't been easy. I did so much want to keep autobiography out of "Learning To Draw". I think I used "I" just twice in 100 pages before I began this section.

I intend to break all the sections up when I am finished and have one continuous verse. That in itself is going to take some doing. Because, like a drawing, my lines cross other lines, other painters, other poets. H.D., D.H. Lawrence, and William Carlos Williams, Thomas Hicks and Thomas Jefferson. I have Big Harpe and Little Harpe, Benjamin West and Walker Evans. I can't forget Bryher, Freud, and Rothschild. And don't forget the ocean that laps against both shores. Richard Serra understands that one. I know he does. Serra's Torques are grounded in space as a luxury liner floats in water. A lesser artist would tell you more, would be more literal as to where the curves and walls begin and end. But Serra has a different kind of ambition. His ambition is art, pure and undamaged.

The second printing of my book *Warp Spasm* came a week ago. Much sooner than I expected. The cover colour is a little off. Selby's blurb is on the back. It's strange but of late more than one person has said what Selby says about me in his blurb. He says Basil King gets lost in his paintings.

Get rich. Be rich. Get Rich. Be rich.

The family's row house is comfortable and is situated in a residential area that is appropriate to their income and status. Their one car is garaged in a local indoor parking lot. They lack for nothing. And after supper, after the children have gone to bed, the couple drink a few glasses of wine. Then they go to their bedroom, and sometimes they don't turn off the light.

On September 11, she didn't phone her husband. She left her job to pick up the children from school. They had had a nanny for the children. A nice woman who had children of her own. When the children came of age the husband and the wife both agreed that they needed the company of other children. The nanny was dismissed and the children were enrolled in a private school.

At home there was one message on the answering machine. Every day her husband came home at the same time, he never phoned. She was about to push the button on the answering machine when the doorbell rang. One of the children yelled, "I'll get it." Her husband came into the kitchen. She gave him a cup of coffee and passed him the milk. His hands were shaking and he had a hard time drinking the coffee. She waited for him to say something. He didn't say a word. She knew he'd come in his pants. She didn't say anything. They have been married for ten years.

He'd seen men and women taking advantage of the confusion. He'd watched them stealing everything they could carry. Watches, female underwear, Coach House bags. He'd watched and he'd done nothing. He'd forgotten his coat and briefcase in the office. He gave up the idea of trying to get them.

Melding into the crowd he walked across the Brooklyn Bridge wondering if his secretary was okay. Had she gotten out. He'd forgotten her children and her husband's names. He realized he couldn't phone her because he didn't know where she lived, and he began to cry. He said his wife's name out loud. Then he remembered his children and to himself he said forgive me and he began to fantasize.

He wants to paint his wife green. He wants to paint his children, his house and himself green. He wants her to understand that he isn't deferring to the dead when he wants to repaint the house green and eat $1, $5, $10 and $100 bills for breakfast. He wants her to know that he has always been afraid of flowers. Of those who dislike flowers, like Mondrian, and those who adore flowers, like Gaudi. He's afraid of them. He wants his wife to know domesticity is the wildest.

> Get rich. Be rich. Get rich, be rich.

Rothko's paintings "Black on Maroon" with their selection of ten commanding colours resembles a wall that interprets every Jew's emotional angst. Rothko remains sitting with his back to us. His concerns are ancient. Justice, Beauty, Intellectual Fortitude. Maroon's starkest Black depresses a beautiful surface.

In front of Rothko facing his painting a group of young men have their backs turned towards him, and as they pray they chant their disapproval. Democracy distributes wealth. Modern life gives equal rights to women. Democracy destroys purity and initiates disobedience.

The young Jews who are praying have no feeling of kinship for the young Moslems who committed suicide. They should. They also believe the modern world is a sin. A place where Satan thrives unchecked. The orthodox Jew and the orthodox Moslem do not see that purity runs next to Satan's side. Always watching, always aware, the two of them cannot exist one without the other. Brown and Black in Reds. Satan relishes his position. He has Moslems, ideologues, and artists wanting to destroy him. Moslems have cut him up into little pieces; ideologues have tried fire and brimstone to eviscerate him. Rothko covers Satan with blankets of oil paint hoping there will come a time when Orange, Wine, or Grey or Plum would saturate his veneer and destroy his false blessings.

Pause

Rothko was ill when the horizon line refused to yield divide and guide him as it had always done. He felt betrayed. His surface had become a Trojan horse that released unbearable monsters. No colour could appease them and they pecked at him as if he were the lowest barnyard runt. Rothko committed suicide.

Casper David Friedrich turned his back on modern life. The orthodox Moslems, Jews and Christians turn their backs on modern life. Every one's ego is in crisis.

I insist light abstracts the smallest thing. And because I believe this I believe the miniature is as powerful as a mural.

Get rich. Be rich. Get rich. Be rich.

Walking over to Donna Cameron's house a few weeks after September 11th I passed one of the churches on Seventh Avenue. The fireman's casket was being carried to the hearse. I began to cry. I wasn't crying for him, I was crying for the mother I never trusted. I was crying because I'd hated being in Halifax, Canada and having to relive some of my childhood.

Halifax, Canada is full of monuments. To the fisherman of Gloucester, Mass. To the sailors who ran the German Wolf Packs' gauntlet during the Second World War. To the dead of the *Titanic*. Halifax sent two cable ships, under the charter of White Star Line, and recovered 328 bodies, 150 of which are still buried there. And the Halifax Maritime Museum commemorates the Halifax explosion. The explosion occurred December 6, 1917 when the French steamship "Mont Blanc" and the Belgian steamer "Imo" collided in the harbour. Nineteen hundred people were killed instantly, over 9,000 injured, many permanently. Two thousand of them were made blind by flying glass.

The Maritime Museum has a documentary made in 1939 showing English citizens boarding ships to take them home. I didn't wait to see if my mother and I were in the movie. We had been on one of the convoys and we had been torpedoed. We were fortunate. We were put into a life boat with a lot of other people and picked up hours later. In Halifax I felt sick not because we had been torpedoed, but because I remembered. A few weeks before we left Detroit for Halifax my mother let her sister, my aunt, wash out my mouth with soap. I had wanted the three-quarter violin that was perched high above on the top of a bureau. I put chairs together and climbed up and got it, and then my aunt told me I couldn't have it. I can't remember what I said. I was four years old and I wanted to play the violin. I wanted music. I remember I wanted music.

I have fought death for as long as I can remember. Having had to, my ego has learnt to forage for small, not always delicate things. Thousands of drawings and over four hundred of my paintings are in storage. I am, as my ego says, an independent. I paint when I want. I write when I want.

Pause

In the early 1960s, John Manning asked me if I'd like to team up with him on a contract to paint and hang signs for the Big Apple, a chain of supermarkets. Most of the markets were outside of Manhattan, on Long Island. We'd arrive before the store closed for the night with templates, wooden letters, large cardboard apples with aisle numbers on them, our brushes, and a large nondescript bag filled with crumpled paper. We dragged this bag as if it were heavy. The stores usually closed at 9p.m. and the manager would let us out the next morning at 7a.m. The freezers had peculiar music – low, demanding – they were as if from another planet, and John and I were disturbed by them. Chickens, pigs, and cows. It was painting by numbers. We had templates, instructions, and premixed colours. We applied all this to the white walls. Then we'd take a break and decide what meats and canned goods we were going to put into the now empty bag. A week's provisions for our families.

One night we were to paint a huge basket of eggs. We made three different whites which we distributed Albers-like. Some eggs came forward, some went back. About a week later, we got a call. The manager of the store was getting complaints from customers who said when they looked at that basket of eggs they got dizzy. The manager didn't know what was wrong – but we'd better fix it fast. One coat of white and safety was restored.

Pause

Death has recently taken four old friends: Jack Rice, Fielding Dawson, Pete Voulkos, John Wieners. I'd known all four of them at Back Mountain College. I didn't know anyone who was killed in Viet Nam. I don't know anyone who was killed at the World Trade Centre. I've known people who were killed in car accidents. Artists who were killed by the chemicals they used in their work. Friends who were killed by cancer, heart attack, illnesses, and old age. People you love have strokes, they drown. People don't only die from illness and war. They die from loss, and their hearts break.

She had photographs of him in his fireman's uniform on the walls of their bedroom. She thought he was handsome and the uniform turned her on. She loved going to bed with him. He had strong hands. He wasn't afraid of her, and she wasn't afraid of him. The children knew this. Their house exuded a sexual generosity that made many of their friends nervous. They talked about her getting a job. But he had odd days and hours at the firehouse and she wanted to be there for him when he came home. In all the years he'd been a fireman he'd never gotten as much as a scratch on the job.

He hadn't come home and she was being told by the Mayor and the press that he was a hero. She'd never thought of him as anything but a fireman who did his job. It was a week after the 11th and her mother had come to stay with her. What was she going to do. She slumped and her mind wandered. Did the Moslems who had flown the jets into the towers have wives. What were their mothers and fathers feeling. She straightened up. Why should she give a shit about what their wives and parents were feeling. She hated all of them.

Pause

In 1983, I didn't know Casper David Friedrich. I knew Rothko. I knew he grieved. His horizon lines never had beautiful nudes stretched out smiling. His horizon lines were always devoid of human likeness. He would never allow himself to paint a deformed figure. His layered surfaces are monuments to bitter times.

Loss and gain can't be measured in a Rothko painting. We have to settle for his colour and our self-hate. Each day the news reports more killings, more death.

Justice has had her breast covered over. How can we win.

The surreal knocks.

BASIL'S ARC

Who affects you. What affects you. Does war. Does peace. Nations fight nations, the good guys and the bad guy.

Who becomes the wholesale killer whose many layered surfaces contrast war's violence.

Who goes to war. Who is able and willing to fight. Do you know and if you do what do you remember. There are no solutions in dying. Death is too final.

I write about all of the above because there are men and women who still think war not peace is a solvent, a cleanser.

Was it a cleanser at Agincourt on October 25, 1415, when Henry V defeated the French and killed 10,000 Frenchmen. Does killing answer any question.

The English lost 125 men. Does that answer. Does that justify not answering the questions that are hard to answer.

Does this preclude that we have to have another war?

Pulling out or going in – the sexual overtones cannot be ignored. Who is the male. Who is the female. No child is being produced. No dialogue, prose or theatrical presentation is equipped to produce an answer.

In Iraq as it is in any war, retrogrades and perverts deny the fact that men, women and children are made lame. That men, women and children fall into the water and die.

Their deaths do not give me any distance from the greed that I cannot avoid. On the contrary greed provokes. And the nightmare returns.

Not one of us lives in a natural environment. Not anymore. Not even the wild animals that inhabit the jungle. We all live in compounds. Some of us can say we are free, others can't.

The animal world is being traumatized by a species that still denies that we are all animals.

The artist Henri Rousseau without shame or apology meticulously recorded his fear of not being accepted.

Love me. I want to be loved. I want Paris to love me. I want France to love me. I want all the artists and all the poets to love me.

Rousseau wasn't an intellectual but he was a thinker. The French, the English, and the German public loved the jungle. This is what the colonies had to offer the imagination. Every aristocratic family had a Tarzan. Every jungle had a great Ape, Black cats, Lions, Tigers, Monkeys.

Henri Rousseau seized the jungle and its inhabitants. He brought them home with him. Gave them seats in his studio and he watched them, and he petted them and he talked to them.

And when he got to know them he began to paint.

He might not understand why his libido was aroused. Or why his intuition told him the jungle and its inhabitants have their own rules and manners. Your rules and theirs are different from one another and a distance has to be maintained between them. Otherwise the vision will be lost.

Rousseau frequented the Zoo of the Jardin des Plantes. He absorbed the popular magazines that featured the jungle's wild creatures.

He wanted the public to adore his paintings.

Unfortunately for him the oversized leaves are the oversized hands of the women and the men Rousseau paints. This approach to the subject isn't decorative and it isn't academic or entertaining. In its originality, its power challenges Picasso.

By bringing the jungle into his living room Rousseau's distortions are anti-colonial. Rousseau's manipulations of the figures come directly from his own vision. They are not appropriated as Picasso's are from African sculpture.

Rousseau's work is awkward, quirky and disturbing. It has been said he is a primitive and not to be taken seriously. But Rousseau was not an outsider.

On the contrary he was smack dab in the centre.

Rousseau's paintings gave many of the younger painters permission to pursue their own obsessions. Max Beckman, Edvard Munch, Kandinsky,

Delaunay. Yes, and Picasso. In November 1908, a young Picasso, who had just completed his "Demoiselles de Avignon," stopped in his tracks upon seeing Rousseau's large "Portrait of a Woman" in a bric-a-brac shop.

He bought the painting for five francs and never parted with it: "The first work by Le Douanier that I had the occasion to buy grew inside me with an obsessive power… It is one of the most truthful French psychological portraits," he later told Florent Fels.

Rousseau may have grown inside Picasso and stayed with him all his life. But Picasso needed to know what comes next. And it wasn't Rousseau.

Rousseau disturbs, he never titillates, he never shocks, he places his subject in front of you and you are. You are alone. You are not alone. The psalm replaces religion.

Picasso didn't invent the twentieth century but he understood it.

Since Picasso, art, modern art, has had to shock.

POW! The Cubist sensibility retires to a surface of moving parts. The conveyer belt never stops. Picasso. The name became a business producing paintings, sculptures, drawings, prints, and ceramics.

His son who is the executor of Picasso's estate says they are still counting.

Picasso saw that mass production was changing everything. What we eat what we wear and where we live have changed our politics and the way we think.

What Picasso did invent was collage. From the excesses of the industrial revolution. Assemble the waste. The bits and pieces that remain after the feast has taken place. Assemble the family and crown your lovers. Buy them houses and give them your paintings and drawings.

Minutiae surrounds you, you sleep with crayons. You sleep and you dream and you discover African sculpture. The result is startling. Africa's culture and religion are usurped and forgotten. In its place she saw that she had more than two eyes.

And her mouth.
What did her mouth say yesterday.
And what about her nose.
The mirror is given new meaning.

Yes, I always cross my legs.
But I didn't know that my hands are, are they.

Yes, what Picasso paints is immediately more recognizable than Rousseau's slow changes. Rousseau brings the outside into his home. And by so doing he says, domesticity is the wildest.

Awake or asleep Rousseau has sharp teeth.
The Tiger is caught in a storm.
The Lion eats the Antelope.
Sex can be dangerous.
Black can be dangerous.
War can be dangerous.

Henri Rousseau's painting of "WAR," 1894, is as terrifying and as brutal as any one of his portraits.

> Black birds,
> leaves,
> tree limbs.
> Black alone frightens the Blue Sky.
> Nothing is incidental.
> The tangle
> of bodies.
> The sparse
> amount of Red. Blood.

War calculates. As she rides a horse through the landscape displaying her hate she bares her teeth. She is a child, and she can't stand it that she isn't able to have her own way.

Centuries before Rousseau's painting of "WAR," 1894, and long before there was an Ad Reinhart there was Titian's "Virgin and Child with Saints Catherine and Dominic," 1513-1514.

Titian's painting is an abstract sensation of Black shapes and straight lines interacting with Red figures, Blue, and a landscape.

Titian's asymmetrical composition uses so many of the same colours as Henri Rousseau's 1894 painting of "WAR." But Titian's Black and all the other colours he uses are non-violent.

To the figures in fervent interaction with one another Black is a theatrical backdrop. And we who live within nature's complications have a calming of air.

> Narcissus looked into the pool and saw himself.
> Ad Reinhart's colour Black is transparent.
> We see. But we do not see.
> We are told. But we are not told.
> There is no mention of war.
> There is no mention of peace.
> We are alone. But we are not alone.
> Everything is as language is.
> Is our conscious an undefined shape
>
> In Reinhart's Black the void is a verb.
>
> A motion that changes with or without
> the four seasons consumes.
> It doesn't consume. I want a drink.
> I do not want a drink. I want to eat.
> Help me Gertrude.
> I see. But I do not see.
> I am told. But I am not told.
> I do not want to eat.
> There is no mention of war.
> There is no mention of peace.
> I am alone. But I am not alone.
>
> Ad Reinhart's colour Black is layered.
> One floor after another floor triples
> up and down. The building is both horizontal
> and vertical. The building has no stairs
> and no windows. Distances are impossible
> to judge. There are questions.
> But there are no answers.

The last time Martha and I visited MOMA we saw the Dada show. Martha said she would like to come back and see the show again. I checked the Museum's calendar and found the show was closing that day. It had stopped raining and the sun came out. We went outside and sat down by the pool in MOMA'S sculpture garden.

There was a sick bird in the water. A guard used a baseball cap to scoop the bird out of the water. He placed the bird in the surrounding shrubbery.

Every time he did this, the bird would leave the greenery and obstinately waddle back to the edge of the pool and fall in.

There was no mention of war. There was no mention of peace.

Dada triumphs.

What the Dadaists did wasn't easy. Every one of its members personally scrutinizes the rules and manners of their day.

It takes courage and a lot of humour to go against the tide. I am forever grateful to these men and women for their ethics and their integrity.

You can be at war with yourself, with your parents, your children, with politics or aesthetics. Who goes to war. Who is able and willing to fight. Who is willing to fight their parents, their children. Who affects you. What affects you. Does war. Does peace.

Do you remember and if you do what do you remember. Nations fight nations, the good guys and the bad guys. Who becomes the wholesale killer whose many layered surface contrasts with violence.

Was the First World War a cleanser.

Henri Rousseau had already painted his "WAR," 1894, when in 1914 a huge fist came down and crushed the hopes of the twentieth century.

After 1918, Cubism, Dada, collage, new music had no effect on the men who were full of resentments. In fact these arts fuelled their fears and heightened their sense of purpose. Stop the change. Stop the poem, stop the exposure, stop the courageous. We must have limits.

1936, one year after I was born, the Spanish Civil War began. Since then there has been one war after another. War, not peace, has been the norm. My experience is that war perpetuates arrogance, spite, and meanness.

I was nine when British Tommies with machine guns told us to leave the lavatory in Victoria Station so the German officers they were guarding could use the toilets. The German officers marched past us wearing long grey coats, shiny leather boots, and gloves. They didn't look defeated. On the contrary, their arrogance cited spite and a meanness I have never forgotten.

I think of it as a responsibility to do something more than simply remember this event that has haunted my memory for over sixty years.

A face is a face as a tree is a tree except when they become something else, and when they do there is no way of predicting what will happen. But when a change happens, believe it.

In Edward Hicks' "Peaceable Kingdom" animal faces change, trees change. In his "Noah's Ark," his hollow trees and Bosch's hollow tree in "The Temptation of Saint Anthony" *record* a failure of confidence.

In Ryder's deliberate attempt to change his loveless life, the sky and the sea are consumed by things that hide behind the moon.

And Gauguin, dear Gauguin, his "Yellow Christ" forgives the peasants for not wanting to change. But he had to, and instead of going forward he stepped back. So did Rimbaud. POW! They retreated.

These two brilliant men retreated into what had passed. Colonialism was already over as they insisted western culture and only western culture deserves attention. That everything else takes place before Adam and Eve's expulsion from Eden.

In the Brancascci Chapel of Santa Maria del Carmine the young Masaccio's "Expulsion of Adam and Eve from Eden" has a naked man and woman looking back at something that horrifies them. They are fleeing from their home without clothes or possessions.

They have had to abandon everything. They are not running away from a war zone or an oppressor who wants to kill them. They are running away from guilt. Will they leave it behind. Have we.

Have you, have I, fought as hard as Edvard Munch did. He painted youth and old age and all the stages between grief, love and death. He kissed the lips, the hands, the mocking knowledge that he too could be taken.

On the left side of a tree in Edvard Munch's "Fertility" a clothed woman holds a basket full of fruit, vegetables. On the right side of the tree a clothed man sits. Here there is peace and plenty. Is there guilt.

Vegetation blooms in abundance in a field grounded by the tree that gives no sign of being a threat. The man wears a hat and has a walking stick by his left side. There is no way of determining the couple's ages. There is no way of determining what is the ending to this bucolic story. I can only say a short story has no ending.

But there is another side to Edvard Munch: He has a Viking temperament.

He can be fierce when he is angry. He wants his "Madonna" and when he can't have her he screams *and* writes an epic poem.

It does not please him but he knows that he is capable of murder. As *The Book of Common Prayer* (Church of England) says in its Litany, "from the fury of the Norse Men, Good Lord deliver us."

Deliver us from Munch's painting "Metabolism."

A naked woman with long red hair and a slipper on her right foot stands next to a tree trunk. She is going through some kind of change. On the right side of the tree there is a naked man. He too is going through a change.

The man and the woman might be Adam and Eve and then they might not be. Whoever they are they are frightening.

The frame that surrounds the painting has a skull and bones carved into the wood. Black circles circle both of their eyes. They are dying and everything they covet will die with them.

Behind the man and the woman there are smaller trees and behind the trees a blue sky and an inkling of lights from a town we cannot see. Munch is a master of distance.

The placement of a tree. The body, be it male or female, is placed between good and evil. Between light and dark Munch immerses his inhibitions. He wars with the devil, with the obscene cruelties that fear frustrates. He appropriates only what is needed. He is personal with his motif. And at the same time he knows he has to step back and give himself distance.

Remember the last time you were in pain. Remember how you had to distance yourself from it. Munch painted pain. Munch the master of distance taught us distance, that most essential being, is given to all of us.

Distance, that most essential being, is given to all of us. When we use it, we are capable of doing crazy things.

The composers Felix Mendelssohn, Gustav Mahler, and Arnold Schoenberg converted to Christianity to further their careers. In 1898 at the age of 24 Schoenberg became a Lutheran. But in 1933 when Hitler came to power he converted back to Judaism. Mendelssohn's family converted when he was seven. Mahler became a Catholic when he was 37 and was appointed Kapellmeister at the Vienna Hofper two months later.

The conductor Herbert Von Karajan, age 25, joined the National Socialist Party, and the singer Elisabeth Schwarzkopf became a member of the German Nazi Party when she was 21. They joined so they could practice their art.

Now Günter Grass is being condemned for having joined the Nazi's Waffen SS when he was 17. People are saying that Grass is only now telling what he kept secret for over half a century just to promote his new book. Maybe, but Grass is the only one who knows and he isn't telling.

Grass isn't ashamed of what he did at 17 any more than any of the artists mentioned above are ashamed of what they did. Grass's thinking after the war was as calculated and as hard-headed as Picasso's. POW! What comes next.

Consider Grass's position. Weren't there enough ambitious Germans after the war ended confessing to what they did during the war. It made some of them heroes.

Grass didn't want to be that kind of hero. He wanted to be a great artist with all the accolades that go with being established and successful. Grass is a snob.

Most artists are.

For Grass, the artist, the artist's obligation is to tell it before it happens, whilst it is happening, and then tell it again after it has happened.

Grass has become an old man and is it not so strange that the old artist Grass now has to shed his Waffen SS uniform. So that he can continue. He has worn it for a very long time. It has become threadbare and is unrecognizable.

Because he remembers at 17 the past seemed reluctant and too lazy to change. As for the future, there really is no future. Everything is now. Now I want. Now. I must have it now.

And now we have another war. Pulling out or going in, the sexual overtones cannot be ignored. Who is the male. Who is the female. No child is being produced. No dialogue, prose or theatrical presentation is equipped to produce an answer.

Retrogrades and perverts deny the fact that men, women and children are being made lame. That men, women and children fall into the water and die. Their deaths do not give me any distance from the greed that I cannot avoid. On the contrary greed provokes. And the nightmare returns.

I write about all of the above because there are men and women who still think war not peace is a solvent, a cleanser. Was it a cleanser at Agincourt on October 25, 1415, when Henry V defeated the French and killed 10,000 Frenchmen. Does killing answer any question. The English lost 125 men. Does that answer. Does that justify not answering the questions that are hard to answer.

I had already gone to war. I wake up in the morning not knowing which one of the seven people who inhabit me I am going to be.

For years I fought to make myself be one person.

No more do I do this.

It's complicated; they are my toons, my seven selves. They live in my house with Martha and me. They sit at our table and I feed them.

With fourteen eyes I desire.

Then there are the times when all seven go blank and I can't remember names, dates, eyes or faces.

I remember what you are wearing, the colour of your shirt, your pants, your skirt and the cut of your blouse. I remember what you told me two years ago. I remember stories the ones that have no ending.

It was in the nineteen sixties and Martha and I met with my mother's cousins the Lapsons. Yahuda Lapson had a position with the Israeli government or one of its Jewish-American affiliates.

I remember that I liked him and his wife. I remember that the food was good and that we all talked. I told them that we'd seen photographs in newspapers and magazines showing armed Israeli soldiers patrolling the streets of Jerusalem and Haifa.

It was beyond me: Israeli soldiers, Jews, patrolling the streets with guns.

He said they had to protect themselves. They had no choice. The Arabs couldn't be trusted. I remember saying, "Yahuda, this is not good. Guns, armed soldiers. Isn't this a bad beginning. Jews imitating European nationalists. It's retrograde. There must be another way. It will end badly."

He listened and said, "What else can we do."

Did the Kennedys tell us what they were doing in Viet Nam. The Harvard boys entertained us. If it weren't for the Kennedys we would never have had Beatlemania or Andy Warhol's wigs. The Kennedys displayed a social and domestic upper class ease that had never been seen in an American political family in the 20th century. They looked like they belonged.

A generation of artists, my generation, said they belonged. The POP artists didn't want to change society. Toothpaste, coke, cars and the movies; they had come to terms with the commercial world.

When I rehash the Kennedys' actions I have to admit to myself the Kennedys had arrogance, meanness, and spite.

President Bush wants the country to think of him as an uneducated Texas cowboy. A workingman, a man of and for the people. POW! Whereas the Kennedys were proud to say they were educated. Were proud of their intellectual contacts. But their performance and behaviour was as shameful as anything the Bush administration does.

They too gave themselves permission to destroy everyone and everything that stood in their way.

Unchecked, artless hierarchies that mimic South American dictators cannot be called democratic. We are not alone in creating wars in creating misunderstandings that inflict terrible things, horrible disasters.

Not one of us live in a natural environment, not anymore, not even the wild animals that inhabit the jungle. We all live in compounds. Some of us can say we are free, others can't. The animal world is being traumatized by a species that still denies that we are all animals.

We animals need to eat and sleep with some guarantee that we will not be woken up in the night and be hauled off to a place we do not know, that nobody knows. That we will not be tortured by other animals that do not know us or care about who we are or what we do.

This is not science fiction. It's a surreal haemorrhage, and it's not a dream. We know that this happens. Even the newspapers confirm it. Just as the newspapers confirm that Israeli soldiers walk the streets with guns.

Yesterday in the paper there was a photograph of a left-handed pitcher. He is going to be my next painting. The last time I painted baseball must be twenty years ago. I already know that I will approach this pitcher differently.

I've been looking at the photograph and the canvas for days.

Sized canvases are beautiful. I have a hard time making that first mark. After that my excitement becomes concentrated.

Beyond that there are times when I put the sized canvas on the wall and begin without hesitation to employ destruction.

The surface of the canvas gets a barrage of materials practically thrown at it. Charcoal, moulding paste, chalk, and oils.

Who goes to war. Who is able and willing to fight. Do you know and if you do what do you remember. There are no solutions in dying. Death is too final.

I write all of the above because there are men and women who still think war not peace is a solvent, a cleanser.

Remember de Kooning could have unloaded Europe, its culture and its landscape. Instead he surprises everyone. POW! Bill paints the figure.

She is like no figure we have ever seen. She doesn't resemble Aphrodite. Her violence makes the Venus of Willendorf blush. She doesn't look like any of the women Picasso painted. She is a fighter. She has purpose. Her ancestors gave birth always wanting, always wanting.

Paint created her
So that she could
Destruct and be
Born again.

Were we all born in paint.
On a brush. On a staircase.
In a conception
Depending on paint.

Death is never mentioned.
War is never mentioned.
Peace is never mentioned.

Remember Europe, the coast of Holland. The Pacific Ocean, Southampton.

The tides refuse compromise. De Kooning wiggles his toes. He is beautiful. He looks like a woman.

Death is never mentioned.
War is never mentioned.
Peace is never mentioned.

The "Clam Diggers"
Divulge the violence
Of their occupation
Their migrant status
Their loss of innocence

Has America ever lost a war.

Will America ever lose its faith in sentimentality.

Who will you kiss.
Who will you hold.
Who is willing.

It was early morning. I was coming from the West side crossing Washington Square to go east. Bill de Kooning was sitting on a bench. I waved, he waved, I walked over and I sat down. We talked. He said he'd been painting all night and he couldn't sleep. I asked him if he'd seen the Venus of Willendorf. He said he hadn't but he'd seen photographs. I told him that Charles Olson had introduced us to her in one of his classes. We talked about Black Mountain. He and Elaine had been there for a summer.

We walked down Eighth Street and he said, "Let me do something for you." We were standing under the El on Third Ave and I said that's all right I'm going home. And he said, "I insist." He said, "You wait here." He came back with a black woman who wasn't much older than me. He said, "You go with her. It's all right I've paid her."

           Blue
  Blue

Willem de Kooning like his mentor Arshile Gorky traced and retraced Picasso. Lines became layered, paint thickened, and the surface became impersonal.

There was no way that the truth could be told.

There was no way that Gorky could bring up his past and bring it into the front of the painting as Ryder was able to do. Gorky needed his mother. His mother sits beside him and it is she who creates a space that mutes the heaviness of contemporary life.

In Gorky's space lines and shape seduce the unattainable.

Can we ever be that delicate again.

Can we tell our mothers what Gorky told his.

Willem de Kooning is coming to supper.
He is bringing his mother.
And she is a Dutch woman.
Her wooden shoes are
as hard as her tongue.
Her story is not like yours.
You remember flowers.
Armenian "Summer Snow."
You remember the Turks
and the husband who left
and went to America.
de Kooning's mother
remembers the Germans
the beer, the sausages
the soft feet of her children.

The migration of birds.

Willem de Kooning's women walked, took trains and buses and crossed Europe's borders before immigrating to America. And when the women arrived in America they brought with them embroidered into the fabric of Europe's art the memory of all the wars that Europe had fought.

The great Pieter Bruegal (1525/30-1569) fought "The Battle of Carnival and Lent," "Children's Games." "Anger." "Gluttony." "Avarice." "Pride." "Envy." "Lust" and "Sloth."

In "Mad Meg," 1561, a war-like woman stands with a sword in one hand and the spoils of pillage in the other. Death and destruction surround her. Men and women and soldiers are fighting for a place that does not exist. Hell has two enormous eyes. Hell's hideous open mouth is an entrance. Once in no one will return. Bats, naked couples, torn limbs, disfigured gnomes and fires consume things we cannot see. Misery and hatred dismantle the daily lives of crowned heads and high-church dignitaries. They all mingle in the cauldrons of Hell with common people, just as people of all stations are admitted to Heaven.

Bruegal's integrity always shows in everything that he draws and paints. "The Wedding Feast." "The Beggars." "The Peasant's Dance." "The Blind Leading the Blind." What they depict is accurate, even if we do not understand all their meanings today. The blind are really blind. Winter is winter and in summer the Beekeepers really keep bees.

Bruegal analyzes the human condition.

No one is innocent. Not even the guilty.

Coda

For love.

Robert Creeley

Would put a candle behind your eyes.
Would hold you until you scream.
Would tell you to go and talk to Dr. Williams,
To Robert Duncan and Charles Olson.
Would tell you the darkness surrounds us.

Believe it. Believe Whitman and Frank O'Hara.
Believe the poets. Believe Dante
And don't forget Chaucer.
Don't forget the language, it's all we have.
War has oblivion.

To destruct what no one else
Is willing to destruct. Creeley
Moves into a position where he can
Always see. No comma drops.
To please the subjective Creeley marries.

To augment the conservative
He drives from Buffalo to New York City
And on the way back he stops.
The sequel to Mary Shelly's Frankenstein
Is a de Kooning extension

Armour he wears.
The paint he eats.
She sups with you.
She takes him.
She rows a boat,
Rides bicycles
and is full of contradictions.

If it fails begin again.

A book of 135 poems that riff off other painters' paintings I call *77 Beasts/ Basil King's Beastiary*. It is my first anthology. As I was selecting the poems for the book I began to paint what Kim Lyons titled, "Basil's Arc."

"Basil's Arc" does not copy. It grafts paintings of other painters into my painting.

When I asked the gardener in the Brooklyn Botanic Garden, "Do you have a particular section of the garden that you take care of," he replied, "We all have our own devotions." And it is with devotion that my Arc grafts surrealism, the abstract and the surreal comedians into its hold.

Louis Kahn's monumental faith.
Diane Arbus' introspections.
Kafka laughed at his own jokes.
Sandy Koufax read Spinoza and the next day went out and pitched a perfect game.

Unlike Noah's Ark my Arc is not coupled by animals. My Arc holds photographs, poems, architectural wonders, and paintings, beloved paintings. All are stored in my Arc. I have over thirty paintings completed for it and there are more.

But after writing this I'm not sure. Am I making my Arc because I am becoming old. Because these continuous wars so frighten me that I need to collect and store everything that I love before I too am taken.

I know I am a violent man and if I hadn't fallen in love with art when I was very young I despair thinking about what I would have become.

PURPOSE

I was sitting with Charles Olson on the mound in front of the Studies Building at Black Mountain College and I said, "My generation of Europeans will never go to war."

I remember Olson's silence.

I was fourteen when I saw Gorky's "Betrothal" on the cover of *Art News*. I fell in love. The following year I saw a small show of Jackson Pollack in the Detroit Museum. And one year later I stepped into Black Mountain. Having turned everything upside down everything has become magnified.

Justice as a Flavin light with a mix
Of expectations covers the canvas
BMC had a purpose and that was to
Pursue purpose

Justice not honour
Justice not pain

                          Pause

Draw a three dimensional figure

Charles Olson standing in front of the blackboard
With a cigarette
The cigarette always looked dwarfed
In his large hand
The residue of bygone wars
Have formed a crust on the surface
Of an engraved name that says

Lo, the line comes from outside
Waterfalls are vertical
Discontent is horizontal
Altruism like Justice
Cannot exist
One without the other

Leave home. Meet strangers. And learn to draw.

PURPOSE

We went with my father's brother Uncle Lew his wife Aunt Jenny and their daughter cousin Renee to my father's uncle's house. The family was sitting Shiva. Their son a brilliant student at Oxford had been recruited to parachute into Germany or was it Poland. He was caught. He was a spy and the Germans killed him. My relatives were very orthodox. All the mirrors were turned to the wall. There was brown paper on the floors.

My father held my right hand my Uncle Lew held my left hand. I was a little boy. I walked between them into a room where there was no furniture. My cousin Renee was with the women in another room. Men were sitting on the floor praying. We sat down and my father and my uncle began to pray. The emotional tones and the overwhelming sorrow frightened me I couldn't cry I was terrified.

Pause

I was about to cross the Manhattan Bridge into Brooklyn when I remembered it was Rosh Hashanah. There was an orthodox synagogue a few blocks from the bridge. I parked my car and walked to the synagogue. Men were milling around the entrance. "I'd like to go inside for a few minutes." "Do you have a ticket." "No, I'm a Jew and I just want to go inside for a few minutes." "You can't go inside you don't have a ticket." The man shook his head and said there was nothing more to say.

Shall I tell my mother
Shall I tell her
What I have told you
I had no ticket
And without a ticket
I am not a Jew
Nothing comforts
My mother
Shall I tell my father
He has a ticket
Shall I tell him
What I'm going to tell you

I got back in the car and drove across the Manhattan Bridge. Parked my car in front of my house and walked to the Reform Temple that is six blocks from my house. Men were milling around the entrance and I repeated what I had said to the man at the door to the orthodox synagogue. "You can't go in without a ticket." I couldn't believe what I was hearing. And I said. "I'm a Jew and I can't go into temple and be with my people for a few minutes on Rosh Hashanah because I don't have a ticket. What does a poor Jew who can't afford a ticket do." He didn't answer and I walked home.

Pause

I walked home
To my house
My wife isn't Jewish
She comes from a long line
Of Celts
And as one of our daughters
Was to say
I am half Jewelish
The other half
The Southern half
Feared Catholics
And oh
The Yankees
And Oh
The Greenbergs
And oh
The Black Mammy
If she is not
A mother
Why wear Black
And mourn
All those
You never knew

    Leave home. Meet strangers. And learn to draw.

Dylan Thomas informs us
I was 20 when
I published my first
Book of poetry
And I was a success
Dylan Thomas informs us
It was harder
Than I thought it would be
To be Dylan Thomas

Dylan Thomas came from a middle-class Welsh family. He didn't see any need to contradict the Sitwells when he heard them read his poetry. His father was a schoolteacher and Dylan was overcome. And at the same time Dylan thought if I misbehave if I hold court and sing irregular notes and I pronounce and drop the subjective Shakespeare will sit me on his lap and smile. Dylan forgot Shakespeare was the master of the cruel and a defender of the monarchy.

On Friday
The Monarch says
He isn't afraid of beauty
On Monday
The Monarch raised an army
Crossed the channel
Defeats the French
And asks Shakespeare
For more vocabulary
Shakespeare obliges
And whispers into
The Monarch's ear
My lord

Waterfalls are vertical
Discontent is horizontal
Altruism like Justice
Cannot exist
One without the other

> Lo, the line comes from outside

Around the corner Courbet's "The Young Ladies on the Banks of the Seine (Summer)" lie in wait. He fucks her in the ass. He doesn't want to see her face. He puts his foot on the gas pedal. Goes to a place that has connections, phone numbers, voice mails, Agincourt. Who is missing. They will be found. They trespass on the city's pavements. They knock on doors. They canvas the beleaguered. They will change their clothes and move to another city. There they will find jobs and begin again.

In this town that shall be nameless Flaubert's Madame Bovary sits in a parked car. She is waiting. She whispers to herself. She wants to see his face. She wants a channel she wants to end the separation.

> Pause

Wales was free of glaciers by 10,250 B.C. And people would have been able to walk between Continental Europe and Great Britain until about 7,000-6,000 B.C. when the post-glacial rise in sea level led to Great Britain becoming an island, and the Irish Sea formed to separate Wales and Ireland.

What if there had been no separation between Continental Europe and Great Britain might Rimbaud and Verlaine have walked to London where as Celts Rimbaud's vowels might have cracked their cheeks and pulled down their vanity.

Pause

Dylan came to America and gave readings. He was an enormous success. But Dylan didn't know how to take care of himself. His wife had left him and there was no one to take care of him. Dylan's muse was a very bright child sometimes impulsive sometimes arrogant. Dylan and his muse had no intention of ever growing up. He loved childhood and the admiration of adults.

On one of my visits to New York City a woman in the Cedar Bar told me just about every night Dylan Thomas drank in The White Horse Tavern.

The White Horse Tavern was crowded. I got a pint and found a seat. Dylan was surrounded. He'd have a drink say something and fall off his stool the crowd would laugh he'd get up and they would feed him another drink. Dylan was a poet he wasn't a boxer and if friends had told him not even poetry has the power to cure pain I don't think he would have believed them. When Dylan got up from the floor there was no referee to stop the abuse. I don't think it ever crossed his mind that if he went too far with his excesses his audience would turn and mock him. Dylan had lost the ability to control himself and he had become a geek. Some people have the constitution to be a public figure and tolerate flattery and abuse. Fame is a responsibility. Dylan didn't. I sat watching this evil display of unconscious envy and fear and I asked myself do these people find lynching appalling are these the same people who believe in civil rights.

Lo the line comes from outside

I woke up one morning and I didn't want to be a third generation abstract expressionist. I didn't know what to paint and I broke down and for two years I didn't paint.

Walking down Second Avenue in 1965 I passed St. Marks Church and I said to myself, "You're a painter who's never been." I turned around and went into a stationery store and bought 500 sheets of cheap paper.

The table was round the paper was 8½" x 11" and I drew circles on the paper. And when 500 hundred sheets were filled with circles I went out and bought 500 more. I drew circles day after day I can't remember how many sheets I filled with circles. Martha began to worry. Then without thinking I drew a line and the line became a leaf and the circle became a flower a Sun Flower a memory of childhood.

I have never thought of myself as an environmentalist but I do hate waste. I love leftovers. I use them when I cook. In the 1970s I started a Black Mountain Cook Book. It would contain recipes and anecdotes of Black Mountain College. The problem is I don't cook the same thing twice the same way.

What I experienced forty-five years ago was not comparable to a Blake and Kitty euphoria. I saw shavings on the floor of a carpenter's shop. They were the leftovers shavings of unfulfilled periods beginning with the caves and up to the present these shavings contain unused powers, mathematical mysteries, organic forms (Muscles and Triangles) abstract and emotional gestures, edges, curves, I wanted those shavings and I succeeded and we dovetailed and found a mutual purpose. Forget originality for its own sake.

Chicken feathers
Shoes and an old
Jacket
Pork Chops
Onions and Apple
Sauce
Sidewalks
Pigeons
Flowers
A memory
Of childhood
Pass the pepper
And the salt
Pass the butter
The jam
And a pink
School figure

I didn't paint flowers I painted organic shapes. Visceral shapes that so disturbed one gallery dealer that he told Mike Goldberg after being at my studio he went home took a shower and changed his clothes.

Lo the line comes from outside
It comes bent by oracles
Vast acres of unwashed
Irritations – Gemini splits

Bring in daylight-shells
Towers and finger-tips
Touch the canvas the oil
The face of beans
Cooking in a crockpot
Reinforce the intentions
Of a cook who feeds the fish
Every morning

Pause

Every morning for weeks I went to the merchant marine cooks school located in the kitchen of the San Francisco Board of Education. At first I did nothing but peel potatoes. I know I peeled hundreds and hundreds of potatoes before I moved to the next step. The chief the master cook had forearms larger than my thighs and he had no trouble kneading fifty pounds of hamburger to make a meat loaf. I was the only member of the class who wasn't a felon. There was the time a couple of the men locked another man they were mad at in the freezer. When we served the Board's employees and their guests lunch we'd wear a white tunic a white apron and a chefs hat.

To finalize my ticket I had to take a medical. I didn't get enough sleep the night before so Martha dug into her supply of pills that she had brought with her from UNC Medical Library in Chapel Hill. Martha had worked on the floor where all the doctors' offices were. Pharmaceutical companies sent the doctors samples and the doctors dumped samples into a large cardboard container in turn. Martha helped herself to whatever she wanted. Whatever that pill was I got a hard-on. It lasted throughout the examination somehow I manage not to lose my cool and I got through and I passed. On my way back to North Beach I stopped and had two for the price of one Martinis. My hard-on lasted into late afternoon.

Pause

1957. I was in a bar waiting to board a six-month tour on a merchant marine ship when I looked up and down the bar and I said to myself, "Some day some night you will say something to these guys and they will throw you over board." I went up to the boson and said, "Scratch me." He said, "Don't do it kid you'll never get another boat." I said, "That's okay." And that's the entire history of me going to sea.

Just the other night I met a man in our local bar. He's from New Zealand and a lawyer. He had gone to sea when he was a young man and among the many stories we told each other I told him of my decision and he told me I was absolutely right. He said, you're volatile and I'm not but even so the crew I sailed with found out I was a Jew and if it hadn't been for the cook who everyone was afraid of I would have been in trouble.

Pause

What I said to Charles Olson when I was a teenager was wrong. My generation went to war. Not too much passes through men and women with small livers. Greed and its first cousin bigotry denounce democracy and exercise entitlement. The site of 9/11 has been called hallowed ground. It is not a blessing that three thousand people were killed on that site it was a crime. Some crimes go unpunished.

London was not the only city to suffer heavy bombing and civilian casualties during World War ll. Hundreds of thousands died and many bodies were never recovered. Should we say all that ground is hallowed.

I was a boy of five when the Blitz took place over London and I witnessed some of the destruction that now is shown in documentaries.

Twenty or was it twenty-two thousand people were killed in London and there were thousands who were killed in the bombings of Antwerp, Dresden, Hiroshima and countless other cities in Japan, Soviet Union, China and Europe.

Every time I am on the East River Drive I am reminded I am driving over my childhood. American ships that brought Lend Lease to England had on their return nothing to fill their holds. So for ballast the ships were filled with London's rubble. The rubble was used as fill for the new roadway.

Rubble
The unwanted discarded creativity
Of something having been used
Or destroyed by persons
Known or unknown

Add a totem made
By men and women
Who remember you came
This way before
Before the waters
Rose over your head
You walked on ice

With persons
Known or unknown

        Be Rich. Get Rich. Be Rich. Get Rich.

There was a knock on the door it was 1958-59. It was the FBI. The man came in and said I hadn't registered with my draft board. He said I had forty-eight hours to make up my mind. I could go next door or I could go to jail. Martha and I lived at 32 Whitehall Street the draft board was right next door. I was what you can call a janitor to an empty building that was waiting to be sold. Martha and I had a small apartment. The owners had a wall knocked down between two offices and that space became my studio. My job was to keep the lights running in the hallways of all three floors sweep the floors and polish the handles on the front doors. I also had a day job carving frames at Dain & Schiff.

        Pause

During the Blitz we lived on the third floor of an apartment building. The stairs to the courtyard were constructed on the outside of the building. There was a metal railing a concrete floor and the stairs were metal like a fire escape. When the air raid siren sounded I'd go down to the second floor and take the old blind lady by the hand and walk down to the air raid shelter. When the all-clear sounded I'd walk her up the stairs to her apartment where she lived with her daughter. Her son-in-law was in the army.

The FBI agent said I had two days to make up my mind. If I didn't go to the induction centre he would come and get me and send me to the lock-up in New Jersey. From our window we'd see young men in handcuffs getting into buses to New Jersey. The agent asked me where Martha was. "I don't know but I think she'll be home soon."

He waited and Martha came home.

Two days later I kissed Martha and went to the induction centre. Took the intelligence test and sometime after that we were told to take our clothes off and piss into a bottle.

We were all bare-arse moving single file and holding our vial of piss. I put my piss bottle on a shelf and proceeded to walk up and down the line asking if anyone had seen my piss bottle. A sergeant told me to cut it out and get another bottle and go piss. I did and got back into line. Eyes, ears, throat. I didn't say anything until I was asked by a young doctor wearing a Navy uniform to bend over I said, "You've got to let me in the army. I was too short to play basketball but I can kill, I want to kill Germans." He looked horrified.

We were getting dressed and I was told to report to a room upstairs. It was a large room with a few chairs and an elderly man sitting behind a desk told me to sit down and he asked me if I had friends, if I liked girls and what I did for a living. And then he asked me to walk across the room and he screamed, "Halt." I didn't and he asked me why didn't I stop and I said "I didn't want to. I don't stop for anybody." Then he said, "Go downstairs collect your tokens and go home."

That was the second time Martha welcomed me home. The first was when I didn't go to sea.

Be Rich. Get Rich. Be Rich.

Some time ago I had a dream. I was driving in a beautiful Green coloured Bugatti with a Black top and a very intelligent woman told me "The sky's the limit."

This room that I write in we are going to raise its roof. It has a low peaked ceiling and there is no room for bookshelves. This may seem incidental to what I have written on all the previous pages. But I equate raising the roof with the dream that I had.

Lo, the line comes from outside

Waterfalls are vertical
Discontent is horizontal
Altruism like Justice
Cannot exist
One without the other

My cousin died because he wanted to do something to change the despair that surrounded Europe in 1940. My purpose is not to despair. I raise my roof I paint and I write and I use ambiguity in response to the sentimentality that is shown to things that are disturbing. Intolerance misleads our best intentions and we look for purity when nothing can be truly pure.

www.ingramcontent.com/pod-product-compliance
Lightning Source LLC
Chambersburg PA
CBHW020634220526
45464CB00001B/141